Urban Teaching
in America

To my amazingly supportive and understanding family,
Robert and Shirley Stairs, and Lily, Sara, and Paul Burgos

—Andrea

To my children, with whom learning is so joyful,
Carson Donnell Hall and Zoe Donnell Hall

—Kelly

To my parents, David and Helen Hadley,
who first taught me to love learning, and to my husband,
John Dunn, who teaches me more each day

—Alyssa

Urban Teaching in America

Theory, Research, and Practice in K–12 Classrooms

Andrea J. Stairs
University of Southern Maine

Kelly A. Donnell
Roger Williams University

Alyssa Hadley Dunn
Georgia State University

Los Angeles | London | New Delhi
Singapore | Washington DC

Los Angeles | London | New Delhi
Singapore | Washington DC

FOR INFORMATION:

SAGE Publications, Inc.
2455 Teller Road
Thousand Oaks, California 91320
E-mail: order@sagepub.com

SAGE Publications Ltd.
1 Oliver's Yard
55 City Road
London EC1Y 1SP
United Kingdom

SAGE Publications India Pvt. Ltd.
B 1/I 1 Mohan Cooperative Industrial Area
Mathura Road, New Delhi 110 044
India

SAGE Publications Asia-Pacific Pte. Ltd.
33 Pekin Street #02-01
Far East Square
Singapore 048763

Acquisitions Editor: Diane McDaniel
Editorial Assistant: Theresa Accomazzo
Production Editor: Libby Larson
Copy Editor: Sarah J. Duffy
Typesetter: C&M Digitals (P) Ltd.
Proofreader: Jenifer Kooiman
Indexer: Millis Indexing Services
Cover Designer: Gail Buschman
Marketing Manager: Katie Winter
Permissions Editor: Adele Hutchinson

Copyright © 2012 by SAGE Publications, Inc.

Printed in the United States of America

Library of Congress Cataloging-in-Publication Data

Stairs, Andrea J.
Urban teaching in America : theory, research, and practice in K–12 classrooms / by Andrea J. Stairs, Kelly A. Donnell, Alyssa Hadley Dunn.

p. cm.
Includes bibliographical references and index.

ISBN 978-1-4129-8060-9 (pbk.)

1. Education, Urban—United States—Research.
2. Teachers—Training of—United States. 3. Urban schools—United States. 4. Teaching—
Social aspects—United States. I. Donnell, Kelly A.
II. Dunn, Alyssa Hadley. III. Title.

LC5119.8.S83 2012
370.9173'2—dc23   2011019179

This book is printed on acid-free paper.

11 12 13 14 15 10 9 8 7 6 5 4 3 2 1

BRIEF CONTENTS

DETAILED CONTENTS

PREFACE

The Promise and Possibility of Urban Teaching

I've never been to public school. . . . I had the image of Dangerous Minds. . . . I had all these misconceptions about public high school. Well, you look at this stuff that you see in the movies and then television shows, so you think that there's going to be guys dealing drugs outside the classroom. I thought it was going to be absolutely absurd, and actually student teaching in an urban school washed away all of these misconceptions, and I met a lot of talented kids, kids that have a lot of potential. (Preservice teacher in an urban high school)

*S*tand and Deliver. Lean on Me. Dangerous Minds. The Ron Clark Story. *Freedom Writers. Waiting for "Superman."* If you have seen any of these films, then you have witnessed the Hollywood version of "urban schools." They are violent, unpredictable, overcrowded centers with kids and parents who don't care about education or the future. Because the kids don't want to learn, all they need is to be inspired by a hero teacher who shows them that education is the way out of their urban contexts (Ayers, 1996). This sensationalized, stereotypical portrayal of inner-city children is both misconstrued and dangerous. So, then, what is urban teaching like in reality?

WHAT IS URBAN?

"Urban" doesn't mean the exact same thing everywhere. It will vary from context to context. Even within the federal government, urban varies based on the defining body. For example, according to the U.S. Census Bureau (2005), urban means "a continuously built-up area with a population of 50,000 or more. It comprises one or more places—*central place(s)*—and the adjacent densely settled surrounding area—*urban fringe*" (p. 12–1). It classifies locales as urbanized areas, urbanized clusters, and urban growth areas, all based on population size. The Council of the Great City Schools (2011) also uses a quantitative approach, defining urban schools as those "located in cities with populations over 250,000 or student enrollment over 35,000 . . . [or those] located in the largest city of any state" (para. 3). While we are also concerned with the large number of students in urban schools, we also understand that such institutions are about qualitative differences as much as quantitative differences. These qualitative differences are related to urban student characteristics and characteristics of the districts themselves.

Weiner (1993) argues that urban schools are characterized by large, impersonal, bureaucratic school systems hampered by excessive rules and regulations; inadequate funding, overcrowded classrooms, and insufficient numbers of faculty and staff; the greatest concentration of poor, immigrant students who experience hunger, homelessness, and violence in their everyday lives; teachers who do not reside in their students' neighborhoods and are socially isolated from them; curricular and instructional decisions made in central offices; and the most culturally and linguistically diverse student bodies of any school context. Weiner suggests we define "urbanness" on a continuum ranging from the largest cities (New York City and Los Angeles) on one pole to the least urban communities (small, wealthy White suburbs) on the other. Further, Weiner suggests that the qualities of urban *schools* are a different, albeit related, problem from the cultural and academic characteristics and needs of diverse *students*. Clearer definitions of what is meant by urban teaching that encompass all of these issues related to schooling, students, and location are necessary in order to more fully prepare new teachers for urban contexts. Indeed, the "savage inequalities" (Kozol, 1991) within our public school systems, such as minimal financial resources, inadequate facilities and materials, and underqualified staff, as well as the influence of urban systems and school bureaucracies on classroom life, should have a direct connection to how we prepare teachers in teacher education programs.

In this book, we make a concerted effort to distinguish between the commonly interchangeable terms *urban* and *diverse*. As Weiner (1993) notes, by using *inner-city* and *urban* to describe poor minority students, educators have inadvertently encouraged confusion about what makes urban schools, and the preparation to teach in them, special. Part of the confusion comes from the fact that cities have always had the greatest concentrations of poor, immigrant students and of children described at different times in the nation's history as "culturally deprived," "disadvantaged," or "at risk" (p. 13). We do not see *urban* as a culturally acceptable code for black and brown children, but instead as a unique context in which to teach and learn.

It is out of the complexity of the definition of *urban*, and how we see teaching in urban schools as different from teaching in other contexts, that we felt it was important to create this book.

WHY THIS BOOK? WHY NOW?

The purpose of this book is to provide you with an overview of urban teaching. There are so many complex topics with which students new to education should be familiar that these topics are oversimplified and, therefore, misunderstood by students. This text elaborates on questions that all teachers must learn to address, but here the answers specifically focus on the urban context. Our goal was to compile the work of urban education theorists, researchers, and practitioners into one place. The treatment is more succinct than expansive, though multiple topic areas in urban teaching are addressed, and the text blends conceptual and practical approaches. Some may hope to find a "how to" for urban teaching, but we believe that the topic is more complex and that texts that compile a "toolbox" for new urban teachers may do a disservice to the complexity of urban education. Though you may encounter some people who think that teaching in urban schools is too great a challenge or that there is something inherently wrong with urban students, this text is based on the assumption that urban students bring many resources to the school context and serve as a primary source of their teachers' learning about successful and effective education. We have aimed for a thoughtful and thought-provoking book that discusses specific teaching strategies without outlining them as a prescription for improving urban schools and teaching. In this text, we focus on the promise and possibilities of urban teaching.

In our previous work, we argued that "urban teacher learning is not represented by discrete pieces of knowledge but by teachers' grappling with professional decisions that take into account all of their knowledge, skills, commitments, and dispositions while situated within their social context" (Stairs & Donnell, 2010, p. 192). This grappling can be a difficult and lengthy process, but while reading this text, we intend for you to feel prepared to challenge, rather than maintain, the status quo. Urban teachers who defy existing social and bureaucratic structures are especially important now, as we enter into a new decade with a renewed federal focus on high-stakes accountability, testing, and competition. In order to challenge these structures, we feel now, more than ever, that urban teachers must engage in true *praxis,* or "action and reflection . . . upon their world in order to transform it" (Freire, 1970, p. 466).

WHY DID WE CONCEPTUALIZE URBAN TEACHING AROUND EIGHT QUESTIONS?

In our years working and researching in urban schools, we have consistently come back to these eight essential questions that guide our thinking about and understanding of urban teaching.

1. How do urban teachers build upon the resources and attributes students bring to the classroom in order to improve teaching and learning?

2. How do urban teachers create positive learning environments?

3. How does culturally responsive pedagogy improve teaching and learning in urban schools?

4. How do urban teachers best support English language learners?

5. How does taking an inquiry stance on teaching support urban teachers' resilience and success?

6. How do urban teachers teach to the standards without standardizing the curriculum?

7. How do urban teachers work within and around the bureaucracy of urban schools?

8. What is the role of social justice and equity in urban teaching?

As an urban teacher, you will be making connections among *yourself, your students, your commitments, and your context*, which is why we have organized the questions into these four main categories. The figure here depicts the conceptual framework that guides this text. We remind you of each chapter's essential question by including it as the first focus question at the beginning of each chapter.

HOW IS EACH CHAPTER ORGANIZED?

Each chapter begins with a **vignette** about a real teacher, illustrating how current educators synthesize theory, research, and practice. After a series of **focus questions**, we guide you through the theory, research, and practice for each essential question. The **theoretical section** helps you frame conceptual issues. The **research section** focuses on the empirical base and assists you in

Figure I.I Conceptual Framework for Urban Teaching in America

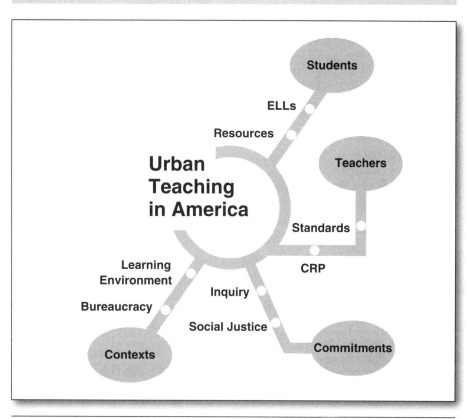

Source: Conceptual framework created by Faith Burgos.

recognizing key questions and current findings. We see theory and research as inextricably linked, so in the theory section, you may see examples of research. We do not intend to share a review of *all* the literature in each area. The studies we highlight in the research section will instead serve as examples of the type of work being done on this topic and what big ideas are coming out of the field. It should be noted that the empirical research base is uneven for each of the chapter topics. We have carefully selected as many representative studies as possible from urban research settings. Some of the research studies include hyperlinks, or a permanent link to an online journal article freely available for you to gain a more in-depth understanding of a particular study and findings.

Each **practice section** is written by two urban teachers who focus on successfully translating theory and research into practice in urban classrooms. We conclude each chapter with a **wrap-up** and two types of **extension activities** (Reflection and Action). One assignment offers all readers the opportunity to reflect on their new knowledge, while the other assignment offers readers working in the field a way to move beyond reflection and apply their learning. Each chapter concludes with **suggested resources** and **references** to enhance your understanding of urban issues.

An important aspect of developing into a successful urban teacher is viewing learning to teach as an ongoing process over one's professional career. We hope that this text helps you acknowledge the challenges while highlighting the promise and possibilities for successful and fulfilling urban teaching. We conclude with a reflection from a preservice teacher in an urban school:

> *This whole year we have learned about how hard things are in urban schools. And it's scary to think about the challenges; will I be overwhelmed and cry every day? I guess that's possible, at first, but I think the more I learn about urban schools, the more I get excited by it, too. There's so much potential and room for hope.*

REFERENCES

Ayers, W. (1996). A teacher ain't nothin' but a hero: Teachers and teaching in film. In W. Ayers & P. Ford (Eds.), *City kids, city teachers: Reports from the front row* (pp. 228–240). New York, NY: New Press.

Council of Great City Schools. (2011). *Fact sheet.* Retrieved from http://www.cgcs.org/about/fact_sheet.aspx

Freire, P. (1970). *Pedagogy of the oppressed.* New York, NY: Seabury Press.

Kozol, J. (1991). *Savage inequalities: Children in America's schools.* New York, NY: Crown.

Donnell, K., & Stairs, A. (2010). Conclusion: Developing synergy between learning and context. In A. J. Stairs & K. A. Donnell (Eds.), *Research on urban teacher learning: Examining contextual factors over time* (pp. 191–197). Charlotte, NC: Information Age.

U.S. Census Bureau. (2005). *Geographic areas reference manual.* Retrieved from http://www.census.gov/geo/www/garm.html

Weiner, L. (1993). *Preparing teachers for urban schools: Lessons from 30 years of school reform.* New York, NY: Teachers College Press.

ACKNOWLEDGMENTS

Urban Teaching in America is the work of many minds, and we are forever grateful to our contributing authors. These practicing teachers remind us about the promise and possibility of urban teaching, and their dedication continues to inspire us. We gratefully acknowledge Andrea Eifrid Avery, Karen Coyle Aylward, Katrin A. Beinroth, Jim Conti, Michael Coppola, Dennis Groenke, Sarah McGee Hess, Tracey Kareemo, Gillian Maimon, Lauren McKinley, Brenda A. Murphy, Danielle Richardson, Laura Rosenfield, Beth Sullivan, and Aileen M. Zeigler. Thank you, too, to the educators who allowed us to share glimpses of their classrooms through each chapter's opening vignette: Lisa Garcia, Melodie Miranda, Brenda A. Murphy, Mei Ou, Susie Planert, Katie Plemmons, Danielle Richardson, Stephanie Reiss, and Virginia Stephenson.

We would also like to thank our SAGE editor, Diane McDaniel; her editorial assistants, Ashley Conlon and Theresa Accomazzo; our production editor, Libby Larson; and our copy editor, Sarah Duffy. Thank you, Diane, for your honest feedback and guidance throughout the publishing process.

Additionally, many thanks to graduate research assistant Monica Chenard at the University of Southern Maine for her professionalism, dedication, and diligence. Monica's scholarship greatly enhanced the research sections of this text. Faith Burgos was our incredibly talented graphic designer (and is Andrea's niece) whose creative and meaningful visual representation serves as our text's conceptual framework. Thank you, Faith.

We appreciate the critical commentary and suggestions of all reviewers, including our anonymous reviewers and the following people:

Paula Arvedson, California State University, Los Angeles

Elinor Brown, University of Kentucky

Cynthia Chapel, Lincoln University

Russell Coward, St. John Fisher College

Glenna Gustafson, Radford University

Janna Jackson-Kellinger, University of Massachusetts, Boston

Virginia Keil, University of Toledo

Kathleen Kesson, Long Island University, Brooklyn Campus

Peg Kritzler, Northwestern University

Cynthia Leung, University of South Florida

Kay C. Reeves, University of Memphis

Amanda Smith, Concordia University, Chicago

Finally, we are indebted to our many colleagues at Boston College, Emory University, Georgia State University, Roger Williams University, the University of Southern Maine, and the University of Tennessee. To our friends and students who choose to teach in urban contexts and make these schools better places: thank you for doing the work that so greatly needs to be done and for doing it with such passion and commitment.

CHAPTER 1

BUILDING UPON STUDENT RESOURCES AND ATTRIBUTES

VIGNETTE: A RESOURCE APPROACH IN ACTION

As the bell rings, Ms. Miranda's high school social studies students are settling into their seats. It is the winter of 2006, and she is about to begin a simulation that transports students to another time period through role play. She begins by handing out and projecting that day's assignment on the overhead: "It is 1880, you are a recent immigrant to New York City, and it is your first day at work in a factory. You, your spouse, and your children all have to work. You enter the factory quietly and await orders."

In a booming tone, Ms. Miranda says, "I'm the factory manager. You are to create shirts on an assembly line. One of you will cut out the shirts, one of you will attach the buttons, and one of you will neatly fold and package the shirts for shipment." She hands out large manila envelopes that include paper photocopies of shirt outlines, pre-cut paper buttons, and glue. The small groups get to work as Ms. Miranda role-plays the manager well, berating them for not working efficiently, for cutting corners, for making only one shirt in the first few minutes. One boy exclaims, "I feel like a slave! Do it yourself!" to which Ms. Miranda replies, "You're fired!" Angered, the student continues, "How am I going to tell my 10 kids I got fired?" The other students giggle at the spontaneous and intense role play by their teacher and classmates. Another boy says, "I'm protesting. Give me paper and a pencil." The girl next to him provides both and asks, "Immigrant, do you know how to read and write?" He makes a sign that reads, "We Need Freedom," tapes it to a ruler, and begins marching around the room. Ms. Miranda encourages him to walk out on the job because she has plenty of immigrants waiting in line outside the door who can take his place.

After several more minutes, Ms. Miranda ends the role play and invites students to express their feelings about being an immigrant in the late 19th century. The conversation takes a turn to modern-day immigration, and the teacher and students focus the rest of the lesson on the struggles and achievements of U.S. immigrants.

Teaching in an urban school with many first- and second-generation immigrants, and being a first-generation immigrant raised in the city herself, Ms. Miranda shares personal stories and invites her students to elaborate on their own experiences or those of their family and close friends who have emigrated to the United States. The lesson is a huge success, drawing students into the class with an entertaining simulation activity that resonated with many of them. Ms. Miranda's lesson reveals her respect for students' lives and their knowledge developed outside of school as an asset for instruction in school.

FOCUS QUESTIONS

- How do urban teachers build upon the resources and attributes students bring to the classroom in order to improve teaching and learning?
- What does it mean to view urban students through an asset lens versus a deficit lens?
- What do successful teachers of urban students know about bringing out the best in their students?
- How might teaching and learning look different when students' lives are valued in the classroom?

Tell some people that you are a new teacher in an urban school and you may hear comments like, "Sorry to hear that. I'm sure that if you just put in your time, you'll get a better job with smarter kids someday," or "That's too bad that someone as intelligent as you has to work with troublemakers who don't appreciate all that you can teach them." In truth, many experienced urban teachers will tell you that there is nowhere else they would rather teach than a city school. Given the negative assumptions and generalizations that abound about urban students, how are some teachers able to thrive? Successful urban teachers recognize the resources and attributes of their students—their gifts, talents, struggles, and dreams—and they use this knowledge to make teaching and learning most effective for all students. This recognition and utilization of students' knowledge is known as a **resource approach** to teaching.

Oakes and Lipton (2007) describe the resource approach in this way:

Teachers who seek to build their teaching on the strengths of communities must question commonly accepted beliefs and practices surrounding ability, race, class, gender, language, difference, and so on. They must sit at the intersection of theory and practice, constantly asking, "Why do we do it this way?" "What assumptions about the communities and cultures of my students underlie these practices?" "Whose interests does this practice serve?" "How might the cultural resources of my students contribute to achieving our educational goals?" (p. 492)

Questioning the status quo is the first step toward building upon students' resources and attributes in order to improve teaching and learning.

Anyon (1997) argues that educational change for urban schools is related to social change. She states that "until the economic and political systems in which the cities are enmeshed are themselves transformed so they may be more democratic and productive for urban residents, educational reformers have little chance of effecting long-lasting educational change in city schools" (p. 13). Though Anyon may be right, urban teachers cannot wait for fundamental social changes to occur. They remain responsible for doing their best to improve students' learning and success in school and life, and most take this responsibility very seriously.

In this chapter, we will consider urban students' lives and family experiences, deficit versus asset perspectives, the concept of meritocracy, the funds of knowledge that urban students bring to the school setting, and special education in urban schools. After presenting relevant research studies, the chapter closes with the stories of two teachers who build upon students' resources to improve teaching and learning.

THEORETICAL FRAMEWORK FOR A RESOURCE APPROACH

Urban Students' Lives and Families

Who are urban students and their families? What constitutes their lives outside of school? Teachers can capitalize on what students bring with them from their homes and communities when they learn more about them. Of course, it is difficult to generalize about any student's day-to-day life outside of school, but demographic and economic trends do shed some light on the lives of typical urban students and their families. The key for a new teacher in an urban school is to understand general trends for families who live in cities and students who would attend city schools, then get to know more about individual students and families (discussed further in the section on funds of knowledge).

About three quarters of PK–12 students in the United States live in cities, which include large or midsize metropolitan areas and the urban fringe of these areas (Chou & Tozer, 2008). Poverty is a challenge for many families living in these urban areas. For example, recent information from Chicago, one of the largest school districts in the country, reveals what conditions outside of school may be like for city students. Chicago enrolls 85.3% low-income children with a 24.8% mobility rate (Chou & Tozer, 2008). This means Chicago schools have an extremely high concentration of poor children, of whom about one in four move between or out of Chicago schools each year. Related to poverty is the highly segregated nature of U.S. cities. Though the Supreme Court ruled to desegregate schools in 1954, U.S. cities have become more segregated over the past two decades. Orfield and Lee (2004) confirm the trend toward segregation in large and small central cities and their suburban rings, citing five states with the most racially segregated schools in the nation: New York, Michigan, Illinois, California, and Texas. More than half of Chicago's schools are over 90% Black or Latino, and 78% are predominantly Black or predominantly Latino. As Chou and Tozer (2008) argue, "This segregation reminds us of an old and tragic lesson: Where separateness prevails, inequality is rarely far behind" (p. 10).

Black children today are significantly more likely to attend a segregated school than they were in any year since 1968, according to Orfield and Lee (2004).

The economic factors that urban families experience present serious challenges to school success. Joblessness is prevalent in urban areas, as are low-wage employment opportunities and poor living conditions (Kopetz, Lease, & Warren-Kring, 2006). The homeless child population grew rapidly in the past few years to one million in 2009 (Salopek, 2010). One in five children has an immigrant parent, and these children are much more likely to live in poverty, possess limited English proficiency, and have parents who have not earned a high school degree (Oakes & Lipton, 2007). This translates into few opportunities for urban students to view models of highly educated, skilled workforce members in their local communities, resulting in a feeling of learned hopelessness about economic security and future life chances among many urban students and their families (Kozol, 1991). Educational opportunities in school can seem unrelated to the actual and potential life paths of urban students.

Weiner's (2006) scholarship and experiences teaching in New York City are valuable when considering urban communities. She argues, "Teachers and students bring attitudes and behaviors to school that they've acquired in living in particular places, and cities are no different from other locales in making their mark on the way we view life and respond to it, in ways that are both potentially positive and negative in a school setting" (p. 60). For example, some urban students may react defensively, either verbally or physically, if they feel they are threatened in any way. This reaction may be dismissed by a teacher as an inherent character flaw, but it may be an understandable, learned response for children who have experienced the harshness of poverty and city life.

Weiner (2006) also explains that there may be legitimate tensions between urban teachers and the students and families served by urban schools.

A teacher's higher social and economic status, as well as position in a school system that for most of its existence legally and openly discriminated against racial minorities, can make teachers appear to be supporters of the status quo, even if they are not. I think that in order to persuade your students and their parents that they will benefit from what you and the school can offer, you must understand their perspective. You need not share their viewpoint, but you need to acknowledge its existence. Generally speaking, you can win their confidence by making intellectual and social space in your classroom for cultural differences, acknowledging that all students bring life experiences, beliefs, and ideas that are no less worthy of examination than your own or those of classmates. (p. 66)

Though there may be obvious differences in worldviews stemming from different life experiences, teachers, students, and families can acknowledge the differences and respect each other's backgrounds and what each brings to the schooling experience. Ignoring these differences benefits no one, least of all the students who need to have teachers who understand them as learners and human beings. (Further discussion of this tendency to ignore differences, often known as **colorblindness**, is presented in Chapter 3.)

Murrell (2001) argues that an accomplished practitioner in an urban setting is a **community teacher**. Community teachers "draw on a richly contextualized knowledge of culture, community, and identity in their professional work with children and families in diverse urban communities" (p. 4). He maintains that any teacher candidate may become a community teacher if given the opportunity to develop and learn from practice-oriented, community-dedicated, and urban-focused teacher education experiences with the guided assistance of more skilled urban practitioners. The notion of the community teacher is grounded in the belief that students bring valuable resources and assets to their classrooms that teachers should acknowledge and incorporate into teaching and learning. It is an example of viewing students, their families, and their communities not from a deficit perspective, but from an asset perspective.

Deficit Versus Asset Perspectives

A **deficit perspective** is held when teachers maintain negative assumptions about students, when they presume that "young Americans who are not white and middle class come to school with deficits that make their school success extremely difficult" (Oakes & Lipton, 2007, p. 55). Teachers who believe that certain students cannot succeed in school because of particular attributes (e.g., they are Black or Hispanic, poor, or non-native English speakers) operate from a deficit perspective. They may also write students off before they come to school or believe that parents and students need to change to fit into an educational system that is assumed to work (Garcia & Guerra, 2004). Some have argued that deficit thinking pervades schools and society to such an extent that some educators may not even realize they hold deficit perspectives.

Donnell (2010) has written about the deficit perspective in this way:

Those who engage in deficit thinking regard student failure as a result of alleged internal deficiencies, such as a lack of intelligence, or socially linked shortcomings such as dysfunctional family situations. The popular "at risk" construct views urban children and their families as responsible for urban school failure. The deficit paradigm is highly counterproductive and fails to capitalize on the positive and powerful opportunities available in urban education. When we acknowledge that there is nothing "wrong" with urban students or their families or their communities, we must ask if the problem has been in the type of schools we have been providing for them. (p. 162)

What Donnell stresses here is that what is "wrong" may be within the curriculum and the system of urban schooling, not with the students. Donnell's perspective reminds us that operating from a deficit paradigm allows teachers only to see what is "wrong" with their students rather than critiquing the system and building upon what is "right."

How do teachers develop deficit perspectives about urban students? Teaching has been described as autobiographical (Bullough, Knowles, & Crow, 1991; Nieto, 2003) and research suggests that teachers' beliefs may be difficult to alter or change (Clift & Brady, 2005; Kagan, 1992; Pajares, 1992). Therefore, teachers may have deeply personal and ingrained assumptions about schooling based on their individual experiences, including cultural expectations about schooling. When these experiences do not match the reality of their teaching context, the mismatch can lead to deficit views. Urban teachers may also be socialized into stereotypical, deficit models from the school culture, context, and conditions in which they operate. We believe that individuals go into urban teaching because they care about children and educational opportunity and equity, not because they hold inherently negative views about children in urban schools. Therefore, it is important to help new urban teachers examine their own autobiographies, question their related beliefs and assumptions, and develop new ways of viewing difference that move from deficit to asset paradigms.

An **asset perspective** is characterized by teachers recognizing the resources students bring with them and believing they can and will succeed in school. These teachers do not view their students as deficient or see their families and communities as problems. They recognize the assets students bring to school and build upon them. For example, one urban teacher recognized that her high school seniors possessed strong literacy skills in their first language and were still striving toward literacy skills in English (Stairs, 2010). She modified curriculum and instruction to allow first language use in her classroom in a state that required English be the only language used for instruction. She continued to speak English only with her students, but she allowed them to use academic search engines to find literary criticism articles in their native language, write early drafts of papers in their native language, and share their ideas with partners who spoke the same language. By paying attention to the literacy skills her students possessed rather than assuming they were incapable of the assignment, she allowed her students access to high-level academic work that may not have been possible without recognizing and building upon their assets. The same could be said for Ms. Miranda, the teacher whose vignette opened this chapter. Ms. Miranda knew that many of her students were first- or second-generation immigrants and that some had family members working low-wage factory jobs. Rather than seeing this as a problem that would inhibit their learning, she used this information to help students access concepts of late-19th-century immigration and the industrial revolution.

To underscore the importance of the asset perspective in urban teaching, Donnell (2010) applies an **ecological orientation**. The ecological approach "views school life and classroom teaching as occurring within interconnected webs of settings and institutions that transcend classroom and school borders" (p. 162). This orientation underscores how isolated factors do not influence schooling so much as the whole of the socially and culturally organized environment. If the students are at the center of the web of factors (the classroom, the family, the school, the community, the society), teachers' positive view of their assets is the critical starting point for improving their educational experience.

Weiner (2010) suggests that "school practices and assumptions emerging from the deficit paradigm often hide student and teacher abilities. An impersonal, bureaucratic school culture undercuts many of the teaching attitudes and behaviors that draw on student strengths" (p. 70). Therefore, it is imperative that urban teachers recognize deficit thinking, critique the underlying assumptions of the perspective, and move forward with a positive perspective that focuses on students' assets to improve teaching and learning.

The Myth of Meritocracy

The term **meritocracy** refers to the assumption that, with hard work and determination, all individuals can achieve whatever they desire. As the name implies, success directly correlates with **merit**, defined as observable and demonstrable competence. It is more colloquially known as the "pull yourself up by your bootstraps" philosophy: If you work hard enough, you can achieve anything. Those who do not display the same level of talent and competence should not expect the same levels of success. Some argue that meritocracy is a natural result of a democratically organized society. However, others argue that meritocracy neutralizes real historical and institutional factors that privilege some individuals while systemically discriminating against others. McNamee and Miller (2004) assert that the principle of meritocracy is closely related to the concept of the "American Dream."

Unlike European societies historically dominated by hereditary aristocracies, the ideal in America was that its citizens were "free" to achieve on their own merits. . . . Reflecting the reality of their life circumstances, nonwhites and those with less income are more likely to identify "family background," "who you know," and "discrimination" as relevant factors in where people end up in the system. (p. 2)

The **myth of meritocracy**, then, refers to a critique of the overarching notion that hard work always leads to success. Oakes and Lipton (2007) explain:

The problem with the myth of merit is that it presumes a basic equality of opportunity and resources for success, and that the only variable is that of individual merit. . . . The United States is plagued by inequalities, such as disparities in safe neighborhoods, decent housing, adequate health care, and sufficient school resources; many of these inequalities are in domains that affect children's success in school. Notably, even the most meritorious schoolchildren have very little control over these structural inequalities. So, although meritorious qualities occur with no less frequency in low-income families and among blacks, Latinos, and immigrants, inequality limits the degree to which members of these groups can parlay qualities like determination and hard work into school success and enhanced life chances. (p. 52)

One example illuminated in recent years is college admissions in the United States. Though colleges have been attempting to "level the playing field" and allow more students from more backgrounds the opportunity to achieve a higher education degree, elite schools are still primarily admitting upper-middle-class and wealthy students, sometimes as a result of their parents having attended the college. These students, known as legacies of the college, have a distinct advantage in admissions. Students who come from homes where their parents have not attended or completed college, including many urban students, are at a distinct disadvantage by not having the same connections. This calls into question the notion that a meritocracy exists in American education and underscores the importance of admissions policies that aim to diversify college campuses. (See Wise, 2003, about how racial preference did not arise from affirmative action programs in college admissions, but rather has a long history of privileging Whites in society more generally.)

Another example of the myth of meritocracy relates directly to urban education and opportunity to learn (defined below; Darling-Hammond, 2010). It has been well documented that the quality of education in urban and suburban

Many believe that meritocracy exists, but in reality legacy admissions and other opportunities often tip the scale in favor of students whose parents and families are socially connected, rather than provide a truly equal playing field for students from all backgrounds.

schools is quite different in inequitable ways. Urban schools are more likely to offer "test-prep pedagogy" (McNeil, 2000) as a matter of course, where preparation for high-stakes tests becomes the curriculum, rather than the rich, meaningful, authentic learning opportunities typical of suburban schools. We have often heard our urban teacher colleagues bemoan the fact that they work tirelessly to get their students accepted and enrolled in postsecondary education, only to have those students return home the next year sharing how underprepared they were for the intellectual and creative demands of college-level work. Feeling unable to keep up with their classmates, the teachers tell us that their former students leave college and enter the workforce with only their high school diplomas for a credential. These students worked hard to earn a place in college, but the lack of consistent opportunities for high-level, college-preparatory curriculum, instruction, and assessment in K–12 urban education has left them unable to compete with other students who had multiple, varied opportunities to learn in ways congruent with college expectations. Recent research has confirmed what urban teachers have told us all along (e.g., Carey, 2008).

Many scholars focus on **opportunity to learn** (OTL) as a critical factor in school success. Darling-Hammond (2010) has been advocating for OTL standards in addition to state content learning standards. OTL standards would include "the availability of well-qualified teachers; strong curriculum opportunities; books, materials, and equipment (such as science labs and computers); and adequate facilities" (pp. 309–310). If urban students do not have access to these opportunities that support content learning, it is less likely they will succeed even though they may work very hard.

Hardworking, capable, determined individuals may end up succeeding more often in school and in society, but the real question for urban students is whether they are afforded the same opportunities to work hard and display their competence and capabilities as students who come from more privileged backgrounds. MacLeod's (2009) ethnographic study of low-income boys provides an excellent critique of schools and American society as meritocracies. MacLeod followed two groups of neighborhood boys from their teenage years into adulthood and middle age. His research revealed how poverty is perpetuated and social inequality is reproduced from generation to generation. Effective urban teachers deconstruct the myth of meritocracy that pervades American society in order to help their students understand the challenges and opportunities available to them.

Funds of Knowledge

The term **funds of knowledge** refers to "a systematic and powerful way to represent communities in terms of resources, the wherewithal they possess, and how to harness these resources for classroom teaching" (Gonzalez, Moll, & Amanti, 2005, p. x). It represents an asset perspective on what families pass on to their children explicitly or implicitly. The assumption that underlies this approach, as described by Gonzalez et al., is "based on a simple premise: People are competent, they have knowledge, and their life experiences have given them that knowledge" (p. x). These scholars argue that a primary purpose of approaching teaching from a funds-of-knowledge approach is "to alter perceptions of working-class or poor communities and to view these households primarily in terms of their strengths and resources (or funds of knowledge) as their defining pedagogical characteristic" (p. x). They believe that, even in the face of current accountability demands and high-stakes testing pressures, this approach to pedagogy is relevant and useful. As a result of their ongoing research over the past two decades, they have produced some of the seminal research on this topic.

In Moll, Amanti, Neff, and Gonzalez's (1992) work, teachers were invited to be coresearchers in conducting household studies and examining the funds of knowledge possessed and accessed by Mexican families in the southwestern United States. The researchers explain how families' funds of knowledge were broad and diverse. For example, families possessed knowledge of agriculture and mining, as evidenced by their experiences with ranching, farming, soil and irrigation systems, crop planting, and timbering. Families possessed knowledge of economics, as evidenced by appraising, renting and selling, and familiarizing themselves with labor laws, accounting, and building codes. Families possessed knowledge of contemporary and folk medicine, as evidenced by first aid procedures, midwifery, and herbal knowledge. The funds-of-knowledge paradigm views these and other forms of knowledge as important in their own right, not simply as support for or "add-ons" to the sanctioned school curriculum.

Lee (2007) and Weiner (2006) have extended the funds-of-knowledge approach in education. Lee's **cultural modeling theory** is an anti-deficit model positing that out-of-school knowledge should be used to acquire in-school knowledge (Howard, 2010). Weiner (2006) has applied the funds-of-knowledge concept to teaching in urban schools. She has been critical of calling urban students "street smart" because it assumes that "the astuteness and maturity that children have developed living in a demanding environment aren't applicable to the learning that should occur in school" (p. 61). Weiner advocates for teachers learning about and being respectful of students' city lifestyles. She says that teachers who do so may describe their students not as "street smart" but simply "smart." This approach legitimizes the knowledge that students bring with them to school.

Brian Schultz (2008) provides an example of creating curriculum along with your students by capitalizing on their funds of knowledge. When he was a teacher at a Chicago public school located next to the Cabrini Green housing project, he engaged his fifth-grade students in a class activity to identify problems affecting them. After coming up with 89 problems they felt impacted their day-to-day lives in the city, the students decided the most pressing issue for them was their inadequate school building, and they wanted a new school. Schultz describes how "the students' action plan became the epicenter of the entire curriculum for the remainder of the school year" (p. 7). Students and teacher engaged in cross-curricular learning in authentic ways, all because the teacher valued what students knew about their neighborhood and their lives outside of school and invited this knowledge into the classroom to further their learning. Schultz's students told him that prior to their fifth-grade year with him, their strengths and abilities learned outside of school were not valued or nurtured. Schultz argues, "If education was measured by the students' successes in their neighborhood via their own lived experiences, many would outperform their more affluent peers, not to mention their teachers" (p. 6). By using students' funds of knowledge, he transformed the curriculum, and students learned about the potential of political and social action.

Scholars have acknowledged that some school subject areas may draw rather seamlessly from students' funds of knowledge (e.g., social studies, language arts), but other subject areas may not be so easily incorporated (e.g., mathematics, science). Gonzalez, Andrade, Civil, and Moll (2001) say, "We had found that a linear transference of mathematical knowledge from household to classroom was problematic. Yet, we were aware that deep and rich mathematical processes were being tapped in the forms of constructions, buildings, landscapes, gardens, and clothing" (p. 120). They explain the mathematical processes involved with sewing as an example of how advanced mathematical processes are used by seamstresses, though not recognized as such. The potential for learning from day-to-day lived experiences is possible even with math, though perhaps not in the same linear ways math is taught in school. The funds-of-knowledge approach respects local knowledge and uses it to enhance and improve teaching and learning.

Special Education in Urban Schools

One group that is often marginalized and viewed from a deficit rather than an asset perspective is students identified for special education services. The Individuals with Disabilities Education Improvement Act of 2004 (known as IDEA 2004) reauthorized the original IDEA law requiring that students with disabilities receive a free and appropriate public education in the least restrictive environment from birth to age 21. This means that students should have the support they need to work on curriculum materials alongside their nondisabled peers as much as possible. Morse (2001) argues that curriculum and instruction for special education students look different depending on the school context—urban, suburban, or rural. He argues that "inner cities face unique challenges" (p. 5), such as how to provide the least restrictive environment when full inclusion of special education students in general education classes requires additional resources in an environment where resources are especially scare. Resources that provide for certified teachers, paraprofessionals, and planning time are necessary for inclusion settings but often cannot be fulfilled by urban districts.

Additionally, there continues to be evidence that poor, African American, and Latino students—who primarily populate urban schools—have been disproportionately placed in special education programs. Blanchett (2009) argues that "special education is the new tool for the resegregation of African American and other students of color in special education" (p. 370). For example, in Georgia, while Black students made up 39% of the special education population in 2009–2010, they made up 47% of students classified as having emotional or behavioral disorders and 57% of students classified as having intellectual disabilities. Are there urban students who need special education services? Absolutely. But why is it that the number of urban students who are identified for special education is disproportionately high compared to students in other schools?

Some believe that minority students are overidentified in special education, particularly classified as mentally retarded or emotionally disturbed, as a result of systemic racism and that minority students who *are* properly designated for special education services receive poorer services than White students (Losen & Orfield, 2002). Data have revealed that urban special education students are more likely to be taught in separate classrooms rather than educated with the general education population, which is troubling as special education students included in general education classrooms tend to perform better than peers in pull-out settings and have higher achievement test scores, among other positive educational outcomes (Kozleski & Smith, 2009). Urban special education students need culturally responsive practices in both pull-out and general education settings as well as highly prepared, fully licensed special education teachers, who are often in short supply (Blanchett, 2009).

One issue receiving recent attention is how to determine whether an English language learner (ELL) needs special education services. Many school-based personnel have a difficult time distinguishing a language disability from normal second language development. This results in some ELLs being overidentified or underidentified for special education services. Zetlin, Beltran, Salcido, Gonzalez, and Reyes (2010) argue, "An equitable, culturally and linguistically sensitive assessment plan should include evaluation of background variables such as first and second language proficiency (including receptive and expressive assessment in both languages), language dominance, and educational history including exposure to bilingual and/or ELD models, immigration pattern, socioeconomic status (SES), and cultural background" (p. 61). This comprehensive assessment plan is often not in place, presenting many challenges to appropriately identifying ELLs with or without special needs. Urban teachers should work closely with other school personnel to advocate for effective and comprehensive assessments of ELLs who may need special education services and ensure that they are placed in classrooms where their learning needs may be met.

Morse (2001) states that "urban school personnel can be assured that they will continuously be challenged to create a comprehensive curriculum that meets the presenting needs of urban special education students" (p. 15). We agree, and we suggest that it is critical for urban teachers to consider how special education students are advantaged or disadvantaged in their schools and to advocate for equitable, nondiscriminatory practices for identifying, instructing, and assessing these students.

WHAT THE RESEARCH SAYS
ABOUT A RESOURCE APPROACH

The body of research on adopting a resource approach to teaching in urban schools is still developing. Research has confirmed several benefits to a resource approach (Donnell, 2007; Gay, 2010; Love & Kruger, 2005; Quartz & TEP Research Group, 2003; Storz & Nestor, 2008):

- Activating students' prior knowledge increases learning.
- Drawing upon students' interests improves engagement.
- An asset perspective creates an inclusive classroom climate and a sense of belonging.
- A resource approach challenges the status quo and creates democratic classrooms.

This section reviews some examples of representative research on resource approaches toward teaching. Cucchiara and Horvat (2009) investigated the involvement of parents in urban schools. Through a qualitative investigation and comparison of two urban elementary schools, it was noted that there is variation in both amount and type of parental involvement. This involvement ranged from a collective approach to an individualistic approach. Also, parents of students in urban schools were identified as possible catalysts for positive change in the school environment. Donnell (2007) investigated, through a longitudinal interview method, the means by which urban teachers learn to teach. Beginning teachers in urban schools that focused on the mutual learning of teachers and pupils developed a strong sense of efficacy that holds with them throughout their teaching careers. Moll and colleagues' (1992) study of low-income Mexican American households examined funds of knowledge available for developing innovations in teaching that drew upon the knowledge and skills found in the households. By visiting homes and documenting the wealth of knowledge available in the community, teacher researchers discovered that teachers and parents could equally share their family and school expertise. K. Schultz, Jones-Walker, and Chikkatur (2008) followed four teachers from the same teacher education program over two years to determine how they implemented a "listening stance"—using knowledge of students' strengths and needs to plan classroom instruction. The teachers in the study struggled to enact what they learned about students in the face of standardized core curriculum in math and reading; however, "teachers negotiated small moments of time to bring students' voices and interests into the classroom" (p. 181). Upadhyay's (2005) study of one urban elementary school science teacher using students' funds of knowledge for teaching reveals how the framework can be applied with science content. Upadhyay found that students' experiences and knowledge paired with science content led to enhanced learning. Finally, Whitney, Leonard, Camelio, and Camelio's (2006) study shares students' perspectives about good urban teaching. See Table 1.1.

Table 1.1   Research Studies on Taking a Resource Approach in Teaching

Author(s)	Purpose	Findings	Implications	URL
Cucchiara & Horvat (2009)	Researchers aimed to discover what motivates parent involvement in urban public schools; how this involvement affects the teacher's methods, classroom management and relationships; and how it affects students' success in the classroom.	Parents fell along a continuum, ranging from strongly individualistic to collective when interacting with the school. Parents were found to bring a variety of resources to urban schools; one of the most significant was that they acted as catalysts for change. Collective approaches were more successful in improving children's school-related experiences.	This study indicates that parent involvement in urban schools can bring significant resources to the school. Their commitment to the well-being of all of the children, values, and social justice points to the importance of parent involvement in urban schools.	http://aer .sagepub.com/ content/46/4/974 .full.pdf+html
Donnell (2007)	The researcher explored how beginning teachers learn to teach in urban	Teachers who were able to learn both with and from their students	Teachers preparing for urban schools should be given support in	http://uex .sagepub.com/ content/42/3/ 223.full .pdf+html

Author(s)	Purpose	Findings	Implications	URL
	schools and to connect their learning to their daily practice.	experienced a greater sense of efficacy. Beginning teachers in urban schools benefited from individualized support in generating knowledge regarding teaching in these schools.	learning both about their students and from their students, while at the same time providing these students with an education. Student achievement in urban schools rests on urban teachers' transformative teaching practices. These practices can be developed via various initiatives in teacher education for both preservice and practicing teachers.	
Moll, Amanti, Neff, & Gonzalez (1992)	Teacher researchers sought to develop innovations in teaching that drew upon the knowledge and skills found in local households.	Learning about low-income Mexican American families' household funds of knowledge allowed teachers to see beyond stereotypes and experiment with practice.	It is feasible and useful to have teachers visit households for research purposes. By assuming the role of learner, teachers establish new, more symmetrical relationships with parents.	

(Continued)

Table 1.1 (Continued)

Author(s)	Purpose	Findings	Implications	URL
K. Schultz, Jones-Walker, & Chikkatur (2008)	Researchers conducted a two-year ethnographic study to examine how four new elementary teachers listened to students and made decisions about instruction.	The teachers listened to individual students, the rhythm and balance of the classroom, and the community and cultural contexts, but struggled to find ways to adapt mandated curricula and transform their teaching practice.	New teachers must be explicitly taught how to negotiate the multiple demands and contradictions of urban teaching.	
Upadhyay (2005)	The researcher observed one fourth-grade teacher to determine how she integrated her students' life experiences with her own to make science meaningful for them.	The teacher made her students feel that their questions, ideas, experience, and knowledge were integral to science learning. The teacher used students' funds of knowledge to introduce new science concepts and recognized that science involves connections between many concepts and everyday experiences.	The science curriculum available may have an impact on how well teachers draw upon students' funds of knowledge. (The "Linking Food and the Environment" curriculum was successful.)	

Author(s)	Purpose	Findings	Implications	URL
Whitney, Leonard, Camelio, & Camelio (2006)	Researchers surveyed urban high school students to determine attributes of teachers they admired and classes they felt most comfortable in.	Students' responses indicated three themes about good teaching: personal connections (teachers know students), universality (teachers help all students learn), and balance (teachers are strict but firm).	Urban teachers should access their students as experts in identifying strengths and areas of improvement for schools and teacher education programs.	

PRACTICE

In this section, practicing urban teachers **Dennis Groenke** and **Gillian Maimon** reflect on how they build upon the resources and attributes students bring to the classroom in order to improve teaching and learning. Dennis teaches middle school science in Knoxville, Tennessee, and Gillian teaches first grade in Philadelphia, Pennsylvania. Their firsthand accounts illuminate the theory and research that were reviewed earlier in this chapter.

Dennis explains how he uses what he knows about students' strong community ties to enhance his science teaching.

Dennis: Many of my students live in the same neighborhood in close proximity to the school. More than half of them walk to school. Therefore, they tend to have strong social networks outside of the school that I can build on in my classroom. My students hang out with each other in neighborhood public parks or laundromats, for example, so they develop social bonds. Mostly this is positive (sometimes negative), but either way there are communally shared experiences that the students bring to my class. They know each other's families, histories, stories. They are used to being together, and this camaraderie is something I build on in the classroom to create positive learning experiences. For example, I have the students work a lot in cooperative lab groups—to look at microscope slides, discuss cell parts, prepare lab reports. I use my evolving understandings of students' out-of-school social relationships to make decisions about groupings. I tend to let friends work together, as I've found this promotes more engagement and participation. Also, I like to draw from the students' knowledge of and awareness about their neighborhood and community landscapes to create teachable moments. As an example, recently a corner appliance store burned down, exposing a hillside that had been excavated to make room for the building. I took pictures of this and used them to teach science concepts (e.g., erosion, sedimentation, types of rock, phototropism). This really engaged the students, as they all recognized where the building had been. After the lesson, some students walked by the hillside to see it for themselves.

I also spend some time with students trying to get them to take pride in their communities and neighborhoods. During our conservation unit ("Reduce, Reuse, Recycle"), we adopt our school grounds as a "green zone." We collect all loose debris; sort everything we collect into paper, plastic, or scrap metal; weigh it; and then recycle it. This makes an impact—I hear students complain about how fast the school gets "trashed" again.

Like Dennis, as Gillian determines her students' assets and resources, she considers what she knows about students, their families, and their communities. Here she reflects on one particular experience the day before school started for the year.

Gillian: As I worked to prepare the classroom for the arrival of the children the next day, a mother walked into the room. She asked if I was Teacher Gill and I told her yes. She may not have known me, but she had been on my radar screen for years. My first year at the school was also the year that her oldest child had entered kindergarten. The boy immediately attracted the alarm of his teacher because, at the age of five, he was not yet toilet trained. This fact, as well as other developmental delays and signs of neglect, prompted a great deal of concern about the child's home situation. When the mother began making surprise visits to the classroom, her emaciated appearance and unfocused eyes left little doubt about one of the sources of problems at home. Over the years, we have been able to chart the status of the mother's heroin addiction simply by eyeballing her physical state. On this day, her coloring appeared good and she was carrying more meat on her bones than I had observed in the past.

This year, I was to be the teacher of Danny, her second son. Her third child, a daughter, was in a different teacher's first-grade room. Because Danny had spent two years in kindergarten, he was now in the same grade as his sister, though the girl was a year younger than her brother. I confess that, at the end of last year, when I saw Danny's name on my new class list, I asked our principal if it might be possible to assign him to a different classroom. It was not that I worried about teaching the child. (From all I had seen of him, he appeared to be an eager learner.) Rather, I had concerns about my ability to treat the mother with patience and respect.

This was hardly the first time that I had taught the child of a drug-addicted parent. What was new for me in this circumstance was that the mother happened to be White. I had not been aware of the numb resignation with which I regarded non-White addicted parents until this mother evoked in me such a visceral sense of revulsion. Clearly my repugnance for this parent was not an appropriate reaction (nor, for that matter, was the remove I had felt from the non-White parents), but it was a true one. Perhaps the greatest peril (and, at times, the greatest reward) of the work that I do is that I cannot help but be human in the way that I experience each day. It would be a challenge to keep my emotions from contaminating my interactions with this parent.

As it turned out, the mother had simply come to request an advance copy of the supply list I would be sending home with the children on the first day of school. She intended to go shopping over the weekend and wanted to make sure that she made the appropriate purchases. I was both relieved that her request was such a reasonable—indeed productive—one and ashamed that I had feared it might have been otherwise.

Gillian's ability to look inward and be honest about her negative assumptions reveals her highly developed reflective stance, a necessity for a successful urban teacher. She also has purposefully committed to school rules that do not align with rules of the neighborhood, as she shares in the next excerpt.

Gillian: My rule against hitting back is sometimes at odds with what children are told at home. When a child tells me, "But my mom told me that if somebody hits me, I should hit back," I say, "Then hit him back at your house, because the rules here at school are different." This is one instance when I do not attempt to build a bridge between school and home. I recognize that there are good reasons that some children's parents advise them to deal with problems in this way, not the least of which is that, in the context of the neighborhood, a child who doesn't fight back is seen to be a ripe target. But school should be a place in which revenge need not be a child's only way to feel defended. Children should be able to trust that their teachers will step in and deal with any child who is causing them physical harm. I know that as students get older, teachers have less and less power as authority figures and hence are less effective defenders of children. But in an elementary school like mine, in which even the hardest-headed children still want to be loved by their teachers, there is no reason for the code of the neighborhood to supersede the school's determination of what defines appropriate behavior.

Gillian clearly understands that life in city neighborhoods may require children to develop some defensive tactics in order to survive, but to create a school environment where students can thrive, she explains the different code of conduct she expects. She is teaching her students how to behaviorally "code-switch" depending on the context. She is also creating a safe, loving climate where kids can feel protected. New urban teachers can learn from Gill's thoughtfulness when making decisions about teaching and learning.

Dennis also reveals thoughtfulness as he decides that his middle school science students can appropriately engage with popular culture to enhance their learning.

Dennis: Another resource my students bring to the classroom is their keen knowledge of popular media. Again, sometimes this can be both positive and negative (as we don't want kids watching too much TV). But I have learned I can build on this knowledge to engage students and teach science concepts. For example, lots of my students like the show *Dirty Jobs* on the Discovery Channel. In each episode, host Mike Rowe takes on some of the dirtiest jobs in the country, such as making homemade cheese and cleaning zoo cages. In one episode, Rowe took on the job of collecting owl pellets (which is owl vomit). The pellets are sold to schools for science dissection activities. I do an activity with owl pellets and show the episode before we start. Students love it. The show is funny, but perhaps more important, the students see how the pellets are obtained, cleaned, and processed. And they feel the lesson is immediately relevant. This is probably one of the more popular activities I do all year. I pair up with the language arts teacher and we teach Carl Hiassen's young adult novel *Hoot*, which is about an endangered species of owl. This is a nice way to bridge content areas—students learn about the anatomy and digestion habits of owls and then read about owls and their increasingly endangered habitats in the book.

Another media source popular with students is cartoons. When I showed an excerpt this year of Al Gore's *An Inconvenient Truth* during a conservation unit, many students recognized the cartoon *Futurama* that Gore uses to make points about global warming. The fact that my students knew a cartoon that Gore was using seemed to validate the content for them. They recognized the media source and seemed to connect to the information. I referred to the cartoon several times as we moved through the unit, building on these connections.

Dennis's excerpt reveals his attention to students' prior knowledge when designing his curriculum units. By building bridges between known information and new information, all students can experience success in school. Gillian and Dennis are two urban teachers who recognize students' assets and resources to be utilized in their teaching.

WRAP UP

This chapter has focused on putting a resource perspective at the forefront in urban teaching. You have read about the realities of urban students' lives and families, the difference between deficit and asset perspectives, the myth of meritocracy, funds of knowledge, and the overrepresentation of urban minorities in special education.

Certainly there are real challenges, struggles, and disappointments evident in urban education today. There are teachers, administrators, and other school personnel who view urban students and their families from a deficit perspective and believe that American society truly operates as a meritocracy. Effective urban teachers can be mindful of the challenges while, at the same time, making a concerted decision to focus on the assets their students bring from their homes and communities into the classroom. Real-life experiences can improve teaching and learning in urban schools, and new urban teachers can successfully connect with their students and promote learning. Cornbleth (2008), who conducted a study of novice urban teachers, shares our worldview on the potentials of drawing upon student resources in the urban classroom: "Rather than add-ons or a 'bag of tricks,' think of tailoring teaching to better fit our students and build on their strengths, teaching as custom-made or 'designer' rather than mass-produced or 'off the rack'" (p. 145). We believe that each urban teacher has the potential to create a designer classroom where all students thrive and succeed.

EXTENSION ACTIVITIES

Reflection

1. Reflect on your prior schooling and life experiences. How would you describe your opportunities to learn? Were there ever moments when you noticed discrepancies between your opportunities and those of students in other classrooms, schools, or districts? Do you think you operated in a meritocratic system, or did you or others you know have advantages without seemingly working hard for them? Provide specific examples to support your response.

Action

1. What are some resources and assets your current students bring to the classroom? How can you adapt your curriculum to draw on these assets and enhance your instruction? Provide specific examples of student resources and the related curricular modifications you will make and why.

2. Conduct a modified Equity Audit of your school. Find all the data available about teachers, programs, and achievement. Look for teacher experience, mobility, and education; demographics for special, gifted and talented, and bilingual education, as well as discipline referrals; achievement test performance (state and SAT/ACT/AP/IB tests), dropout rates, and graduation tracks. Analyze what the data reveal about equity and learning opportunities in your school. How might you draw upon local communities to make your school more equitable? Create a plan of action. (See Skrla, McKenzie, & Scheurich, 2009, for a full description of Equity Audits.)

SUGGESTED RESOURCES

Books

Gonzalez, N., Moll, L. C., & Amanti, C. (Eds.). (2005). *Funds of knowledge: Theorizing practices in households, communities, and classrooms.* Mahwah, NJ: Lawrence Erlbaum.

McNamee, S. J., & Miller, R. K., Jr. (2004). *The meritocracy myth.* Lanham, MD: Rowman & Littlefield.

Valencia, R. (Ed.). (1997). *The origins of deficit thinking: Educational thought and practice.* London, UK: Falmer Press.

Weiner, L. (2006). *Urban teaching: The essentials.* New York, NY: Teachers College Press.

Websites

The Council of the Great City Schools (www.cgcs.org)
A national organization exclusively representing the needs of urban public schools since 1956. The website offers many resources, including a link to the organization's newsletter, *Urban Educator.*

Rethinking Schools (www.rethinkingschools.org)
A progressive education journal that balances classroom practice with theory and emphasizes socially just solutions to urban school problems.

Teaching Tolerance (www.tolerance.org/magazine/archives)
An award-winning magazine dedicated to reducing prejudice and promoting equity.

REFERENCES

Anyon, J. (1997). *Ghetto schooling: A political economy of urban educational reform.* New York, NY: Teachers College Press.

Blanchett, W. J. (2009). A retrospective examination of urban education: From Brown to resegregation of African Americans in special education—it's time to "go for broke." *Urban Education, 44,* 370–388. doi:10.1177/0042085909338688

Bullough, R. V., Knowles, J. G., & Crow, N. A. (1991). *Emerging as a teacher.* London, UK: Routledge.

Carey, K. (2008). *Graduation rate watch: Making minority student success a priority.* Retrieved from http://www.educationsector.org/research/research_show.htm?doc_id=678433

Chou, V., & Tozer, S. (2008). What's urban got to do with it? The meanings of urban in teacher preparation and development. In F. P. Peterman (Ed.), *Partnering to prepare urban teachers: A call to activism* (pp. 1–20). New York, NY: Peter Lang.

Clift, R. T., & Brady, P. (2005). Research on methods courses and field experiences. In M. Cochran-Smith & K. Zeichner (Eds.), *Studying teacher education* (pp. 309–424). Mahwah, NJ: Lawrence Erlbaum.

Cornbleth, C. (2008). *Diversity and the new teacher: Learning from experience in urban schools.* New York, NY: Teachers College Press.

Cucchiara, M. B., & Horvat, E. M. (2009). Perils and promises: Middle-class parental involvement in urban schools. *American Educational Research Journal, 46,* 974–1004. doi:10.3102/0002831209345791

Darling-Hammond, L. (2010). *The flat world and education: How America's commitment to equity will determine our future.* New York, NY: Teachers College Press.

Donnell, K. A. (2007). Getting to we: Developing a transformative teaching practice. *Urban Education, 42,* 223–249. doi:10.1177/0042085907300541

Donnell, K. A. (2010). Beyond the deficit paradigm: An ecological orientation to thriving in urban schools. In A. S. Canestrari & B. A. Marlowe (Eds.), *Educational foundations: An anthology of critical readings* (2nd ed., pp. 161–167). Thousand Oaks, CA: Sage.

Garcia, S. B., & Guerra, P. L. (2004). Deconstructing deficit thinking: Working with educators to create more equitable learning environments. *Education and Urban Society, 36,* 150–168. doi:10.1177/0013124503261322

Gay, G. (2010). *Culturally responsive teaching: Theory, research, and practice* (2nd ed.). New York, NY: Teachers College Press.

Gonzalez, N., Andrade, R., Civil, M., & Moll, L. (2001). Bridging funds of knowledge: Creating zones of practices in mathematics. *Journal of Education for Students Placed at Risk, 61,* 115–132. doi:10.1207/S15327671ESPR0601-2_7

Gonzalez, N., Moll, L. C., & Amanti, C. (Eds.). (2005). *Funds of knowledge: Theorizing practices in households, communities, and classrooms.* Mahwah, NJ: Lawrence Erlbaum.

Howard, T. C. (2010). *Why race and culture matter in schools: Closing the achievement gap in America's classrooms.* New York, NY: Teachers College Press.

Individuals with Disabilities Education Improvement Act of 2004, Pub. L. No. 108–446. (2004).

Kagan, D. M. (1992). Implications of research on teacher belief. *Educational Psychology, 27,* 65–90. doi:10.1207/s15326985ep2701_6

Kopetz, P. B., Lease, A. J., & Warren-Kring, B. Z. (2006). *Comprehensive urban education.* Boston, MA: Pearson.

Kozleski, E. B., & Smith, A. (2009). The complexities of systems change in creating equity for students with disabilities in urban schools. *Urban Education, 44,* 427–451. doi:10.1177/0042085909337595

Kozol, J. (1991). *Savage inequalities: Children in America's schools.* New York, NY: Crown.

Lee, C. D. (2007). *Culture, literacy, and learning: Blooming in the midst of the whirlwind.* New York, NY: Teachers College Press.

Losen, D. J., & Orfield, G. (2002). *Racial inequity in special education.* Cambridge, MA: Harvard Education Press.

Love, A., & Kruger, A. C. (2005). Teacher beliefs and student achievement in urban schools serving African American students. *Journal of Educational Research, 99*(2), 87–98. doi:10.3200/JOER.99.2.87-98

MacLeod, J. (2009). *Ain't no makin' it: Aspirations and attainment in a low-income neighborhood* (3rd ed.). Boulder, CO: Westview Press.

McNamee, S. J., & Miller, R. K., Jr. (2004). *The meritocracy myth.* Lanham, MD: Rowman & Littlefield.

McNeil, L. M. (2000). *Contradictions in school reform: Educational costs of standardized testing.* New York, NY: Routledge.

Moll, L. C., Amanti, C., Neff, D., & González, N. (1992). Funds of knowledge for teaching: Using a qualitative approach to connect homes and classrooms. *Theory Into Practice, 31,* 132–141. doi:10.1080/00405849209543534

Morse, T. E. (2001). Designing appropriate curriculum for special education students in urban schools. *Education and Urban Society, 34*(4), 4–17. doi:10.1177/00131245 01341002

Murrell, P. C., Jr. (2001). *The community teacher: A new framework for effective urban teaching.* New York, NY: Teachers College Press.

Nieto, S. (2003). *What keeps teachers going?* New York, NY: Teachers College Press.

Oakes, J., & Lipton, M. (2007). *Teaching to change the world* (3rd ed.). New York, NY: McGraw-Hill.

Orfield, G., & Lee, C. (2004). *Brown at 50: King's dream or Plessy's nightmare?* Retrieved from http://www.civilrights project.ucla.edu

Pajares, M. F. (1992). Teachers' beliefs and educational research: Cleaning up a messy construct. *Review of Educational Research, 62,* 307–332. doi:10.2307/1170741

Quartz, K. H., & TEP Research Group. (2003). "Too angry to leave": Supporting new teachers' commitment to transform urban schools. *Journal of Teacher Education, 54*(2), 99–111. doi:10.1177/0022487102250284

Salopek, J. J. (2010). Creating a welcoming classroom for homeless students. *Education Update, 52*(6), 1, 6.

Schultz, B. D. (2008). *Spectacular things happen along the way: Lessons from an urban classroom.* New York, NY: Teachers College Press.

Schultz, K., Jones-Walker, C. E., & Chikkatur, A. P. (2008). Listening to students, negotiating beliefs: Preparing teachers for urban classrooms. *Curriculum Inquiry, 38,* 155–187. doi:10.1111/j.1467-873X.2007.00404.x

Skrla, L., McKenzie, K., & Scheurich, J. (2009). *Using equity audits to create equitable and excellent schools.* Thousand Oaks, CA: Corwin.

Stairs, A. J. (2010). Becoming an urban teacher in a professional development school: A view from preparation to practice. In A. J. Stairs & K. A. Donnell (Eds.), *Research on urban teacher learning: Examining contextual factors over time* (pp. 41–60). Charlotte, NC: Information Age.

Storz, M. G., & Nestor, K. R. (2008). It's all about relationships: Urban middle school students speak out on effective schooling practices. In F. P. Peterman (Ed.), *Partnering to prepare urban teachers: A call to activism* (pp. 77–101). New York, NY: Peter Lang.

Upadhyay, B. R. (2005). Using students' lived experiences in an urban science classroom: An elementary school teacher's thinking. *Science Education, 90,* 94–110. doi:10.1002/sce.20095

Weiner, L. (2006). *Urban teaching: The essentials.* New York, NY: Teachers College Press.

Weiner, L. (2010). Challenging deficit thinking. In A. S. Canestrari & B. A. Marlowe (Eds.), *Educational foundations: An anthology of critical readings* (2nd ed., pp. 64–70). Thousand Oaks, CA: Sage.

Whitney, J., Leonard, W., Camelio, M., & Camelio, V. (2006). Seek balance, connect with others, and reach all students: High school students describe a moral imperative for teachers. *The High School Journal, 89*(2), 29–39. doi:10.1353/hsj.2005.0024

Wise, T. (2003, February 20). Whites swim in racial preference. *AlterNet.* Retrieved from http://www.alternet.org/

Zetlin, A., Beltran, D., Salcido, P., Gonzalez, T., & Reyes, T. (2010). Building a pathway for optimal support for English language learners in special education. *Teacher Education and Special Education, 34,* 59–70. doi:10.1177/0888406410380423

CONTRIBUTING AUTHORS

Dennis Groenke, born in Washington, D.C., and raised in Northern Virginia, is a "product" of an urban school setting. After earning his bachelor's degree in outdoor recreation, Dennis began work as an adjudicate youth counselor at a camp for troubled teens (an 18-month, residential, court-appointed program). He has spent more than a decade teaching in urban schools, both in Virginia and Tennessee. In the 2009–2010 school year, Dennis was recognized as Whittle Springs Middle School Teacher of the Year (Knoxville, Tennessee).

Gillian Maimon is a first- and second-grade teacher in the School District of Philadelphia. She is a PhD candidate at the University of Pennsylvania, where she teaches courses to undergraduate and graduate students that involve utilizing her urban elementary classroom as a site for inquiry.

Melodie Miranda, who is featured in the opening vignette to this chapter, earned her BA in history and education and her MEd in special education at Boston College. She is currently completing a master's degree in literacy at Boston University while teaching ninth- and eleventh-grade humanities at West Roxbury Educational Complex, in Boston Public Schools.

CHAPTER 2

CREATING POSITIVE LEARNING ENVIRONMENTS

VIGNETTE: POSITIVE LEARNING ENVIRONMENTS IN ACTION

Ms. Reiss and Ms. Stephenson walk between students' desks, offering helpful advice and encouraging words to their geometry students. Above the door is a sign describing the mission of the classroom: Teach People, Not Content. The two educators here appear to live by that motto, and during their lesson on special quadrilaterals, students are learning content but also being treated as whole people. The teachers are passionate, and students are immediately responsive. Hands are in the air; students are vying to answer the teachers' carefully worded and analytical questions. Who knew that the many properties of trapezoids and rhombuses could be so engaging?

This is a group of students who, in the eyes of other teachers, administrators, or the system itself, may often be stereotyped as "dumb" or having "behavior problems," but in this room they are equals. The transmission of knowledge is fluid, and teachers and students learn from each other. Students are praised for their participation, even if their answers are not always right; "excellent," "great," and "beautiful job" seem like subconscious remarks from the teachers, but the reactions on students' faces show that the praise is still quite meaningful to them. Student volunteers pass out supplies, collect them, and help other students. It is no wonder they do this, as it is obvious from the teachers' dialogue that this a true community of learners: "Can anybody help him out?", "Do you want to try again? I can help you," "We're going to do this together," "Do your best. I know you can do it," and "If anybody needs help, call us over. But I think you should be able to do it." Students are explicitly and frequently thanked for their help, participation, and focus. Community does not happen naturally, and it is obvious that the teachers have worked diligently to build it.

FOCUS QUESTIONS

- How can urban teachers create positive learning environments?
- What do positive learning environments look like in practice?
- How do teachers offer urban students opportunities to learn in their classrooms?
- How does the balance of power in urban classrooms nurture collaboration and positivity?
- What are the ways that teachers can utilize culturally responsive classroom management and avoid disproportionate disciplinary practices?

The community built by Ms. Reiss and Ms. Stephenson is an excellent example of what a positive learning environment looks like in urban classrooms. Students who may not feel, or have not been, successful in the traditional sense or in other classes are given opportunities to learn, a chance to collaborate and share their ideas, and the respect of their teachers and peers. This chapter builds on the resource model presented in Chapter 1 and lays the groundwork for culturally responsive pedagogy, described in Chapter 3. Specifically, we discuss the ways teachers can create positive learning environments in urban schools and the important impact that such environments have on students and their achievement.

THEORETICAL FRAMEWORK FOR POSITIVE LEARNING ENVIRONMENTS

When we ask our preservice teachers what a positive learning environment looks like, the responses generally involve several adjectives that teachers associate with their own positive learning experiences: "safe," "warm," "caring," and "intellectual." However, when we ask what a positive learning environment looks like in urban schools in particular, comments more commonly reference classroom management and discipline. Yet educational researchers have found that positive learning environments in urban schools are those that move *beyond* student behavior as a defining factor.

This section outlines the theoretical framework for positive learning environments. Specifically, we discuss the ways that such environments can be developed and nurtured through the creation of opportunities to learn; a balance of power between teachers and students; a resistance of disproportionate disciplinary practices while nurturing collaboration, cooperation, and reciprocity; the establishment of a safe, bully-free space for students of all identities;

and a reframing of the deficit paradigm. Within each subsection, we provide evidence from leading researchers in the field of urban education and from real-life classroom teachers that illustrates the necessity of building positive learning environments in urban schools.

Learning Opportunities

As new teachers, you have most likely spent time discussing the age-old question: Can all students learn? Or perhaps conversations have extended to the debate: Do all students *want* to learn? We posit that, as decades of educational research have shown, all students *can* learn and all students *want* to learn. The more salient question is whether all students are given the *opportunities* to learn. **Opportunity to learn**, as discussed in Chapter 1, refers to the conditions within a classroom and school, such as curriculum, instruction, facilities, and resources, that enable all students to learn effectively and efficiently (Darling-Hammond, 2010; U.S. Department of Education, 1994).

In the mid-1990s, the opportunity-to-learn (OTL) movement focused on the development of national and state standards that would ensure all students were taught equitably. A provision that required states to develop OTL standards if they were to receive federal funds was initially included in the Goals 2000 legislation, which extended the findings of *A Nation at Risk* (National Commission on Excellence in Education, 1984) and encouraged states to adopt national standards for curriculum; later, the OTL standards were removed because they were too controversial. While proponents of OTL believed that adoption of these standards would increase accountability and equality in underprivileged schools, critics of OTL believed that national standards would stifle local control and creativity (Elmore & Fuhrman, 1995; Guiton & Oakes, 1995; Stevens & Grymes, 1993; Traiman, 1993). However, as Guiton and Oakes explain, "whether OTL indicators are used to hold schools accountable, diagnose problems, or monitor the status of the system, their use requires agreement" (p. 332) about what equality actually means and looks likes in different contexts. In recent years, OTL has been applied to content areas; that is, what is necessary in a teacher's classroom for students to have the opportunity to learn mathematics or English as a second language, for example. Research in these areas has shown that, if students are given the opportunity to learn in urban schools as much as in wealthier districts, achievement follows (Aguirre-Munoz & Boscardin, 2008; Darling-Hammond, 2010).

What does all this mean for teachers? It means that individual teachers, whether required by national, state, or local standards, must provide opportunities for each student to learn in their classrooms. (See Chapter 6 for more information on standards.) It means guaranteeing that all students have access to the same high-level courses and materials so that they can meet high standards and access good career opportunities; that teachers are provided with adequate time to teach content and real-life skills and use this time wisely to ensure that students are able to engage in mastery learning; and that teachers encourage and model diversity, respect, and collaboration (Schwartz, 1995).

Urban classrooms frequently do not have the resources that wealthy schools possess, thus inhibiting urban students' opportunities to learn.

Balancing Power

Too often, urban schools and classrooms replicate society's injustices (Applebaum, 2003). Instead of using education as a site for transformation and social justice, some schools serve to further disempower urban youth and silence their voices (Delpit, 1988). In her seminal work on the **culture of power** in urban communities, Delpit lists **five components of power that urban** teachers must understand in order to help their students navigate a society in which they may feel powerless:

1. Issues of power are enacted in classrooms.

2. There are codes or rules for participating in power; that is, there is a *culture of power.*

3. The rules of the culture of power are a reflection of the rules of the culture of those *in* power.

4. If you are not already a participant in the culture of power, being told explicitly the rules of that culture makes acquiring power easier.

5. Those with power are frequently least aware of—or least willing to acknowledge—its existence. Those with less power are often most aware of its existence.

Just as in the U.S. government, where the separation of powers ensures that no one entity is allowed too much control, there should be a balance of power in a classroom setting as well. While some teachers are of the mindset "I'm the teacher, you're the student, so deal with it," this attitude is not often effective because it represses students' ideas and feelings in a way that inhibits their achievement.

There are many ways that teachers can maintain the balance of power in their classrooms, the foremost of which is to listen to students. For example, allow them to have some control over classroom routines. This can be as simple as Ms. Ife, a middle school teacher, asking her students at the beginning of the year, "What is one way I can get your attention without making you feel like babies?" The students felt that a teacher flicking the lights or clapping to get their attention was too infantile, so together the group generated novel ideas for ways to regain focus, such as Ms. Ife putting up her hand in a peace sign or a Black solidarity fist. Her students felt like empowered young adults as they worked to come up with a solution to the problem, and Ms. Ife showed them that she is willing to accommodate their ideas in her planning.

Maintaining Equitable Treatment

In addition to allowing students to share in classroom power dynamics, urban teachers should also resist and reject disproportionate disciplinary practices (Nieto, 2003). In the wake of inner-city violence and gang disputes, urban schools frequently practice **zero tolerance**, or a "one strike and you're out" mentality, whereby any infraction of the school's disciplinary procedures results in severe punishment. Some urban schools, complete with metal detectors and locker searches, have "criminalized" the classroom (Mukherjee, 2007). Teachers must resist these practices when necessary in order to ensure that students are not stereotyped and punished disproportionately, meaning that a greater number of poor, urban students of color are punished than their White counterparts.

It may be difficult for teachers in urban schools to reconcile their desire to maintain a positive learning environment with the administration's focus on control and discipline. It is even more difficult when the teachers do not understand the cultural behaviors and patterns of students from diverse backgrounds, as they may assume that these students are "misbehaving" or being "disrespectful" when they are merely enacting cultural behaviors and roles that are familiar to them (Black, 2006; Weinstein, Tomlinson-Clarke, & Curran, 2004). Teachers who respond to students' cultures when developing their management and discipline styles recognize that the goals of such practices are not control, but creation of a positive learning environment. As Sheets and Gay (1996) explain,

> obviously, "get tough" policies and practices of issuing harsher punishments are not very effective in remediating disciplinary problems. Students already believe they will not be treated fairly under the best of circumstances and they expect the worst kind of treatment. When schools "get tough" with these students, their expectations are affirmed but their problematic actions may not be reduced at all. Just as browbeating, attempts at intimidation, and demands for unquestioning compliance to procedures have not succeeded in improving the academic achievement of culturally different students, they will not work with disciplinary problems. (p. 84)

Further, if a teacher needs to punish a student, the punishment should fit the crime, so to speak. Teachers who allow their students to help in the creation of classroom policies and procedures, including the warnings that students will receive before disciplinary action is taken, go far in establishing a positive learning environment because students are involved in the generation of **proportionate consequences** for their failure to behave or participate properly. For example, we witnessed what could be considered student "misbehavior" in two different classrooms and saw two very different results. Stefan, an elementary student, fell asleep in the middle of a lesson. The teacher attempted to rouse him by calling his name, then by touching him on the shoulder. He roused himself briefly each time, but then fell back asleep while the teacher was working with another student at the board. The third time that the teacher noticed Stefan sleeping, she called him to the board and made him stand with his back to the classroom, holding three textbooks in his arms, for the rest of the period. Yes, Stefan was awake, but he was also embarrassed in front of his peers, angry with the teacher, and unable to learn. The following period, when Stefan moved to another teacher's classroom, he dozed off again. This time, the teacher approached his desk, knelt down next to him and asked why he was so sleepy today. "We were moving last night," he said quietly, "We had to move to a new apartment because the other one was too expensive and my mom couldn't pay anymore. But we had to move in the middle of the night, so I was up late." The teacher did not allow Stefan to sleep, even though she knew he had a very good reason to be tired, but instead asked him, "What can I do to help you stay awake and focused today?" He then was allowed to keep a cup of water on his desk and to work with manipulatives for the math lesson, which kept his hands and mind busy. The two teachers in this scenario were met with the same type of behavior, yet the first teacher reacted disproportionately to a behavior that could easily have been stymied by the careful attention and care demonstrated by the second teacher. The second teacher embodied Sheets and Gay's (1996) recommendation for **culturally responsive discipline**, which we believe is a necessity for a positive learning environment: "The ultimate purpose is for teachers to create caring and nurturing relationships with students, grounded in cooperation, collaboration, and reciprocity rather than the current teacher controlling-student compliance patterns" (p. 84).

Creating Safe Spaces

Up to 70% of students have reported a negative impact, in some form, from bullying (Canter, 2005), and the figure rises to approximately 85% for lesbian, gay, bisexual, and transgender (LGBT) students (Kosciw, Greytak, Diaz, & Bartkiewicz, 2009). **Bullying** can take many forms, including physical bullying, verbal or emotional bullying, indirect bullying (spreading rumors), cyberbullying, intimidation, or alienation. Indeed, in recent years it has been nearly impossible to turn on the news without seeing coverage of yet another tragic teen suicide that resulted, in part, because of school bullying. An 11-year-old Georgia student, Jaheem Herrera, committed suicide in April 2009 after being teased because of his accent and being called gay at his elementary school. Pheobe Prince, a 15-year-old Irish student living in Massachusetts, killed herself in January 2010 after three months of verbal abuse, assault, and threats of physical harm because other students were displeased by her brief relationship with another male student. Between September and October 2010, at least 11 teen suicides were covered in the national media—and these were only the ones we heard about. Names like Tyler Clementi's, the Rutgers University student who killed himself after his roommate broadcast his sexual encounter over the Internet, will forever become synonymous with bullying, especially cyberbullying and anti-gay bullying. The media attention even spurred a campaign reminding children that "it gets better," in which celebrities and concerned citizens explain how they too were bullied in school but that there is hope for the future. What, then, is a teacher to do in a world where students seem to be more susceptible to bullying and harassment than ever before?

Bullying can have both short-term and long-term consequences for students' behavior, self-esteem, and achievement.

First, teachers must notice the signs of bullying in their own classrooms and students. In the past, researchers found that teachers were significantly less aware of the prevalence of bullying than were students (Zeigler & Rosenstein-Manner, 1991), but we hope this awareness has increased with colleges' and schools' attention to this serious problem. The effects of bullying and harassment are well known and documented (e.g., Beaty & Alexeyev, 2008; Donohue, 2004). Teachers and families may see signs of stress, fear, depression, and anxiety, such as not wanting to attend school, difficulty focusing in class, avoidance of hallways or bathrooms, physical illness, or a sudden change in personality or behavior.

Is there a way, then, to stop the bullying before it begins? During a recent guest speaker panel in which high school students shared their experiences with bullying with Alyssa's college students, one male student said that the best way for teachers to deal with bullying in the classroom is to "implement zero tolerance—no ifs, and, or buts about it." The type of *classroom*-based zero tolerance to which this young man was referring, a type of zero tolerance that had protected him from anti-gay bullying throughout his schooling, was very different than *school*-based policies (discussed in the previous section) that resulted in harsh punishments for minor infractions. Instead, teachers who refuse to allow any type of harassment—verbal (teasing, taunting), physical (pushing, hitting), or sexual—create safe spaces in their classrooms within which students can be fully themselves without fear of retribution or discrimination. From the first day of school, teachers should make students aware of the school and classroom policies regarding bullying and harassment. It's important to explain that bullying takes many forms, none of which are tolerated in your safe space, and that just because certain forms of bullying are "acceptable" in other spaces does not mean they are acceptable in your community. One common example of this is the use of *gay* as an insult.

Creating an inclusive curriculum can also stem bullying and harassment. Research has shown that, while only approximately 12% of students reported a curriculum that "included positive representations of LGBT people, history, and events," the majority of students in schools with that inclusive curriculum were less likely to hear anti-gay slurs, more likely to feel accepted by their peers, and more likely to feel connected to the school community (Kosciw et al., 2009, pp. 12–13).

Reframing the Deficit Paradigm

In their understanding of classroom discipline in urban schools, teachers must also challenge the deficit paradigm to create a positive classroom climate. As discussed in Chapter 1, the deficit perspective of education sees students' failure as a result of their personal, familial, or cultural deficiencies (Weiner, 2003). In order to reject the deficit paradigm, teachers need to come to terms with their students' unique cultural attributes, but this is often difficult when the students are from cultures different than the teachers' own backgrounds and when the teachers view the students' behavior as problematic (Irvine, 1990).

Weiner (2003) suggests that teachers use the theory of reframing (Molnar & Lindquist, 1989) to avoid being so "vexed" by classroom management in urban schools. Reframing involves looking at a problem behavior in an objective way, thus reframing your involvement in the situation, and changing the "ecology" of the classroom to support more positive behaviors. To illustrate

Figure 2.1   An Example of Reframing

Identify the problem behaviors and describe them in neutral terms.

Kara turns around in her seat and talks to her friends each day for ten minutes at the beginning of class. She talks to two students across the classroom when the class has been assigned individual work.

Explain your current explanation for the behavior, how you have attempted to correct it, and the results.

Kara is a very social student and likes to engage with her peers. I have moved her seat twice, but it has not solved the problem. She appears to want to talk to anyone who is around.

Generate alternative explanations (the "reframing") that are positive for the behavior. (The explanations must be plausible.)

Kara has great interpersonal skills that should be utilized. She may not get much "talk time" elsewhere. The material may be too difficult, so she is talking to others so she does not have to see herself fail. Or, the material is too easy, and she is talking to others because she finishes quickly and is bored.

Act on one or more of the *new*, positive explanations.

Kara can be the class leader. She can be in charge of facilitating discussions for her peers, thus capitalizing on her interpersonal skills.

Do not refer to the problem behavior, even by comparing new, positive behaviors to the old behavior as reinforcement.

the five-step process of reframing, we share an example situation that many new teachers encounter. In the words of one preservice teacher, "There's always *one* kid who doesn't pay attention no matter what I do. He wants to talk and talk about anything but the topic I want him to learn. He distracts other students, and that isn't fair."

Imagine Kara: She talks through the whole class and does not let her friends or neighbors pay attention. You have tried everything you can think of, but she just will not quiet down. You are fed up with her behavior, and you are not thinking about *why* she is disruptive, just that she *is* disruptive. This is where reframing comes in and allows you to think in new ways about Kara's behavior, leading to new, more positive outcomes for you, Kara, and the classroom environment. Figure 2.1 shows Weiner's (2003) recommended steps for reframing, accompanied by examples of reframing Kara's behavior and your intervention to it.

Reframing may seem like a fairly self-explanatory, commonsense tactic to solving problem behaviors. Yet it is often difficult for new teachers to consider alternative explanations for what they see on a daily basis, especially if what they see is disappointing, frustrating, or confusing. It is important that urban teachers do not fall into the trap of using stereotypes and deficit perspectives, or else the learning environment will be oppressive and unjust. In the next section, we describe several research studies that illustrate the ways positive learning environments can be developed and cultivated in urban schools.

WHAT THE RESEARCH SAYS ABOUT POSITIVE LEARNING ENVIRONMENTS

As illustrated above, there is a large body of literature on the causes and effects of a positive learning environment (Baker, 1999; Brown, 2004; Irvine, 1990; Ladson-Billings, 1997; Pajares, 1992). Researchers have shown the following:

- Positive learning environments improve student achievement, attendance, and behavior.
- It is possible for teachers of all races and cultures to create positive learning environments by building on the strengths, cultures, and attributes that their students bring to the classroom.
- Teachers who are willing to differentiate instruction and individualize attention are more likely to create positive environments.
- Teachers' beliefs and attitudes about their students are just as important as teacher behavior; they must be willing to care for, trust, and empathize with students.

Table 2.1 shares the findings and implications of several representative studies. More information can be found by reading the research in its entirety, using the URLs included in the table or the references provided at the end of the chapter. Brown (2004) interviewed 13 urban educators regarding the links between cultural responsiveness (discussed further in Chapter 3) and classroom management. Fairbanks, Sugai, Guardino, and Lathrop (2007) evaluated a behavior management program for second-grade students and found the importance of individualized, targeted attention. Irvine's (1990) classic work uncovers some teacher practices that may mediate school failure for Black students. Scheurich (1998) summarizes an investigation of urban HiPass (High Performance All Student Success) schools and their core beliefs and cultural characteristics.

Table 2.1   Research Studies on Positive Learning Environments

Author(s)	Purpose	Findings	Implications	URL
Brown (2004)	The researcher investigated whether classroom management strategies that used cultural responsiveness addressed students' personal needs.	Findings revealed the need for five components of positive classroom management: developing relationships and mutual respect through individualized student attention, creating caring learning communities, establishing business-like learning environments, establishing congruent communication processes, and teaching with assertiveness and clearly stated expectations.	Combining positive classroom management and culturally responsive pedagogy leads to positive learning environments for urban students. Novice teachers in urban schools should be adequately prepared to use the five components of positive classroom management.	http://uex .sagepub .com/ content/ 39/3/266.full .pdf+html
Fairbanks, Sugai, Guardino, & Lathrop (2007)	Researchers investigated a positive behavior management program's	Targeted and individualized attention, such as the "check-in and check-out" procedures examined in this	There are many ways for teachers to create a positive environment, but one of the primary components is	

Author(s)	Purpose	Findings	Implications	URL
	impact on second-grade students whose problem behaviors were unresponsive to general classroom management practices.	article, can lead to a resolution of students' problem behaviors and increase a teacher's ability to nurture a positive learning environment for all students.	establishing a clear, efficient, and effective classroom management plan. Some teachers have found success using positive behavior support and response-to-intervention procedures. (For more information, see www.pbis.org.)	
Irvine (1990)	The author examines the causes and effects of Black students' school failure, including the ways that teachers mediated common policies and practices that led to school failure.	Teachers must be honorable, caring, empathetic, and trustworthy. Some teachers of color act as "cultural brokers" who translate the culture of power for their students.	Teachers who possess nurturing characteristics and high expectations, and who are able to help their students navigate the world in and outside the classroom, can mediate school failure.	
Scheurich (1998)	The author describes the five core principles of successful high-poverty schools that follow the High Performance All Students Success (HiPass) model.	Five core components led to school and student success: schools are child or learner centered; all children can succeed at a high academic level; all children must be treated with love, appreciation, care, and respect; schools should value a student's race, culture, and first language; and schools exist for, and should serve, the community.	Even if they are not in schools that use the HiPass model, teachers can adopt similar beliefs and expect similar results: high levels of student success on standardized tests, increased student engagement, higher attendance rates, and reduced discipline problems.	http://uex .sagepub .com/ content/ 33/4/451 .full.pdf +html

PRACTICE

In this section, practicing urban teachers **Katrin Beinroth** and **Lauren McKinley** describe positive learning environments in their classrooms and explain how such environments create safe and academically focused communities for their students. Katrin is an elementary teacher in Puerto Rico, and Lauren is a former secondary math teacher in Atlanta, Georgia, who now teaches in the Dominican Republic. Their firsthand accounts illuminate the theory and research reviewed earlier in this chapter.

Katrin and Lauren first describe their vision of a positive learning environment.

Katrin: Kids feel safe and willing to take academic risks. I want kids to look forward to school and to like being there. I work hard throughout the year to build and nurture a classroom community where kids feel comfortable and safe being themselves. This makes for a happy classroom, but allows me to push the kids academically, too. Kids, like adults, are more willing to share their ideas and ask questions if they feel respected and valued. I show them that I care about them as people and students. I work to foster connections among students and build a caring, supportive community in the classroom.

Lauren: Students should feel that they are part of a community. They should be comfortable asking and answering questions even if they are unsure of themselves. Each individual should work toward his or her own success as well as the success of the entire group. This group mentality is often difficult to achieve. Instead, there is a sentiment of "every man for himself." In my opinion, the key to creating a community in which students work together for a collective goal is to convince them you care. Then, you must convince them to care about each other. Unfortunately, there is no step-by-step recipe for success. With some students it will come naturally, and with others it will take more work.

Lauren and Katrin had different experiences when they were students themselves. Lauren attended an International Baccalaureate (IB) program where she felt teachers were able to create a community of engaged and cooperative learners. Katrin's identity as a teacher, however, was shaped by seeing what *not* to do.

Katrin: Let's just say the school I attended from kindergarten to third grade still practiced corporal punishment. Children were paddled in front of the class. I was a quiet "good girl." I did my work and never, ever spoke in class. I was petrified! My next school was an improvement in that teachers were more caring and didn't spank anyone, but they turned a blind eye to the social issues that are bound to happen in elementary schools. For example, I remember a lot of bullying and exclusion happening. Not once did a teacher get involved to speak to us about it. I remember feeling as if I had been left to fend for myself with no tools or skills to handle this. I wished that an adult had stepped in.

There are many ways for a teacher to create positive learning environments in an urban classroom. Much of this creation is informed by the teacher's own background experience and his or her personality, but a key component, no matter what teacher differences exist, is that students must be given varied, contextualized, and meaningful opportunities to learn. Here, Katrin and Lauren describe how they provide students with opportunities to learn in their classrooms.

Katrin: We start the day with a morning meeting and with kids sitting in a circle. During the greeting each day, kids greet each other and me by name. We might do a simple handshake or a more complex greeting, but we do it religiously every day as it really sets the tone. Students also have a day each week to share something and respond to questions and comments from their classmates. If kids need help with this, I might practice or rehearse with them before they share. We also do a group game and respond to news and announcements. While some people might think this is too "touchy-feely," I find it essential to both social and academic learning. I am getting the kids ready to work with each other all day, warming them up, so to speak, in a low-stakes and nonthreatening way. I get the kids talking and practicing using the language I want them to use in the classroom. Through the morning message, I preview or review academic concepts. I consider this a 20-minute investment in making a more efficient and effective classroom where everyone is engaged.

We do a lot of student-centered learning, where kids' ideas are important. In writer's workshop, I teach the kids writing strategies, techniques, and mechanics, but the kids choose their own story or topic to write about. In math, we study different approaches to problem solving, and kids share their thinking constantly. In reading, we make connections with the texts and talk about how the stories remind us of something in our own life or something we've read before. Kids come with a wealth of knowledge and information. I help them connect that to what we are working on in the classroom.

In addition, I differentiate instruction as much as possible. My typical class has about 80% students who are English language learners and 30%

kids who have an Individualized Education Plan and receive support services from special education teachers, so I adapt work to better meet students' needs. I also try to let kids work in a variety of mediums and methods. Some kids may prefer to explain their mathematical thinking through drawings and labels and others may want to write out a narrative. They can often choose how they will show what they know, although I try to help them become competent working in a variety of learning styles.

Lauren: I think it is important to create lessons based upon students instead of hoping that students will like the activities that are forced upon them. This idea of starting with the students ties back into creating a community. A teacher should listen and respond to what students bring to the classroom. I start off the semester by asking my students to write down one topic they are interested in learning more about. I then try to incorporate those topics into the year as much as possible.

I try to make my classroom student driven. This could mean projects, group work, student-driven activities, or teacher-led discussions inspired by students. I have had students study medieval warfare and build catapults during the quadratics unit. They created and ran a store that generated profit while studying systems of equations. They also designed images using equations and painted them on ceiling tiles. These activities do not mean that there is no place for rote problem solving. In fact, many students enjoy this type of work also and need it to fully understand a concept.

Katrin's and Lauren's commentary above shows that positive learning environments are possible for all ages and all subjects. It also reveals a delicate balance of power in which teachers are taking into account the ways their students can contribute to classroom learning and the ways teachers can sometimes step back and allow students to plan, execute, and influence learning. Next, Lauren elaborates on the way she and her students share responsibility for the educative process.

Lauren: It is important to have an open dialogue with students. When dialogue stops, the teacher usually becomes more dictatorial and students are no longer part of the learning process. Instead, they become the learners and the teacher the learned. In my classroom, I do things such as give options: "You must do two projects, and you can choose from this list of five options" or "The following assignments are due by the end of class, and the following are due tomorrow at the beginning of class. You may choose the order in which to work on them. You may work in a group or individually, and I am here to answer questions."

I have found that it is important to show students that you are also learning. Each month I present a mathematician of the month. The person we discuss is usually someone that I only know surface information about. When they ask me more detailed questions, I often have to tell them that I don't know the answer, but we can look it up on the Internet. I have a student go to the computer and look up the answer, and together we learn more about the mathematician.

A critical component of maintaining a balance of power is avoiding disciplinary practices that are disproportionate and disrespectful. Katrin feels it is necessary to establish classroom rules from the beginning of the year and involve students in this process as much as possible so that they have a vested interest in cooperating.

Katrin: At the beginning of the year, the class and I create the class rules, which are limited to three to five easy-to-remember, positively stated rules. We also practice classroom procedures and discuss classroom expectations. For example, we practice moving our chairs in a quiet and safe way; we talk about what the room needs to look and sound like during independent reading. We practice this so that kids know exactly what I expect. From the very beginning, we talk about logical consequences and what will happen if someone doesn't follow a rule. I redirect students and then I use "time out" in my classroom. It's important for me to be consistent with time out. We practice this, and the kids soon realize that no one is immune to time out. It's not a punishment, but rather a chance for kids to redirect their attention and refocus. And honestly, who doesn't need that sometimes?

If a particular student is having a hard time following rules, I'll try to have a social conference with her to try to solve the problem. I'll tell the student what behavior I've noticed and ask if she has noticed it as well, and then we try to identify reasons for that behavior together and try to find a solution. I never punish the group for something one or two students have done, and I try to find a consequence that is related and proportionate to the behavior. I don't disrespect my students and I don't yell. I try to keep a firm, matter-of-fact tone when disciplining students.

The teachers also emphasize the importance of collaboration and cooperation in classroom learning. The stories below provide good examples of ways that collaboration is possible in all subject areas. Some novice teachers feel that collaborative learning is only possible in language arts, or other traditionally discussion-based classes, but Katrin and Lauren demonstrate that collaboration is cross-curricular.

Katrin: I try to create lots of opportunities for collaboration in the classroom. Kids in my class work with each other in many permutations: formal assignments, informal chats, extended projects, and brief encounters. I have kids work in pairs or groups almost every day. I work on building a sense of community in our classroom so that everyone can work with each other.

Our math curriculum often has kids play games together, so that's a good opportunity for them to work with a peer. Also, during writer's workshop, kids are assigned a writing partner for each unit. This extended partnership helps kids build trust in each other and lets them focus on each other as writers. In addition, throughout the day I'll have kids "turn and talk" to summarize something I have just said, make predictions, or otherwise engage them into talking about their learning.

When kids work in groups larger than two, such as in science class or during literature circles, I assign each student a role or job to do in the group, and I periodically ask them to self-assess their group-work skills. Throughout the day, kids are working hands-on. I try to limit "teacher talk" to what's necessary. If I need to model something, for instance in writing, I will, but I try to bring kids up as much as possible and model something with them, or use student work as examples. Kids are usually much more interested in what their classmates are doing than in anything I have to say, so I try to capitalize on that.

Lauren: I think that collaboration and cooperation are integral in creating a balance of power. By allowing students to collaborate, you are giving them a sense of power. They feel that they are now in charge of their learning. For example, when students create a store in my Algebra II class, they are in charge of deciding the necessary jobs and assigning them to students in class. They become much more excited about the project than if I had chosen the jobs and assigned them to people. They are also allowed to decide how the profit from the store is spent.

Another example of collaboration is when you assign a task in which students have to turn in their own work, but they are allowed to discuss the assignment with each other. For example, I give math prompts in which students are asked to explain the answer to a question in two or three pages. Students can discuss their answers and even come to me during tutorial if they have questions. I have found that these assignments force students to understand a topic on a deeper level. They can explain *why* and not just *how*, and this empowers students. I had a student who proudly announced that he could explain why the slope of a vertical line was undefined whereas the slope of a horizontal line was zero and a student in the other advanced Algebra II class could not. He had collaborated with me and other students on his math prompt, and what he learned empowered him to be more confident in his ability as a mathematician.

Sometimes, it is not easy to create positive learning environments because students may resist their own responsibilities. Most often it is because they have become accustomed to teacher-centered instruction and need more practice in a collaborative environment. Katrin and Lauren describe the ways they motivate and engage students in this responsibility-taking process.

Katrin: I teach fifth grade, where students are often becoming more independent and ready to transition to middle school. The best way to motivate kids, I've found, is to plan academic work that is worthwhile and interesting. That means that I choose materials carefully, and I think about the purpose for each lesson. Kids know when you are giving them "busy work." I also have kids complete self-assessments frequently. In writing, most kids have immediate buy-in because they are writing down their stories and ideas and learning how to express those ideas better. In other subjects, such as reading or math, I discuss the kids' progress with them. I tell them what reading level they have reached and how many more words they can read per minute now. I also think it's important to go over the report card/progress reports with kids because sometimes parents won't share them with the student and then the person who most needs to know what's up is in the dark! So I have found this helpful. I have colleagues who invite the student to lead the parent-student-teacher conference, and I am going to start doing that as well.

Lauren: Although motivating and engaging students are two of the most difficult parts of teaching, nurturing students who are responsible for their own learning is, in my opinion, the most difficult task a teacher can undertake. Maybe students have been handed things for so long that they have become accustomed to thinking that things will always work out in the end regardless of whether they put in the work. Not giving answers and having students try out their own before they ask me are two ways in which I encourage students to be responsible for their own learning. When a student asks me a question, the first thing I ask him to do is take out his notes. If he does not have notes from the lesson, I tell him to find a friend who takes good notes and get them copied before I can help. I have seen many students borrow other students' notes and, when I come back to see if they still have a question, they say, "No, I understand it now." All they needed was to look at the notes. I also encourage them to use each other as a resource. Many students become dependent upon the teacher to answer every question they have, but in reality there is a classroom full of students who can help each other.

Lauren's example demonstrates her high expectations for all students, rooted in a caring desire to nurture them. Katrin, too, exemplifies these traits.

Katrin: I start by getting to know my students and their families well. In my school, we do home visits before the school year starts. This is an informal chance to get to know families and kids. But I've also worked in schools where home visits weren't done, so I call parents and talk to them briefly before the school year begins. That way my first contact with families is positive, and the kids already know something about me. I get to know my students through games, activities, academic work, and informal conversation, and I build relationships with each one of them. I try to find something to connect with each student. Once I have that connection, then I can push students more. "I know you can do this!" "Give it a try!" "Say more!" "Prove it!"

I think students consider me quite strict, but fun, too. I have very clear expectations for behavior and work, and I enforce the rules. But I also have several running jokes in the classroom. For instance, there is an old skeleton that I bring out every once in a while to remind kids about what happens when you stay in time out too long, or I might wear a clown's nose one day, or we might have an ice cream party in the middle of winter. This builds community and memories. I had parents visit my room at one point to spend the day in class with their kids, and one dad complimented me by saying my classroom was "structured, but without being authoritarian." I appreciated that comment a lot. I am a structured person, but beyond style, I think what stands out in any positive learning environment is that kids know what is expected of them and that they are valued.

This connection with students' families and home cultures is absolutely necessary in a positive learning environment. Lauren links this connection with her desire and ability to show her students how she cares for them. Caring, Katrin says, is "something you can't fake."

Lauren: I greet them every day at the door and ask them how they are doing. I pay attention to small details such as haircuts, new clothes, change in attitude, and so on. I also make phone calls home for good and bad behavior. I try to make a good phone call home first to establish a positive relationship with the parents and student. I go to their events, baseball games, orchestra performances, and plays. Sometimes I allow them to showcase their talents in class by sharing outside activities. One student was involved in a competition to create a short film. I asked him to bring it into class to share.

I also show my students that I care by having patience. I will re-explain a topic in several different ways until a student understands it. I have made special tutorial times for students who need one-on-one help and cannot afford a private tutor. One student often skipped class, and when she was in attendance she socialized with other students during instructional time. I had conferences with her one-on-one and phone conferences with her mother. Finally, the three of us were able to meet in person. The student was in trouble at home for her grades, attitude in class, and truancy. It appeared that she felt there was no way to get out of the hole she had dug. During our conference, we set up a schedule for individual tutoring. Showing her that I cared enough to offer my personal time for her tutorials helped with her behavior in class and her attendance. She often bragged about our close bond to other students in class.

Another good example of patience and care occurred three years ago. I had a student who had just moved to the United States from India. It was the first day of school, and I had them take a Scantron diagnostic test. This student did not know how to use a Scantron, so I explained it to her. This year, three years later, she told me that my kindness and patience with her on that first day made her feel at ease. She said it meant so much to her that I took the time to explain how to use a Scantron when clearly everyone else had used it before. When she told me this story, I couldn't even remember our first day together. It made me realize that little moments of kindness and compassion can go a long way in someone else's day.

WRAP UP

As this chapter has demonstrated, there are many ways for urban teachers to develop positive learning environments "rather than classrooms being battle-grounds and platforms for power plays between students and teachers" (Sheets & Gay, 1996, p. 84). We have discussed nurturing learning opportunities, the importance of balancing power between teachers and students and maintaining equitable treatment, traits of classrooms that are safe spaces, and how to reframe the deficit paradigm with student behavior.

From the first day of school, teachers should welcome students' ideas and cultures into the classroom, thus exhibiting equitable treatment and creating opportunities to learn for all types of students. If teachers are willing to share the balance of power with their students, the students will rise to the occasion, improving their behavior and their achievement. According to Noddings (2005), "if the school has one main goal, a goal that guides the establishment and priority of all others, it should be to promote the growth of students as healthy, competent and moral people. This is a huge task to which all others are properly subordinated. We cannot ignore our children—their purposes, anxieties, and relationships—in the service of making them more competent in academic skills" (p. 10). Intellectual development will follow if the first priority for urban teachers is to create and nurture a positive learning environment.

EXTENSION ACTIVITIES

Reflection

1. How will you create a positive learning environment in your future classroom? Develop a plan for your first day, using Katrin and Lauren's anecdotes as examples, for the way you can establish a community of mutual respect, collaboration, and a balance of power from the beginning of the year.

2. With the advent of social networking technology, students of all ages have been able to find their former teachers online and may have created testimony pages on Facebook, extolling the ways their teachers from 10 to 40 years ago changed their lives in positive ways. (See Feinstein, 2010, for more information.) Envision your students in 30 years. What would you want them to say about you and the environment you created in your classroom? Create a mock Facebook page in which your "students" write comments about their memories of your classroom. Then, reflect on why you chose those comments as something you would find especially meaningful.

Action

1. Observe the teaching of a colleague whom you believe to be an exceptional model. Examine the ways he or she creates a positive learning

environment in the classroom, and speak to the students to better understand ways that such an environment has impacted their learning and lives. What new strategies or philosophies can you take away from this experience? What are at least three concrete steps you will take in your own classroom to nurture a culture of positivity?

2. Many urban schools utilize what researchers and teachers see as disproportionate and unfair disciplinary practices. Are there any such practices in your school? Develop a plan of action to approach your administration about the ways you see this practice as unfair and suggestions for alternative procedures. If you are unable to do this, develop a way to reward positive behavior in your own classroom.

SUGGESTED RESOURCES

Books

American Psychological Association. (1997). *Learner-centered psychological principles: A framework for school reform and redesign.* Washington, DC: Author. Retrieved from http://www.apa.org/ed/governance/bea/learner-centered.pdf

Delpit, L. (1995). *Other people's children: Cultural conflict in the classroom.* New York, NY: New Press.

Irvine, J. J. (2003). *Educating teachers for diversity: Seeing with a cultural eye.* New York, NY: Teachers College Press.

National Commission on Excellence in Education. (1984). *A nation at risk.* Cambridge, MA: USA Research.

National Education Association. (2007). *Truth in labeling: Disproportionality in special education.* New York, NY: Author.

Noddings, N. (2005). *The challenge to care in schools: An alternative approach to education.* New York, NY: Teachers College Press.

Spencer, S. L., & Vavra, S. A. (2009). *The perfect norm: How to teach differently, assess effectively, and manage a classroom ethically in ways that are "brain friendly" and culturally responsive.* Charlotte, NC: Information Age.

Website

Positive Behavioral Interventions and Supports (www.pbis.org)
Offers research-based practices for implementing positive behavioral interventions at all classroom levels.

REFERENCES

Aguirre-Munoz, Z., & Boscardin, C. K. (2008). Opportunity to learn and English learner achievement: Is increased content exposure beneficial? *Journal of Latinos and Education, 7,* 186–205. doi:10.1080/15348430802100089

Applebaum, B. (2003). Social justice, democratic education, and the silencing of words that wound. *Journal of Moral Education, 32,* 151–162. doi:10.1080/0305724032000072924

Baker, J. (1999). Teacher-student interaction in urban at-risk classrooms: Differential behavior, relationship quality, and student satisfaction with school. *The Elementary School Journal, 100,* 57–70. doi:10.1086/461943

Beaty, L. A., & Alexeyev, E. B. (2008). The problem of school bullies: What the research tells us. *Adolescence, 43*(169), 1–11.

Black, S. (2006). Respecting differences: Diverse learners can blossom in culturally responsive classrooms. *American School Board Journal, 193*(1). Retrieved from http://www.asbj.com

Brown, D. F. (2004). Urban teachers' professed classroom management strategies: Reflections of culturally responsive teaching. *Urban Education, 39,* 266–289. doi:10.1177/0042085904263258

Canter, A. S. (2005). Bullying at school. *Principal, 85*(2), 42–45.

Darling-Hammond, L. (2010). *The flat world and education: How America's commitment to equity will determine our future.* New York, NY: Teachers College Press.

Delpit, L. (1988). The silenced dialogue: Power and pedagogy in educating other people's children. *Harvard Educational Review, 58,* 280–298.

Donohue, M. C. (2004). Back off, bullies! *Current Health, 30*(8), 13–15.

Elmore, R. F., & Fuhrman, S. H. (1995). Opportunity-to-learn standards and the state role in education. *Teachers College Record, 96,* 433–458.

Fairbanks, S., Sugai, G., Guardino, D., & Lathrop, M. (2007). Response to intervention: Examining classroom behavior support in second grade. *Exceptional Children, 73,* 288–310.

Feinstein, S. (2010, July 14). On Facebook, telling teachers how much they meant. *The New York Times,* A23.

Guiton, G., & Oakes, J. (1995). Opportunity to learn and conceptions of educational equality. *Educational Evaluation and Policy Analysis, 17,* 323–336. doi:10.2307/1164510

Irvine, J. J. (1990). *Black students and school failure: Policies, practices, and prescriptions.* Westport, CT: Greenwood.

Kosciw, J. G., Greytak, E. A., Diaz, E. M., & Bartkiewicz, M. J. (2009). *The 2009 national school climate survey.* New York, NY: Gay, Lesbian and Straight Education Network Retrieved from http://www.glsen.org/binary-data/GLSEN_ATTACHMENTS/file/000/001/1675-1.pdf

Ladson-Billings, G. (1997). *The dreamkeepers: Successful teachers of African American children.* San Francisco, CA: Jossey-Bass.

Molnar, A., & Lindquist, B. (1989). *Changing problem behavior in schools.* San Francisco, CA: Jossey-Bass.

Mukherjee, E. (2007). *Criminalizing the classroom: The over-policing of New York City Schools.* New York, NY: American Civil Liberties Union. Retrieved from http://www.aclu.org/files/pdfs/racialjustice/overpolicingschools_20070318.pdf

National Commission on Excellence in Education. (1984). *A nation at risk.* Cambridge, MA: USA Research.

Nieto, S. (2003). *Affirming diversity.* New York, NY: Longman.

Noddings, N. (2005). *The challenge to care in schools: An alternative approach to education.* New York, NY: Teachers College Press.

Pajares, M. F. (1992). Teachers' beliefs and educational research: Cleaning up a messy construct. *Review of Educational Research, 62,* 307–332. doi:10.2307/1170741

Scheurich, J. J. (1998). Highly successful and loving, public elementary schools populated mainly by low-SES children of color: Core beliefs and cultural characteristics. *Urban Education, 33,* 451–491. doi:10.1177/0042085998033004001

Schwartz, W. (1995). *Opportunity to learn standards: Their impact on urban students.* New York, NY: ERIC Clearinghouse on Urban Education.

Sheets, R. H., & Gay, G. (1996). Student perceptions of disciplinary conflict in ethnically diverse classrooms. *NAASP Bulletin, 80,* 84–94.

Stevens, F. I., & Grymes, J. (1993). *Opportunity to learn: Issues of equity for poor and minority students.* Washington, DC: U.S. Department of Education, National Center for Education Statistics.

Traiman, S. L. (1993). *The debate on opportunity-to-learn standards.* Washington, DC: National Governors Association.

U.S. Department of Education. (1994). *Goals 2000: Educating America Act.* Retrieved from http://www2.ed.gov/legislation/GOALS2000/TheAct/index.html

Weiner, L. (2003). Why is classroom management so vexing to urban teachers? *Theory Into Practice, 42,* 305–312. doi:10.1353/tip.2003.0052

Weinstein, C. S., Tomlinson-Clarke, S., & Curran, M. (2004). Toward a conception of culturally responsive classroom management. *Journal of Teacher Education, 55,* 25–38. doi:10.1177/0022487103259812

Zeigler, S., & Rosenstein-Manner, M. (1991). *Bullying at school: Toronto in an international context.* Toronto, Ontario, Canada: Toronto Board of Education.

CONTRIBUTING AUTHORS

Katrin A. Beinroth was born and raised in Puerto Rico, where she now teaches fifth grade. She received her bachelor's degree from Brown University and her master's degree in education from Simmons College. Prior to returning to Puerto Rico, she taught eighth grade in Dorchester, Massachusetts, and third through fifth grade in Pawtucket, Rhode Island, where she also served as a math instructional coach. She has been teaching in urban schools for over 10 years.

Lauren McKinley, currently a math teacher in the Dominican Republic, received her bachelor's degree from the University of Florida and her master's degree in math education from Georgia State University. Prior to moving to the Dominican Republic, Lauren taught ninth- through twelfth-grade math in Atlanta, Georgia. She received Druid Hills High School's PTA Teacher of the Year award in 2009.

Stephanie Reiss and **Virginia Stephenson,** whose story is shared in this chapter's opening vignette, are coteachers in Atlanta, Georgia. Stephanie received her bachelor's degree from the University of Massachusetts–Amherst and her master's degree in education from Georgia State University. Virginia received her bachelor's degree from Radford University and her master's degree in interrelated special education from Georgia State University. Stephanie is the chair of the math department and Virginia is cochair of the special education department at Druid Hills High School.

CHAPTER 3

Using Culturally Responsive Pedagogy to Improve Teaching and Learning

VIGNETTE: CULTURALLY RESPONSIVE PEDAGOGY IN ACTION

Ms. Ou's racially and economically diverse class is engaged in a stimulating conversation about cultural stereotypes. Some would say sixth graders are not capable of such insightful and thoughtful comments, but the students themselves are heatedly debating. Ms. Ou skillfully moderates a student-centered discussion, continuously asking students to bring their ideas back to the texts. Initially, they compare the tone and mood in Amy Tan's short story "Fish Cheeks" and Wing Tek Lum's poem "T-Bone Steak for Ben Tong," but the conversation slowly evolves to a discussion of cultural beliefs and practices.

Ms. Ou shares her personal story of being Chinese American, comparing herself to the characters in the story. She says to the class, as they listen raptly, "When I went back to China, I felt more like a tourist. On the outside, I blended in, but on the inside, I felt more American. I experienced a role reversal." She then asks the students if they ever feel "one way on the inside, though you look differently on the outside." The students discuss their emerging teenager identities, and students from other cultures, such as French and Chinese, share examples of cultural habits that sometimes make them question their own identities. When one student makes a joke about another's cultural practice, Ms. Ou is quick to remind him of the classroom rules of respect and tolerance: "You can't judge someone because their worldview or their culture is different than yours or the way you grew up. Let's look back to the texts to see if we can learn any lessons from these authors."

FOCUS QUESTIONS

- How does culturally responsive pedagogy (CRP) improve teaching and learning in urban schools?
- What are the primary components of CRP?
- Why is it important to address, respect, and incorporate students' cultures into classroom practice?
- What effective teaching practices are associated with CRP?

The seamless connection between the way that Ms. Ou discusses curriculum and culture with her students makes this type of teaching seem effortless, but behind the scenes Ms. Ou reflects and plans continually to ensure that her lessons are rigorous, individualized, and relevant to the students' lives inside and outside the classroom. In today's society, which emphasizes student consumption of media and teacher consumption of test scores, it is especially important that all teachers find ways to make students feel valued in the classroom, emphasizing that their identity is more than what society tells them they are and how school districts label them. As discussed in the previous chapter, maintaining a positive learning environment in which students are respected, challenged, and committed improves not only teaching, but also learning, which is educators' primary goal.

One of the most significant and effective ways to nurture this positive learning environment is by establishing a pedagogy of cultural responsiveness in one's classroom. In the next section, we describe what it means to be culturally responsive by first defining culture and then sharing the key theoretical tenets of this approach to teaching.

THEORETICAL FRAMEWORK FOR CULTURALLY RESPONSIVE PEDAGOGY

Race, Ethnicity, and Culture: What's the Difference?

A key component to the theory of **culturally responsive pedagogy** (CRP) is the very specific definition of culture used by noted scholars in various fields, including education, sociology, history, cultural studies, and others. What is notable about this definition is its distinction from other ideas such as race and ethnicity. While all of the terms are interrelated, it is important to distinguish between their unique attributes to understand how to incorporate culture into one's classroom.

Race is a socially constructed category, not biologically based on physical appearance and attributes, as some believe. The idea of race as a social construction is explained well by Waters (2002):

> These categories vary across time and place . . . [and] reflect shared social meanings in society [and] differences in power relations. . . . Rather than being an immutable fixed characteristic, [social categories like race] are subject to a great deal of flux and change—both intergenerationally, over the life course, and situationally. (p. 25)

Racially, one might be Caucasian/White, Black, Hispanic/Latino/Chicano, Native American, or Asian/Indian, for example, depending on the time and place. Thus, while a Southeast Indian student might be racially constructed as Asian in the United States, he would be racially constructed as Black in Britain (Hall, 2002). **Ethnicity, on the other hand, is a particular group to which one belongs, as determined by an acceptance of cultural mores, origins, and customs.** Ethnicity is about a group's tradition. For example, one may be racially White, but ethnically Irish or Italian. Others may be racially Black, but ethnically African American, Kenyan, or Caribbean.

Culture is often described as a group's way of being in the world. Cultural perspectives and identities shape individuals' worldviews, values, and preferences. For example, mainstream White American culture might be described as valuing individualism and competition. There are many intersecting identities that make up one's culture, including language, religion, and sexuality. It is especially important for teachers to recognize students who may fit into one or more racial, ethnic, or cultural categories and may consider themselves bi- or multiracial, multiethnic, or multicultural. These students may identify with one group more than the others, or they may choose to identify with traditions and traits of both groups. Currently, No Child Left Behind requires school to report scores by racial subgroup, while the U.S. Census asks citizens to report their ethnic origins; thus, sometimes these categories, if used appropriately, can also help to examine discrimination patterns in society.

"I Don't See Race": Eschewing a Colorblind Approach to Teaching

For many novice teachers, especially White teachers, thinking about race and culture is a new experience, something that they may never have confronted before. Howard (1999) calls this the *luxury of ignorance,* building on McIntosh's (1992) notion that Whites have the **privilege** of going through their

Students bring many intersecting cultural identities to the classroom, including race, ethnicity, gender, religion, sexuality, and ability.

lives without needing to defend or prove themselves because of their race. McIntosh sees these privileges as an "invisible knapsack" that Whites carry with them wherever they go, enabling them to peruse a store without being followed, to succeed in life without being seen as a "credit to their race," or even to find a Band-Aid the color of their skin. White teachers may see the acknowledgment of racial and cultural differences as counterproductive, and they often assert what has come to be known as a **colorblind** approach to teaching. For example, we have heard teachers say, "It doesn't matter if my students are White, Black, purple, or green. I treat all students the same way," and "I don't see race. I see individual students, not their skin color."

Colorblindness has become especially popular since the election of President Barack Obama, when supporters and critics alike claimed that his election proved we are in a "post-racial" society. Some scholars, however, disagree that post-raciality is a goal for the common good and see colorblindness as "the new racism" (Bonilla-Silva, 2010, p. 213). Bonilla-Silva argues, "A black man 'in charge' gives the impression of monumental change and allows whites to tell those who research, write, talk and organize against racial inequality that they must be crazy. Whites can now say 'How can racism be important in a country that just elected a black man as its president?' and add 'By the way, I voted for Obama, so I cannot be a racist'" (p. 233). Refusing to acknowledge that racism still exists is similar to the discursive practices that are used to discuss race in a world where discussing race is seen as taboo or incendiary. For example, people may couch racial views discursively by beginning, "I am not prejudiced, but . . ." or "Some of my best friends are Black, so . . ." or "I'm not Black so I don't know, but. . . ." We frequently hear preservice teachers, especially White preservice teachers, begin discussions on race and culture with the caveat, "I don't want to offend anyone, but. . . ."

White teachers' desire or ability to not see race, though, is an example of their cultural privilege. Because they have never been forced to see themselves as racial beings, unlike their black and brown students, they may not understand how central one's race is to one's identity. Thus, colorblindness is a counterproductive technique. By refusing to acknowledge vital components of their students' backgrounds, teachers who assert colorblind ideologies either ignore or undervalue the children they teach. Bonilla-Silva (2010) believes that this colorblindness is even more dangerous for society writ large:

> The "new racism" reproduces racial domination mostly through subtle and covert discriminatory practices which are often institutionalized, defended with coded language, . . . and bonded by the racial ideology of color-blind racism. . . . Compared to Jim Crow, this new system seems genteel but it is extremely effective in preserving systemic advantages for whites and keeping people of color at bay. The new regime is, in the immortal words of Roberta Flack's song, of the "killing me softly" variety. (p. 213)

Cochran-Smith (2004) sees moving *beyond* colorblindness as one of the central ways to combat and erase dysfunctional schooling patterns for children of color.

Colorblindness can have serious, long-term effects on student learning and success. For example, teachers who do not recognize their students' backgrounds may also consciously or unconsciously hold a deficit perspective of their abilities (Irvine, 2003; Sleeter & Grant, 1987). Such a perspective undermines quality education because it allows teachers to blame outside factors for students' failure; instead of taking responsibility for their teaching and instead of acknowledging an unequal structure of power, teachers instead blame parents, "rough" neighborhoods, or a culture that doesn't value education, for example. As a result, they may lower their expectations for and stereotype their students of color. (See Chapter 1 for further discussion of the deficit perspective.)

From Colorblind to Culturally Responsive

Once teachers are able to recognize that race, ethnicity, and culture are salient parts of their students' identities that deserve to be respected and represented in classroom discourse, they can move from colorblindness to **cultural responsiveness**. Scholars have referred to this skill—the ability to teach in a way that validates their students' cultural, racial, and ethnic identities—by many different names, including "culturally relevant, sensitive, [student] centered, congruent, reflective, mediated, contextualized, synchronized, and responsive" (Gay, 2000, p. 29). But common among all research is the notion that students' cultures need to be validated in both *what* they are taught and *how* they are taught, combined with a wider transformative purpose to empower students. Culturally responsive teaching is evident in the way teachers see themselves and others, the way teachers structure their social interactions, and the way teachers view knowledge in their classrooms (Ladson-Billings, 1997, p. 28).

Though these theories have been traditionally used to describe the process needed for White teachers to work with Black children, the same theory can be applied to *any* teacher who needs to be prepared to instruct students of various races, ethnicities, and socioeconomic backgrounds. Whether racial, ethnic, or cultural, any gap between students and teachers can result in a misunderstanding of student behavior, academic ability, and teacher expectations (Irvine, 1991). It is important to remember that simply because a teacher is the same race or culture as her students does not mean she is automatically culturally responsive (Nieto, 2003).

According to Ladson-Billings (1997), one of the foremost scholars in multicultural education, the aim of culturally relevant or responsive pedagogy is to "empower students intellectually, socially, emotionally, and politically by using cultural referents to impart knowledge, skills, and attitudes" (p. 20). She contrasts this type of teaching, which allows students to identify with both academic excellence and their home culture, with **assimilationist** teaching styles, whereby teachers do not consider students' culture or personal characteristics. Assimilationist teachers are concerned with ensuring that students "fit into society" and thus "homogenize students into one 'American' identity" (p. 38). Context needs to be taken into consideration for cultural responsiveness to be effective. If teachers are able to recognize that they are "some person teaching something to some student somewhere" (Irvine, 2003, p. 48), they will be able to view their teaching with a "cultural eye," thus combating the assimilationist perspective that standardizes students and curricula.

This sample lesson asks students to consider their culture's definition of beauty alongside the media's image of beauty, drawing on students' cultural knowledge.

Source: Alyssa Hadley Dunn.

Teachers who are culturally responsive also want students to "fit" into society and recognize that they must provide them with the skills necessary to succeed in dominant society, but they have higher expectations and maintain intellectual rigor in their classrooms (Delpit, 1995; Irvine & Armento, 2001; Ladson-Billings, 1997). As Siddle Walker (1996) has shown, African American teachers historically held high expectations for students of color, and these expectations enabled students to reach "their highest potential," the title of her historical text. Thus, if students of color could succeed with high expectations in the segregated South, there is no reason to lower expectations for them in contemporary society. Intellectual rigor is achieved by carefully "scaffold[ing] instruction and build[ing] bridges between the cultural experiences . . . and the curriculum content . . . to facilitate higher levels of learning" and by using a variety of teaching strategies that encourage dialogue and critical thinking (Gay, 2000, p. 44).

Additionally, CRP makes explicit issues of power and privilege. Teachers who are culturally responsive challenge their own privilege and combat the **myth of meritocracy**, whereby everyone can succeed equally if they desire it enough (McIntosh, 1992). They challenge the "up by the bootstraps" mentality and are willing to discuss these controversies with their students. (See Chapter 1 for more on the myth of meritocracy.) Table 3.1 contrasts what CRP *is* and what it is *not,* providing a summary of characteristics from noted theorists Gay (2000), Irvine and Armento (2001), and Ladson-Billings (1997). Also included is an example of each culturally responsive pedagogical practice in a classroom setting. While there are many more characteristics of culturally responsive teachers, which can be found in the books presented in this chapter's References and Suggested Resources sections, we have chosen only several to highlight here because of their preponderance across theories.

Table 3.1 Characteristics and Examples of CRP

What CRP IS	What CRP IS NOT
Having high expectations for students of all backgrounds to achieve their highest potential *For example:* A teacher of English language learners (ELLs) believes that her first-generation immigrant students are capable of attending college if they desire.	Lowering expectations because of a belief that students of some backgrounds are not capable of high achievement *For example:* An ELL teacher creates lessons that help prepare her first-generation immigrant students for menial labor positions because she does not think them capable of attending college.
Using high-level teaching strategies and encouraging intellectual rigor *For example:* A language arts teacher uses similar teaching strategies, like a Socratic seminar or literature circles, for her gifted class and her general level class.	Using low-level teaching strategies and teaching only basic skills *For example:* A language arts teacher uses project-based learning for her gifted class but uses only test-prep and rote memorization lessons with her general level class.
Making explicit issues of power and privilege *For example:* A social studies teacher discusses residential segregation and gentrification with her history class and provides the historical context for such inequality.	Pretending that issues of power and privilege do not exist or are too uncomfortable to discuss *For example:* When discussing the history of their city, a social studies teacher ignores the history of residential segregation or racism.

(Continued)

Table 3.1 (Continued)

What CRP IS	What CRP IS NOT
Incorporating students' cultures into the curriculum *For example:* A math teacher discusses the evolution of mathematics from Egypt and Babylon, instead of focusing only on Greek math systems.	Teaching curricular content that does not relate to or respect students' funds of knowledge *For example:* A math teacher uses a classic example of a standardized test question about the speed of a boat in a regatta. For urban students who may have no cultural knowledge of sailing, this example is not relevant or responsive.
Providing opportunities for students to engage, cooperate, and collaborate with each other *For example:* A science teacher allows groups of students to develop their own experiment and demonstrate the process and results to the class.	Focusing on teacher-centered instruction that replicates the *banking model* of education (Freire, 2006) *For example:* During a science class, the teacher puts a cell diagram on the board and lectures about each part's function, then requires students to memorize the information for a multiple-choice exam.
Demonstrating that all cultures have value *For example:* An elementary teacher discusses the conflict between Israel and Palestine during a current events unit, presenting both sides of the story and challenging students to form their own opinions.	Valuing some cultural beliefs or practices above others *For example:* During a lesson on the Israeli-Palestinian conflict, an elementary teacher presents only the portion of the story with which she agrees.
Sustaining a commitment to multicultural education throughout the year and throughout curricula *For example:* A Spanish teacher discusses the political movements behind and social implications of Cinco de Mayo, instead of having only a food-centered celebration.	Celebrating only "heroes and holidays" or discussing only "food and festivals," thus encouraging a cursory approach to multicultural education *For example:* A Spanish teacher asks students to bring in tacos and piñatas to celebrate Cinco de Mayo, without discussing any historical or cultural facts.

The Importance of Multicultural Education

A major component of CRP is **multicultural education**. When students and teachers typically hear the term, they think about "add on" lessons or cultural celebrations or months. However, we believe that Nieto's (2003) definition of multicultural education is both comprehensive and significant:

Multicultural education is a process of comprehensive school reform and basic education for all students. It challenges and rejects racism and other forms of discrimination in schools and society and accepts and affirms the pluralism (ethnic, racial, linguistic, religious, economic, and gender, among others) that students, their communities, and teachers reflect. Multicultural education permeates the schools' curriculum and instructional strategies, as well as the interactions among teachers, students, and families, and the very way that schools conceptualize the nature of teaching and learning. Because it uses critical pedagogy as its underlying philosophy and focuses on knowledge, reflection, and action (praxis) as the basis for social change, multicultural education promotes democratic principles of social justice. (p. 305)

Several components of this definition will be discussed in future chapters (reflection and action in Chapter 7 on inquiry, social change in Chapter 8 on social justice). Here, we concentrate on the notion that multicultural education should permeate a school's culture and curriculum, no matter what type of school. Multicultural education, in contrast to **monocultural education**, is indeed important for students from all backgrounds: "Because it is *about* all people, it is also *for* all people" (Nieto, 2003, p. 311). And, as Nieto writes, "it can even be convincingly argued that students from the dominant culture need multicultural education more than others because they are generally the most miseducated about diversity" (p. 311).

One of the ways that you and your fellow educators can evaluate the type and effectiveness of multicultural education used in your school and classroom is by examining Banks's (2004) theory of approaches to multicultural education. Banks lists four approaches in ascending order of effectiveness. The first is the **Contributions Approach**, in which already-planned lessons include minimal discussion of multicultural figures. Colloquially, this is known as the "heroes and holidays" or "food and festivals" approach to multicultural education, whereby students learn about Martin Luther King Jr. and Rosa Parks during Black History Month. This approach "reinforces the notion, already held by many students, that ethnic minorities are not integral parts of mainstream U.S. society" (Banks, 2009, para. 8). The second approach is the **Additive Approach**, which, while an improvement over the Contributions Approach, is still problematic because it introduces isolated lessons or units on specific cultural groups without true integration into the curriculum. This might resemble a social studies unit on Native American reservations, a biology unit on African American scientists, or a literature unit on Asian American writers.

Teachers in urban schools should consistently strive for the top two approaches on the tier of multicultural education. In the **Transformation Approach**, diverse figures and topics become fundamental to and unified with the established curriculum. Instead of cursory mentions or supplemental units, "the center of the curriculum no longer focuses on mainstream and dominant groups, but on an event, issue, or concept that is viewed from many different perspectives and points of view" (Banks, 2009, para. 10). For example, an elementary teacher may structure her entire year's curriculum around the theme of identity and examine multiple and intersecting identities in all subjects from many perspectives.

Finally, the **Social Action Approach**, at the top of the multicultural pyramid, is the most difficult to adopt, especially given urban schools' bureaucratic constraints. At this level, students "acquire the knowledge and commitments needed to make reflective decisions and to take personal, social, and civic action to promote democracy and democratic living" (Banks, 2009, para. 11). Thus, students do not merely consume their multicultural knowledge, but seek to use it in ways that better their school, family, and community. Banks offers some suggestions for ways that students can participate in social activist multicultural education, no matter their age:

> Mak[e] a commitment to stop laughing at ethnic jokes that sting. . . . Read books about other racial, ethnic, and cultural groups. . . . Make friends with students who are members of other racial and ethnic groups and participate in cross-racial activities and projects with students who attend a different school in the city. . . . Participate in projects that provide help and comfort to people in the community with special needs. . . . Participate in local political activities such as school board elections and elections on local initiatives. (para. 12)

When teachers ascribe to the tenets of CRP and seek to include transformative and social activist multicultural education in their classrooms, urban students are more likely to experience success in school and in life. We believe that urban educators are fully capable of being culturally responsive, no matter their own race or background, as long as they are committed to challenging their previously held notions, dedicated to constant reflection and renewal, and willing to involve their students in classroom life and curricular planning. The next section, on research on CRP, demonstrates other ways that teachers can use this pedagogy.

WHAT THE RESEARCH SAYS ABOUT CULTURALLY RESPONSIVE PEDAGOGY

Because of its recent prevalence in critical and progressive education literature and practice, there are numerous research studies that demonstrate the effectiveness of CRP. Findings from research include the following (Gay, 2000; Irvine & Armento, 2001; Ladson-Billings, 1997; Lee, 1998; Ware, 2006; Young, 2010):

- Teachers are perceived as more effective when they implement principles of CRP.
- CRP creates a collaborative, equitable classroom community.
- Culturally responsive classrooms and teachers improve student achievement.
- CRP is most meaningful when combined with teacher reflection.

Four studies are included in Table 3.2 to illustrate the ways that researchers examine cultural responsiveness in practice. Lee (1998), as a teacher researcher, investigated a new curriculum and assessment structure designed to draw on students' funds of knowledge by addressing important community problems through performance-based assessments and technology. (See Chapter 1 for more information on funds on knowledge and Chapter 5 for more information on teachers as researchers.) She argues that such assessments involve higher cognitive abilities and also make cultural sense. Roberts (2010) studied eight successful African American teachers in the Southeastern United States and uncovered the ways they cared for their students. She suggests a theory of "culturally relevant critical teacher care" that improved student achievement and teacher-student relationships. Ware (2006) examined one component of CRP: warm demanders. This type of teaching, often associated with African American teachers of African American students, involves teachers who cares for their students and continuously hold high expectations for students' achievement. Ware found that teachers who viewed themselves through this warm demander lens implemented culturally responsive practices and increased student achievement. Finally, Young (2010) engaged in coparticipatory action research, forming a reflective group with teachers and administrators to discuss the translation of CRP from theory to practice. (See Chapter 5 for more information on participatory action research.) Findings show that teachers must be always vigilant and aware of their cultural biases and work as a collective group to ensure that CRP is translated from theory to practice.

Table 3.2   Research Studies on Culturally Responsive Pedagogy

Author(s)	Purpose	Findings	Implications	URL
Lee (1998)	The researcher worked with faculty at an inner-city high school to implement culturally relevant performance-based assessments (PBAs).	Culturally relevant PBAs make sense both cognitively and culturally, as they improve higher-level thinking skills and encourage students' connections to their home cultures and communities.	Teachers can design culturally relevant PBAs when they link assessment to curriculum and instruction, draw on students' and their communities' funds of knowledge, address a community or political need, and involve collaboration. Lee was a teacher and researcher in the program, thus illustrating that teachers can research their own students and use their findings to improve practice.	
Roberts (2010)	The researcher conducted a case study of eight successful African American teachers and examined how their definitions of care intersected with culturally relevant pedagogy and critical race theory (CRT).	Teachers demonstrated "culturally relevant critical teacher care," which the researcher defined as a blend of traditional care, critical race consciousness, and historical notions of African American education pre- and post-*Brown*.	When working with Black students in urban schools, successful teachers should make attempts to combine important theories (CRP, CRT, and care) in a way that best serves their students and their students' needs. Teachers can learn from the pedagogy of teachers in pre-*Brown* segregated schools.	

Author(s)	Purpose	Findings	Implications	URL
Ware (2006)	The researcher interviewed and observed two African American teachers and analyzed how these teachers described their instructional practices and beliefs and how their backgrounds informed their practice.	Teachers embodied the "warm demander" role in which students believed they did not lower their standards but were still willing to help students achieve. This pedagogy, when combined with CRP, leads to increased student achievement.	Teachers who view themselves as warm demanders, caregivers, and pedagogues can increase achievement, so teachers should consciously embody these different aspects of practice to encourage students.	http://uex .sagepub .com/ content/ 41/4/427 .full.pdf+ html
Young (2010)	Using an inquiry approach and participatory action research, researchers examined how teachers and administrators conceptualized CRP, what efforts were required to actualize CRP, and what challenges arose for both groups.	Teachers and administrators often defined CRP in different ways and continued to allow their own personal biases to inform their implementation of CRP. Teachers found it difficult, given the current political climate, to translate CRP theory into practice.	Teachers need to continually and critically examine their own cultural biases in order to address education's systemic racism. This can be done through peer dialogue, which includes coparticipatory discussion of not just what theories to use in the classroom, but how to implement them in practice.	http://jte .sagepub .com/ content/ 61/3/248 .full.pdf+ html

PRACTICE

In this section, practicing urban teachers **Andrea Eifrid Avery** and **Beth Sullivan** describe cultural responsiveness in their classrooms and explain how adopting CRP has improved their teaching and helped create equitable classroom communities. Andrea is a secondary social studies teacher in Atlanta, Georgia, and Beth is a secondary special education teacher in New York City. Their firsthand accounts illuminate the theory and research reviewed earlier in this chapter.

Andrea and Beth acknowledge that the first step in adopting a culturally responsive stance is to think about what culture means, as teachers and as cultural beings themselves. This includes reflecting on one's own background. Reflecting on her educational history and how her schooling was influenced by culture allowed Andrea to make decisions about how she would teach students of all cultures on her own classroom.

Andrea: I attended public school in Atlanta near Emory University and the Centers for Disease Control. Although my school was always ethnically diverse, it was overwhelmingly middle to upper class. From kindergarten to 12th grade, I watched my schools become "less White." Much of this change was caused by a demographic change in my county and redistricting. By the time I graduated, I had been exposed to greater diversity in my student body. I am extremely grateful that I was educated in a diverse school system. We had international field days and were always asked to research other nations. I feel my school celebrated international diversity, but like many schools, it was usually on the surface level, ignoring deeper interpretations of history and culture. Somehow my schools placed even less emphasis on celebrating local cultures, such as the large Black population in our county. The majority of my teachers were White baby boomers, who were most likely out of touch with the younger Black culture. I now teach at the same school where I attended high school. From what I have experienced during my teaching career here, the teachers now are younger, more diverse, and have a better grasp on the culture of today's students.

Beth also finds herself thinking about her own cultural education when determining what and how to teach. She works in a school for special education students, where she teaches secondary English and social studies in a self-contained classroom. Here, she discusses the way she conceptualizes her background's influence on her teaching style.

Beth: I am making a concerted effort at becoming more aware of how my own culture and values affect and influence my teaching. I currently have the luxury of developing and implementing my own curricula, which frequently leaves me asking myself, "Why do I think this is important to teach them? Am I teaching them this because I was taught it? Am I teaching this because I think I am supposed to or because I believe it to be important for them to learn?" I have found myself struggling with the decision to teach the "classics" versus contemporary authors. While teaching Shakespeare's *The Tragedy of Hamlet,* I began most classes with a five-minute writing prompt directly relating to a theme or idea from that day's reading. The students thoroughly enjoyed talking about their own experiences. Therefore, with the appropriate questioning, a 400-year-old play written by a European became relevant to my modern day New York City teenagers through discussions of love, revenge, murder, parent-child relationships, and friendship.

Andrea and Beth are both passionate about and committed to connecting their students' lives outside the classroom to the world of academic learning. Andrea sees being culturally responsive as learning to speak the "language" of her students.

Andrea: Culture can many times double as language. If you want to communicate with someone, you must speak his or her language. Assuming you and most of your students speak English but do not share similar cultures, you have to use the students' culture to reinforce your message. Otherwise they may not understand or retain the lesson. Outside of school hours, urban students are immersed in a culture that may be very different than yours, and over time they "learn to learn" within the confines of that culture. If you are not using that culture in your own classroom, you are missing out on an opportunity to really engage students so they can truly comprehend and *love* what you are trying to teach them.

The question remains, then, how to turn the theory of cultural responsiveness into practice. Andrea and Beth provide detailed examples of lessons they use with diverse groups of students. It is important to note that Beth's lessons, while designed for a special education population, are no less culturally responsive and certainly no less rigorous than Andrea's lessons, designed for a general social studies classroom. Both teachers demonstrate that connecting to students' cultures is not only necessary but also *possible*, no matter what their academic level, and that this connection improves student learning for all.

Andrea: I wrote a lesson for my American Civil War unit keeping in mind my diverse students and what motivates them. Over the years, I have learned to incorporate a few elements, such as music, art, and competition, into my lessons as much as possible to reach students of all backgrounds. This particular project had a list of 15 Civil War people, battles, and events. The students paired up and chose the type of project they wanted to do on a first-come basis. At least three of the project ideas asked the students to compose a song about their topic. One topic in particular, the Battle of Antietam, called for a rap song. Every year I am amazed at the hard work and talent demonstrated. Antietam was the bloodiest battle of the war, and many times this idea resonates with the students because they are exposed to so much violence in their music and video games and—for some—in real life. Most of the time the students come up with several verses and bring in their own beat. It's awesome, and I guarantee you they will never forget Antietam (or anything else they write a song about)!

At least three of the project ideas asked the students to draw a cartoon or illustration. For example, drawing a cartoon about Sherman's Battle of Atlanta or the Anaconda Plan is great for young artists. I have so many great drawings that I have run out of room on my classroom walls. Having a checklist has helped keep my students from getting fixated on one idea. Also, my students love to win, especially when prizes are involved. For the Civil War projects, the students rated each project (excluding their own), and we held a silent vote for the top two projects.

A second example of a culturally responsive lesson is the map relay I created. Movement is very prevalent in African American culture, so I try to incorporate kinesthetic activity into many of my lessons. However, active lessons work for all teenagers, so it can be useful no matter where or who you teach. Do you have a map or diagram that needs to be labeled? The 50 states? The bones in the body? The layers of the atmosphere? For example, when I needed the students to label the 50 states, I divided the class into small groups and taped blank maps around the classroom. I gave each group five minutes to refresh before the game began, and then I lined the teams up in front of a map with only one pen or marker per group. When I said "Go," each team member had to run to the map, label only one state, and then pass the pen to the next member. They rotated their lines for two minutes, and then whichever team had the most states correct was the winner. In addition to being active and fun, you have given the students other reasons to care. They want to do well for each other. Plus, every student will study the map before the test, which is more than I could claim before the game, right?

Beth: The underlying current of my modern World Cultures senior-level class rests on two concepts: cultural diffusion and globalization. If the students cannot see how the lives of individuals from around the world can impact their own lives, then the lasting effect of a course is easily lost. For example, with a unit on African cultures, my students utilized New York City to help make the connections between their own lives and the lives of millions living in the diverse continent of Africa. (I am certain they now know Africa is not a country.) We went to an African roots dance performance and a Ghanaian restaurant to eat fufu. We analyzed the structure, purpose, and significance of traditional African folktales.

After reading African folktales, I then guided the students in writing their own. They had to creatively explain something about their own lives in the form of a folktale. A couple that students came up with were "My folktale explains why there are rats in the projects" and "My folktale explains why there are cockroaches in my apartment in Harlem." They used their own environments to generate a folktale as it was my hope that they would benefit from gaining a glimpse into the creative process of using stories to answer questions about the world around them. The length and quality of each student's writing grew, and the application of daily lessons to rough drafts showed a genuine desire to strengthen and write meaningful folktales. Draft after draft, the students listened to their peers' feedback and read notes from teacher conferences to improve the quality of their writing and the power of their voice. Some even chose to read their original folktales at our schoolwide "celebration of learning" months later. There was ownership and pride in their work, and equally as important, there was a successful marriage of their New York City lives to traditional African storytelling.

In another social studies class, I have written my curriculum for our study of ancient civilizations with the essential question "What does this have to do with my life?" hanging on the wall. My efforts to connect the students' lives to history were affirmed when a mother emailed, "I wanted to thank you for helping [my son] learn about his own and human history in such a thoughtful, interesting, and exciting manner. I am so thrilled he now can thoughtfully think about how cultures can be similar and different." In order to assess their knowledge and help them make connections to the nomadic lifestyle, I routinely posed the question, "Who cares?" I wanted to humanize the stories we were reading about in history, from the development of agriculture to the development of writing, and in order to do this, the students needed to believe these transformations really happened to real people. For example, after reading the legend of Romulus and Remus, my students wrote legends about themselves. They learned about ancient Rome in history and the components of a legend in English, and then made their own decision as to whether they believed the legend of Romulus and Remus really happened.

I believe doing projects like these improves student learning because they combine important process skills in writing, for example, with the content knowledge in history. Over time the repetitive nature of learning about history and seeing how it impacts the modern world—their world—made it easier for my students to automatically make meaningful connections in their work and to classroom discussions. In general, students are able to connect to the content when they recognize that humans, no matter the time period or civilization, use tools, engage in a form of religion, improve efficiency of lives through inventions, produce influential people, and ultimately share a common prehistory.

In each of the lessons described above, Andrea and Beth reveal that they have high expectations for students of all cultures, abilities, and backgrounds. Beth feels it is important not only to hold high expectations as an individual teacher, but also to communicate these expectations to students and families and to encourage a culture of high standards in urban schools.

Beth: Uncompromised, high, and realistic expectations for all students are the first step toward changing each student's perception of his or her own potential. As one of my seniors wrote me, "This year I found out who I really am." Students of all backgrounds, from all kinds of families and homes, and with varying appreciations for their own history and identity, will fill the seats, whether it's a desk in a Boston public school, a home for incarcerated male teenagers, or a lunch table in Spanish Harlem. For example, on my first day working in a youth prison, one of my male students said, "So you know, Miss, we're not bad people. We just did bad things." I didn't want to know what these teenagers had done to end up in prison; instead I wanted to know where I could take them. Never did I compromise my expectations, and I do believe this attitude is contagious. When one teacher watches another teacher push a student a little further each day, a chain reaction begins. The teachers collectively start to believe, the parents believe, and if you're lucky, the student will then begin to believe he can do more than he has let himself in the past. It's not easy, but when you can help redefine a student's expectation of himself, then the hardest part is over. I have not always been successful at this, but I try. I believe this development of a positive self-image and self-worth needs to start at a young age. Students who continuously struggle both in and outside of the classroom from an early age can begin to develop concrete ideas of their potential, which are harder to mold the older they get.

Expecting the most from urban students is a key component of CRP. These expectations, however, cannot be divorced from the realities of society in which oppression may continuously work against urban students' struggles for achievement. Andrea and Beth discuss how they challenge the myth of meritocracy in their classrooms and do not shy away from discussing issues of power and privilege.

Andrea: A colleague suggested I read and analyze Dr. Seuss books with my high school students to help them understand complex social dynamics. One book in particular, *The Sneetches,* discusses power and privilege and, though originally written as an allegory of the Holocaust, can be applied to any situation where people are oppressed. In this book, the Sneetches with stars on their bellies are oppressing those without the stars. I ask my students to provide examples of people they know of now or in history that would be "star-bellied Sneetches" and "starless Sneetches." It is easy for them to provide answers, such as Whites and Blacks, politicians and the masses, or the rich and the poor. Many times students are more aware of power than we realize. It is important to help them identify where power comes from and how it is used. They can also learn that not everyone with power abuses it, and some may gain power with few resources. This discussion helps the students understand that they may possess more "power tools" than they realize.

Beth: Race, power, and privilege are part of students' daily experiences, from the subway train to school to the conversations at track practice. Providing the students with an opportunity to explore these issues in the classroom helps them develop a full sense of their meanings and historical contexts. In my classroom, we began discussing power and privilege in the historical context of the European colonization of Africa and apartheid. This introduced the topics of race and privilege in a less personalized, less threatening, slightly abstract way. To complement the social studies curriculum, in my English class I had the students read short stories about apartheid written from a variety of South African perspectives, including Whites and Blacks, Jews and non-Jews. Then, to personalize the unit, I asked the students if they had ever been victims of racism themselves. Every hand went up. The anecdotes mostly from male students followed: "She moved away from me" or "She took her watch and put it in her bag when I sat next to her." The students explained why they felt they had been treated unfairly, and usually it was because they felt they were being judged based on their gender, size, and skin color.

In addition to equalizing the classroom community and improving student learning, culturally responsive teachers like Andrea and Beth are also able to see positive changes in their own teaching practice, job success, and personal satisfaction. Urban schools and the challenges they present can often cause teachers to burn out or feel unsatisfied, but culturally responsive teachers are able to see each day how they are affecting their students' lives.

Andrea: Trying to understand my students and their culture has greatly improved my teaching practice and reputation at my school. My students tell me that I "really care" about them. As a first-year teacher, I made the mistake of thinking that I should make my students more like me. After all, I was a well-behaved, hardworking student with "manners"—why shouldn't they be like me? My mistake was that I was celebrating myself, not them. I was selfish and probably misconstrued as elitist or out of touch. As a result, I seemed distant to some of my students and had trouble getting through to them. How could students feel comfortable enough to learn in a class where the teacher thinks she is better than them? It's important to be humble and keep our eyes and hearts open. I had to learn the hard way that I am here to help my students become the best versions of themselves, not me.

Beth: I can see a positive correlation between my attitude toward the lesson and the students' level of involvement. The more I believe in what I'm teaching, the more the students reach the objectives I have set for them. I believe in what I'm teaching when I feel it will help them either process information more efficiently or understand something new about their own world. Therefore, if I did not acknowledge the cultural backgrounds of my students, including their learning styles, relationships with each other, and attitudes toward school, my lacking sense of purpose would pull the overall quality of my teaching down, and with it would go the students' performance.

I am a young teacher who is still learning the art of teaching. I have learned a lot about myself and the world through teaching my students, who over the years have ranged from eight to twenty years old. I've worked in both public and private schools and facilities, and each time I learn about a new experience had by children in our country. Some have learning disabilities while some are gifted; some come from traditional families while others have been shuffled through foster homes. Whatever the experiences the students bring with them when they walk through the school door, they need to know they are going to be respected. They need to know that their lives are important and that their voices are valued.

This chapter has shown why and how culturally responsive pedagogy is a necessary component of success in urban classrooms, for both teachers and students. Though some critics argue that CRP, as a component of multicultural education, is essentially taking time away from a focus on the basics and what children really need to know (Hirsh, 1992), the value of CRP cannot be understated. It is not meant to be an "add-on" to the basic curriculum or a celebration of cultural holidays; it is meant to be a complete reworking and critical interpretation of the existing curriculum and pedagogical methods common in urban schools. Culturally responsive teachers set high expectations for all students, utilize high-level teaching strategies for all students, explicate issues of power and privilege in their lessons, incorporate students' cultures into the curriculum, allow students to cooperate and collaborate with each other, demonstrate that all cultures have value, and commit to year-long multicultural education.

Teachers like Andrea and Beth who utilize CRP in their classrooms are advocates for their students because they know that students learn better when they are cared for, when their voices are valued, and when they are part of an equitable classroom community. They do not ignore the cultures of their students, but instead see these cultures as having intrinsic importance, and they are not afraid to address difficult issues of power, privilege, and oppression in their classroom interactions. Teachers with high expectations who maintain intellectual rigor in their lessons and discussions continue to improve learning for all students. Especially in urban schools where bureaucracy or accountability measures that focus more on test scores than on academic and personal development can seem overwhelming, teachers and students alike can be buoyed by culturally responsive pedagogy that improves teaching and learning.

EXTENSION ACTIVITIES

Reflection

1. A necessary part of establishing cultural responsiveness in your classroom is reflecting on your own education. First, with which culture(s) do you identify? In what ways was your prior education culturally responsive or not? Whose cultures were or were not represented? Did you

realize this at the time, or is it only upon reflection that you realize it? Why is that significant?

2. Consider your future first classroom in an urban school. Based on what you learned in this and other chapters, what will you do to ensure that CRP is evident from your first day? Plan a potential first-day activity for the grade level and subject area of your choice, keeping in mind that it should enable you to get to know your students' backgrounds and cultures while still being academically focused. Share your first-day activity with your peers.

Action

1. Choose one lesson that you have already taught that went *well*. Then choose one lesson that you have already taught that could be *improved*. Write a short analysis of how you did or did not use CRP in each lesson, and focus on how using these strategies and skills in a revised lesson would improve your teaching and your students' learning.

2. Conduct a case study of an individual student in your classroom. Using the characteristics of CRP outlined in this chapter, ask the student how he or she feels his or her prior education has or has not been culturally responsive. (If you are teaching an elementary student, you may need to simplify the language or select specific behaviors/beliefs that are of special interest to you.) Seek out specific examples and stories, and write a brief narrative about how the CRP or lack thereof has influenced your student academically and emotionally.

SUGGESTED RESOURCES

Books

Au, W. (Ed.). (2009). *Rethinking multicultural education: Teaching for racial and cultural justice*. Milwaukee, WI: Rethinking Schools.

Banks, J. (1994). *Cultural diversity and education: Foundations, curriculum, and teaching*. Boston, MA: Allyn & Bacon.

Nieto, S. (1999). *The light in their eyes: Creating multicultural learning communities*. New York, NY: Teachers College Press.

Spring, J. (2006). *The intersection of cultures: Multicultural education in the United States and the global community*. Mahwah, NJ: Lawrence Erlbaum.

Websites

Rethinking Schools (www.rethinkingschools.org)
A progressive education journal that balances classroom practice with theory and emphasizes problems facing urban schools.

Teaching for Change (www.teachingforchange.org)
Offers publications and professional development related to transforming urban schools into socially just communities.

Teaching Tolerance (www.tolerance.org/magazine/archives)
An award-winning magazine dedicated to reducing prejudice and promoting equity.

REFERENCES

Banks, J. (Ed.). (2004). *Handbook of research on multicultural education* (2nd ed.). San Francisco, CA: Jossey-Bass.

Banks, J. (2009). *Multicultural education: Goals and dimensions.* Retrieved from http://education.washington.edu/cme/view.htm

Bonilla-Silva, E. (2010). *Racism without racists: Color-blind racism and the persistence of racial inequality in the United States* (3rd ed.). Lanham, MD: Rowman & Littlefield.

Cochran-Smith, M. (2004). *Walking the road: Race, diversity, and social justice in teacher education.* New York, NY: Teachers College Press.

Delpit, L. (1995). *Other people's children: Cultural conflict in the classroom.* New York, NY: New Press.

Freire, P. (2006). *Pedagogy of the oppressed* (30th anniv. ed.). New York, NY: Continuum.

Gay, G. (2000). *Culturally responsive teaching: Theory, research, and practice.* New York, NY: Teachers College Press.

Hall, K. D. (2002). *Lives in translation: Sikh youth as British citizens.* Philadelphia: University of Pennsylvania Press.

Hirsch, E. D. (1992). *Toward a centrist curriculum: Two kinds of multiculturalism in elementary school.* Charlottesville, VA: Core Knowledge Foundation.

Howard, G. R. (1999). *We can't teach what we don't know.* New York, NY: Teachers College Press.

Irvine, J. J. (1991). *Black students and school failure: Policies, practices, and prescriptions.* Westport, CT: Praeger.

Irvine, J. J. (2003). *Educating teachers for diversity: Seeing with a cultural eye.* New York, NY: Teachers College Press.

Irvine, J. J., & Armento, B. J. (2001). *Culturally responsive teaching: Lesson planning for elementary and middle grades.* New York, NY: McGraw-Hill.

Ladson-Billings, G. (1997). *The dreamkeepers: Successful teachers of African American children.* San Francisco, CA: Jossey-Bass.

Lee, C. D. (1998). CRP and performance based assessment. *The Journal of Negro Education, 67,* 268–279. doi:10.2307/2668195

McIntosh, P. (1992). White privilege: Unpacking the invisible knapsack. In M. L. Andersen & P. H. Collins (Eds.), *Race, class, and gender: An anthology* (pp. 103–107). New York, NY: Wadsworth.

Nieto, S. (2003). *Affirming diversity: The sociopolitical context of multicultural education.* Boston, MA: Allyn & Bacon.

Roberts, M. A. (2010). Toward a theory of culturally relevant critical teacher care: African American teachers' definitions and perceptions of care for African American students. *Journal of Moral Education, 39,* 449–467. doi:10.1080/03057241003754922

Siddle Walker, V. (1996). *Their highest potential: An African American school community in the segregated south*. Chapel Hill: University of North Carolina Press.

Sleeter, C. E., & Grant, C. A. (1987). An analysis of multicultural education in the United States. *Harvard Educational Review, 57,* 421–444.

Ware, F. (2006). Warm demander pedagogy: Culturally responsive teaching that supports a culture of achievement for African American students. *Urban Education, 41,* 427–456. doi:10.1177/0042085906289710

Waters, M. C. (2002). The social construction of race and ethnicity: Some examples from demography. In N. A. Dentton & S. E. Tolay (Eds.), *American diversity: A demographic challenge for the twenty-first century* (pp. 25–49). Albany: State University of New York Press.

Young, E. (2010). Challenges to conceptualizing and actualizing culturally relevant pedagogy: How viable is the theory in classroom practice? *Journal of Teacher Education, 61,* 248–260. doi:10.1177/0022487109359775

CONTRIBUTING AUTHORS

Andrea Eifrid Avery is a native Atlantan who received her bachelor's degree in business administration from Georgia Southern University and her master's degree in history from Georgia State University. She teaches secondary social studies in DeKalb County, Georgia, at the same school she attended. Andrea is also the yearbook advisor and faculty sponsor for the Environmental Club and Model United Nations. For her excellence in the classroom, Andrea was awarded Druid Hills High School's 2008 Teacher of Excellence Award and the 2010 WEDD Teacher Motivator Scholarship Award.

Beth Sullivan, originally from Massachusetts, received her bachelor's degree in elementary education from Boston College and her master's and reading specialist's degrees from Columbia University's Teachers College. She has experience teaching Grades 4–6 in Worcester, Massachusetts, and as a supervisor for graduate students at Teachers College. Currently, Beth is a special education teacher at Cooke Center Academy in New York City, focusing on English and social studies.

Mei Ou, who is featured in the opening vignette of this chapter, earned her bachelor's degree in English and music from the University of Georgia and her master's degree in middle grades English and social studies education from Emory University. An accomplished violinist who is also fluent in Cantonese and Mandarin, Mei previously taught second grade and is now a seventh-grade teacher in Lilburn, Georgia.

CHAPTER 4

SUPPORTING ENGLISH LANGUAGE LEARNERS

VIGNETTE: SUPPORT FOR ENGLISH LANGUAGE LEARNERS IN ACTION

Ms. Murphy waited for him at the bottom step of bus 64. She knew his name, but she wasn't sure how to pronounce it. All the information she had was written on a sticky note: Ms. Murphy's new student—Gashim Otto, first grade—starts today. As she waited for her new student, Gashim, to get off the bus, she wondered what it must feel like to be him. He was in a new country, in a new school where he didn't know anyone, and he didn't speak the language. His family had recently moved to her city from Sudan. They put their son on the bus that day with the good faith that she would take care of him, keep him safe, and teach him. She wanted them to know that their child was in good hands and that she was going to take care of him like he was her own child.

Ms. Murphy's experience is similar to that of many teachers who are accepting newly arrived immigrants into their American classrooms. She was provided very little information about her new student and had to hit the ground running. She knew he was from Sudan, and he could speak one of dozens of languages spoken in that region, depending on whether he was from the north or the south. She specialized in teaching nonnative English speakers in her school district, and she was fully prepared to accept her new English language learner with open arms. It was clear she would treat him with kindness and respect.

FOCUS QUESTIONS

- How do urban teachers best support English language learners (ELLs)?
- How can the theoretical principles of second language acquisition be applied in practice with K–12 ELLs?
- How are ELLs assessed and placed in appropriate instructional settings?
- How do teachers increase the comprehensibility of academic content for ELLs?

ELLs are nonnative English speakers who have varying levels of proficiency in their **first language (L1)** and their **second language (L2)**, English. (For some students, English may even be their third or fourth language.) Sometimes ELLs are referred to as **English learners (ELs)** or **English as a second language (ESL), limited English proficient (LEP),** or **bilingual** students. The number of school-aged students in the United States who speak a language other than English at home and speak English with difficulty increased by nearly 140% between 1979 and 2007 (U.S. Department of Education, 2009). Indeed, ELLs are the fastest-growing population in the country, and they are concentrated in the largest 100 school districts, including those in California and Texas, which provide anywhere from 40% to 55% of their student body with ELL services (U.S. Department of Education, 2008). The U.S. Supreme Court decided in 1974's *Lau v. Nichols* ruling that simply providing ELLs with the same facilities, curriculum, materials, and teachers as other students does not provide for equality of treatment, as students who do not know English are not being provided with meaningful education. Therefore, school districts must provide learning opportunities that meet the needs of ELLs in order to truly provide them with equal access to education.

ELLs represent a very diverse group of students. Some are recent immigrants who have experienced formal schooling and quickly learn conversational and academic English (e.g., political asylum seekers, sojourners). Others have left unstable situations in their native countries where formal schooling was not readily available, and their L1 literacy and language skills are less developed, making learning English a formidable challenge (e.g., refugees, migrant workers). Still others are second- or third-generation Americans who speak a native language other than English in the home; years of formal schooling in the United States have provided some development in English, but more progress is necessary to achieve academically (e.g., long-term ELLs). Urban teachers should keep in mind that "one thing is certain: there is no one profile for an ELL student, nor is one single response adequate to meet their educational goals and needs" (National Council of Teachers of English, 2008, p. 16). It is complex work for teachers to meet the needs of ELLs in their classrooms. ELLs are navigating at least two languages (bilingual) and two cultures (bicultural) in an effort to become literate in both languages and cultures (biliterate; Brisk & Harrington, 2007). For this reason, ELLs are known as **culturally and linguistically diverse (CLD)** students.

Biliterate students must learn to navigate and negotiate two languages and cultures, or essentially two worlds.

Before considering the theory, research, and practice that best support ELLs in urban classrooms, teachers should take time to clarify their views on language itself. Ruiz (1984) has described three prominent perspectives on language: language-as-problem, language-as-right, and language-as-resource. **Language-as-problem** suggests that languages other than English are a social problem in the United States that should be eradicated or somehow resolved, which benefits mainstream, native speakers. **Language-as-right**, a reaction to the language-as-problem orientation, assumes that human beings have a legal, moral, and natural right to identity and language and that society is harmed when nonnative English speakers lose their language and culture. **Language-as-resource**, the orientation Ruiz suggests integrates bilingual education into U.S. language policy most effectively, values multiculturalism and bilingualism as resources that enrich the broader society. We believe that viewing language as a right and a resource is most productive in urban schools.

Alex Dailey (2009), a teacher of **English to speakers of other languages (ESOL)**, believes that educators would show more compassionate understanding toward ELLs if they experienced what it is like being an ELL:

> Teachers and administrators need to experience firsthand the turmoil, fatigue, and frustration that so many ELLs experience daily as they struggle to assert themselves as students and human beings with only limited English. It is not enough to attend a cocktail party in a non-English-speaking locale. It is not enough to take a language course for an hour per day. To better understand ELLs' experience, try a week of total immersion—or a month!—in an entirely new language. I assure you, you will gain newfound patience, admiration, and understanding of the ELLs in your classes. (p. 127)

Of course, many teachers may never have the opportunity to immerse themselves in a new language. Nevertheless, all teachers, and especially urban teachers, must develop their understanding and competence related to issues of language and learning for ELLs. This chapter aims to introduce the theories, research, and practice that urban teachers may utilize to best support English language learners in their classrooms.

THEORETICAL FRAMEWORK FOR SUPPORTING ENGLISH LANGUAGE LEARNERS

Second Language Acquisition Theory

To understand how English language learners can best be supported in urban classrooms, teachers must become familiar with the basics of **Second Language Acquisition (SLA)** theory. Behaviorist theories of second language acquisition assume that external factors are most important for language learning. This means that learners must frequently imitate correct models of L2 and receive immediate and consistent feedback on their imitations. Behaviorists believe that L2 usage will become a habit due to the positive and corrective feedback. However, behaviorist theories are not supported by sufficient research evidence, primarily because the research has focused on directly observable behaviors and not the processes that led to the behaviors (VanPatten & Williams, 2007).

In response to behaviorist theories of second language acquisition, Stephen Krashen (1981) developed the **Monitor Theory** of SLA. In Monitor Theory, Krashen presents acquisition and learning as two distinct concepts. **Acquisition** occurs when learners use language in natural communication and are not consciously aware of their acquiring L2. **Learning** occurs when explicit instruction is provided in rules and error correction. It is called Monitor Theory as the learner becomes a monitor of L2 use, employing the acquired system of the L2 picked up in communication events along with the formal, conscious learning of the language either before or after an utterance to make meaning in L2. This positions the learned knowledge as useful only to the extent that it helps the learner purposefully and accurately use the acquired language. Humans have an innate ability to acquire and learn language, and there is a natural order to L2 development. **Comprehensible input,** that is, receiving understandable messages in L2 (explained in more detail in the next section), as well as a positive attitude toward language learning, are also constructs that support Monitor Theory (VanPatten & Williams, 2007).

Krashen's (1981) theory, originally intended to describe adult second language acquisition, has also been drawn upon widely by second language scholars in education. More recently, two other theories have gained prominence in SLA: **Universal Grammar (UG)**, which argues that learners' unconscious knowledge and learning of language derives from an innate understanding of language and need not be explicitly taught (White, 2007), and **Sociocultural Theory**, which argues that SLA occurs as a result of participation in social contexts, leading to internalization of language (Lantolf & Thorne, 2007). As SLA theories proliferate, teachers should keep in mind the basic principles of learning a second language:

1. Learners progress naturally through stages of language development.

2. Comprehensible input matters for acquiring new language learning.

3. L1 proficiency influences L2 learning.

4. Social and academic languages possess important differences.

Stages of Language Development

Anyone who has tried to learn a new language knows that language develops naturally over time, though at different rates for different learners. Many language scholars suggest a stage theory of language development. Krashen and Terrell (1983) list five stages. **Teachers of English to Speakers of Other Languages** (**TESOL**), the global professional education association for English language teaching, and the **World Class Instructional Design and Assessment Consortium (WIDA)**, a nonprofit group that develops ELL standards and assessments, have conceptualized language proficiency similarly, with five and six levels of English proficiency, respectively. In Table 4.1, notice the overlap of stage names and ELLs' knowledge and behaviors.

Table 4.1   Stage Theories of Language Development and Proficiency

Stage	Krashen and Terrell (1983)	TESOL (1996–2007)	WIDA (2007a)	ELLs' Knowledge and Behaviors
1	Preproduction	Starting	Entering	Possess limited or no understanding of English and respond nonverbally or with simple words/phrases (also called the "Silent Period")
2	Early Production	Emerging	Beginning	Understand phrases and short sentences and communicate in simple, everyday situations using short, memorized phrases
3	Speech Emergence	Developing	Developing	Speak in simple sentences; understand more complex speech; and produce longer phrases or sentences, though incorrect
4	Intermediate Fluency	Expanding	Expanding	Possess adequate language skills to communicate day to day, answer higher-level questions with increasing grammatical accuracy, and read independently with occasional comprehension problems
5	Advanced Fluency	Bridging	Bridging	Possess near-native levels of speech; use fluent and spontaneous expressions in English for personal, general, academic, or social purposes; and command technical and academic vocabulary and idiomatic expressions and colloquialisms
6			Reaching	Attain highest level of English proficiency and appear to be a native speaker; use specialized content area language proficiently

Other organizations and scholars conceptualize English language proficiency on different scales, represented by three to six levels. The most important point is that teachers must understand their students' levels of proficiency on whatever scale they use in their district and plan curriculum and instruction accordingly.

It should be noted that within these stages, learners pass through predictable phases of grammatical learning. For example, SLA scholars claim that learners naturally acquire certain grammatical constructions before others, such as questioning skills before negation skills and how to use *-ing* endings of words before knowing how to use *-s* endings of words (the third person singular *-s* ending in English is considered one of the most challenging concepts for ELLs to grasp; VanPatten & Williams, 2007).

Many scholars have argued that maintaining one's native language is critically important to learning a new language. For example, Cummins's (1981) **Common Underlying Proficiency** theory represents the importance of L1 to L2 development. He believes "experience with either language can promote the development of the proficiency underlying both languages, given adequate motivation and exposure to both, either in school or in the wider environment" (p. 25). This theory negates commonly held assumptions that ELLs who are deficient in English need instruction in English only, what Cummins terms **Separate Underlying Proficiency**. Essentially, developing language skills in a learner's L1 and L2 are *interdependent*. This suggests that teachers must encourage students to continue to use their L1 in order to anchor new information and language skills developed in their L2. The transfer of language skills from L1 to L2 is expected.

Comprehensible Input

Comprehensible input is necessary for ELLs to successfully acquire English language skills. Krashen (1985) describes comprehensible input as language delivered in L2 that is understandable to the learner. He argues that language acquisition occurs when ELLs are exposed to comprehensible input that is just beyond their current ability (comprehensible input + 1, or *i* + 1). The importance of comprehensible input is widely accepted by SLA scholars, and providing context for instruction is one of the best ways to provide comprehensible input:

Cummins (2000) explained that language constructions such as casual conversations and rote tasks are cognitively undemanding, whereas other constructions, such as participating in academic conversations or writing academic papers, are cognitively demanding. Cummins theorized that context improved the comprehensibility of even cognitively demanding tasks. (Colombo & Furbush, 2009, p. 39)

When teachers are knowledgeable about the English proficiency of their ELLs, they can provide input that encourages second language acquisition.

Social and Academic Language Proficiency

Students in small groups, led by a more experienced English speaker, can acquire conversational fluency alongside discrete language skills and academic language proficiency.

Second language acquisition theorists often distinguish between social language, or **Basic Interpersonal Communicative Skills (BICS)**, and academic language, or **Cognitive/ Academic Language Proficiency (CALP;** Cummins, 1981). Cummins (2003) outlines three dimensions of language proficiency that are interrelated and develop concurrently: conversational fluency, discrete language skills, and academic language proficiency. **Conversational fluency** (BICS) develops in one to two years and represents a learner's ability to carry on a conversation using social language, high-frequency words, and simple grammatical constructions. In contrast to conversational fluency, which is acquired due to language exposure either in or out of school, **discrete language skills** are learned early in language development as a result of direct instruction in grammar, letter sounds, and decoding of texts. This most often occurs in a formal school environment. **Academic language proficiency** (CALP) refers to learning more content-specific, less-frequent vocabulary and producing more complex language both orally and in writing. Academic language is rarely heard in regular conversations and can take at least five years (and usually more) to develop.

Collier (2008) explains what distinguishes academic language in school contexts:

Academic language includes technical terms specific to content areas (such as science or math vocabulary); higher-level concepts and terms not used in everyday conversation (such as "personification" or "compare and contrast"); and words that may have one meaning in everyday talk but mean something else in a classroom (such as "table" or "round"). (p. 10)

It is important for urban teachers to consider the differences among language proficiencies as the general public and some education stakeholders often misunderstand these differences. When a teacher hears a student speaking nearly fluent English during class discussions, it may be assumed that the student is proficient in English. However, knowing that academic language takes many more years to develop than social language, teachers can support students to develop the content-specific vocabulary and writing style and syntax typical of the field to ensure academic achievement (as discussed later in this chapter). Additionally, teachers may distinguish between literacy and proficiency:

When evaluating literacy of bilingual students, it is important to distinguish between literacy (i.e., being able to function as a literate person in either language) and specific proficiency to read and write in a particular language. A group of first graders are at grade level in literacy, as well as in proficiency, in both languages if they read at grade level in both languages. On the other hand, if eighth graders can only read first-grade level books in English, while they can read eighth-grade content-area books in Chinese, they have an eighth-grade level of literacy, but only a beginner level reading proficiency in English. (Brisk & Harrington, 2007, pp. 4–5)

Urban teachers who understand concepts of second language acquisition are well informed to support bilingual, bicultural, biliterate learners in their classrooms.

Assessing ELLs' Language Proficiency and Programming for ELLs

It is important that ELLs be properly assessed and placed in programs that will appropriately support their development from one level of proficiency to the next. WIDA (2007b) describes itself as a "non-profit, cooperative group whose purpose is to establish and promote standards and assessments for English language learners that meet and exceed the goals of No Child Left Behind" (para. 1). More than twenty states belong to the consortium and employ its assessment measures for determining English language proficiency.

Figure 4.1   WIDA Assessments

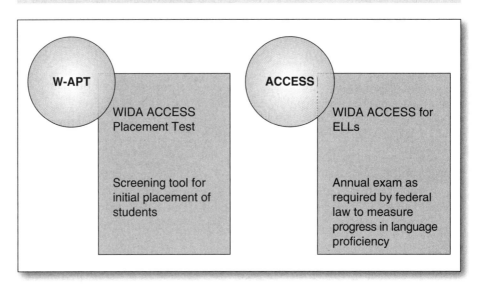

W-APT
WIDA ACCESS
Placement Test

Screening tool for
initial placement of
students

ACCESS
WIDA ACCESS for
ELLs

Annual exam as
required by federal
law to measure
progress in language
proficiency

Two commonly used WIDA assessments include the **WIDA ACCESS Placement Test (W-APT)** and the **WIDA ACCESS for ELLs**. ACCESS stands for Assessing Comprehension and Communication in English State-to-State. These two assessments are summarized in Figure 4.1. Other commonly used assessments in schools include the **Bilingual Verbal Ability Test (BVAT)**, which measures verbal and cognitive results in L1 and L2 (visit www.riversidepublishing.com for more information), and the **LAS Links K–12 Assessment**, which measures listening, speaking, reading, writing, and comprehension (visit www.ctb.com for more information). States may use a commercially available assessment or create their own, as many states have done, as long as the test aligns with state language proficiency and content standards. Teachers should learn about the assessments used in their districts for initial screening and progress monitoring of ELLs' language proficiency in order to properly support ELLs' language development.

After English language proficiency is determined, students are placed into one of the commonly used instructional arrangements to support their learning. **Two-way bilingual education (TWBE)** programs include native and nonnative English speakers learning content in both languages (e.g., English and Spanish). These have been shown to be the most effective in terms of English language achievement (Hudelson, Poynor, & Wolfe, 2003) and encourage bilingualism, biliteracy, and biculturalism. However, with the pressure and legislation to use English only for instruction in many states (e.g., Arizona, California, Massachusetts), these programs have come under attack. **Sheltered English**

immersion (SEI) classes are separate classrooms where students learn English and academic content simultaneously before transitioning into mainstream classrooms. Whereas TWBE is meant to foster bilingualism among native and non-native English speakers and is designed for multiple-year placements (five or six years, typically), SEI programs are meant primarily to improve English proficiency and academic learning for nonnative English speakers and are designed to be one-year placements (sometimes extended for a second or third year). The ultimate goal is for ELLs to experience academic success in English and transition to mainstream classrooms, where they may still be supported by ESL teachers who work closely with regular classroom teachers. See Table 4.2.

Table 4.2 Programs for ELLs in U.S. Schools

Program	Goal	Language of Instruction	Approximate Time in Program
Two-Way Immersion	Bilingualism and biliteracy for ELLs and native-English speakers	English and native language	Generally at least six years and may continue throughout student's education
Maintenance Bilingual	Bilingualism and biliteracy for ELLs	English and native language	Generally at least six years and may continue throughout student's education
Transitional Bilingual Education (TBE), late exit	English proficiency	English and native language	Generally five years
TBE, early exit	English proficiency	English and native language	Generally not to exceed three years
Sheltered English Immersion (SEI) and/or Specially Designed Academic Instruction in English (SDAIE)	English proficiency	English	Varies—one to three years is often the norm, but this can be extended
English to Speakers of Other Languages (ESOL) alone[a]	English proficiency	English	Varies depending on proficiency levels of ELLs on entry into the program

Source: Colombo & Furbush, 2009.

a. ESOL consists of two models: a pull-out model, in which ELLs leave mainstream classrooms for instruction, and a push-in model, where the ESOL/ELD teacher provides support within the mainstream program.

The best educational programs for ELLs are categorized as additive, meaning they "add to the language abilities of ELLs; program goals include bilingualism, biliteracy, and biculturalism" (Colombo & Furbush, 2009, p. 11). On the other hand, some programs offered to ELLs are subtractive, meaning they "focus only on the development of English language proficiency and ignore the value of bilingualism and biliteracy" (p. 11). TWBE programs are considered to be additive, while SEI programs are considered to be subtractive. However, school- and district-level implementation of educational programs varies, and the quality of implementation matters as much as the type of program offered.

Content-Based ESL and the SIOP Model

One recent area of focus in teaching ELLs is **content-based ESL**, also known as **content-based instruction (CBI)**, whereby teachers design language instruction through content. Though scholars argue that ESL teachers in sheltered or mainstream classrooms should remain language teachers first and foremost, they recognize that teachers of ELLs need to become aware of the efficacy of teaching language through content: "CBI often calls on teachers to rework their notion of grammar instruction from being an adjunct to content to being closely tied to content" (Bigelow, Ranney, & Dahlman, 2006, p. 41). Sound language objectives that are explicitly met alongside content objectives for lessons and units lead to language learning through content.

Brown (2004) suggests several benefits to content-based ESL. First, students learn age-appropriate content knowledge and progress with building background knowledge similar to their native-English-speaking peers. Second, ESL students read authentic texts, not contrived texts written for ESL courses. Third, language learning becomes more purposeful as students are learning the language through content, not just learning about the language in decontextualized language lessons. Finally, students learn technical vocabulary in meaningful ways, which can improve their academic language skills and success.

Echevarria, Vogt, and Short (2007) explain the **Sheltered Instruction Observation Protocol (SIOP)**, a commonly used research-based model for teaching ELLs content and language. Originally created for use by ESL teachers in SEI environments, it has been widely adapted in mainstream classrooms. The SIOP model focuses on eight areas of effective lesson planning for ELLs: preparation, building background, comprehensible input, strategies, interaction, practice/application, lesson delivery, and review/assessment. In preparing to teach a SIOP lesson, teachers clearly define not only content objectives, but also language objectives. Teachers often select appropriate content objectives for lessons from their district's scope and sequence for curriculum or from their state's standards. The SIOP model asks teachers to consider what language objectives might also be met in the lesson and to consider how language practice can be part of the lesson.

For example, a social studies teacher might state the following content objective: "Students will be able to identify and distinguish among the three branches of the United States government." A language objective for this lesson might be: "Students will be able to explain the three branches of the United States government in writing and orally with a partner." Both objectives should be explained by the teacher and displayed in the classroom before beginning the lesson. In addition to these planned opportunities for language instruction and practice, the teacher may notice other language opportunities that were not planned for, such as a student asking a question about whether "House of Representatives" means legislative branch members live together in the same house. Preparing in this way reminds the teacher to be conscious of language learning opportunities in every lesson, planned and unplanned.

After explaining the objectives, the teacher should build background knowledge to enhance learning of the new concepts with prior learning and life experiences. Then, the teacher can include multiple instructional strategies for practice with the new concepts, including clarification of new concepts in students' L1 if necessary, and with attention to providing comprehensible input and plenty of interaction. In the practice/application stage, hands-on materials are often used to give students a means for applying new knowledge in class. Activities at this stage should integrate listening, speaking, reading, and writing. As the lesson winds down, teachers should evaluate the effectiveness of lesson delivery by determining whether students were engaged at least 90% of the time, the content objectives and instructional strategies were congruent, and the pacing was appropriate. Finally, student comprehension is assessed to conclude the lesson, with review of key vocabulary and concepts. The SIOP model supports ELLs through attention to content and language simultaneously with a structured lesson delivery system that increases comprehensibility.

Developing Academic English and Teaching Vocabulary

Research has shown that ELLs must develop their academic language (CALP; Cummins, 1981) to experience success in school. CALP refers to vocabulary and phrases that are discipline specific. Some examples include *simile, metaphor,* and *alliteration* in English language arts; *circumference, radius,* and *diameter* in math; *cells, protons,* and *neutrons* in science; and *executive branch, legislative branch,* and *judicial branch* in social studies.

Teachers should explicitly teach vocabulary to their ELLs, especially academic language that is uncommon in daily social encounters.

Academic vocabulary instruction is enhanced by teaching contextualized words and allowing for repeated exposure to these words throughout a lesson and unit of study. Colombo and Furbush (2009) cite several research-based techniques for teaching academic language to ELLs. First, teachers must make choices about which words are worth serious investment of time for "rich word instruction" (p. 190) and which words ELLs could learn contextually through exposure rather than needing direct instruction. Teachers can accomplish this by classifying potential vocabulary words for instruction into three categories: content-specific terms, academic content-area words, and high-utility words (p. 191). **Content-specific words** are specific to a single discipline and perhaps a specific unit within the discipline, and they should be explicitly taught. **Academic content-area words** are those that are unlikely to be heard in social conversations and are found in one or more content areas. Coxhead (2000) has identified 570 word families of academic content-area words called the **Academic Word List,** which is helpful for teachers to reference. (See Victoria University's website listed in the Suggested Resources section of this chapter for the list as well as resources for teaching these words.) **High-utility words** are used in social language and academic language, can be learned in context and through accessible reading, and are easily explainable and translatable from the L1.

Second, teachers must provide explicit vocabulary instruction visually, orally, and in written form (Colombo & Furbush, 2009). Systematic, focused instruction that builds on what students know and connects the new to the known can lead to successful learning of academic English. As Brisk and Harrington (2007) argue, "When students are working in their second language, choosing familiar topics can have a dramatic effect on their performance" (p. 6). Semantic mapping is one way to accomplish this. A semantic map includes a core question or concept at the center of the visual, strands that emanate from the central concept and are subordinate ideas that help clarify the concept, and supporting details that are related to each strand (Vacca & Vacca, 2005). Semantic mapping requires that relationships among concepts be made specific in visual form and can be more helpful than simply sharing traditional dictionary definitions of words out of context.

Bridging Home and School, Culture and Identity

One of the challenges that urban teachers face is how to foster parental connections that support ELLs' language and academic achievement. Research has shown that engaging families makes a difference with students' academic success. Moll and Gonzalez's (2003) research suggest many benefits for learners when families' *funds of knowledge* are tapped into and honored as an essential part of teaching and learning. (See Chapter 1 for further discussion of funds of knowledge.) In fact, research supports the notion that culture and language are deeply intertwined, and many people do not separate the two when considering their identities (Menyuk & Brisk, 2005). Therefore, when a teacher admonishes students for speaking their native languages in the classroom, this critique is often viewed as a personal affront on students' cultures and identities.

Clayton, Barnhardt, and Brisk (2008) explain the relationship between language and identity:

> In this country, if English has been our first language and we have had access to being well schooled in that language, we hold a certain type of identity— one that is quite powerful and privileged. On the other hand, people who were born in the United States who do not speak Standard English as their first language or who have immigrated to this country without speaking English tend to be positioned by society in a less positive light. (p. 37)

This example reminds us that identity is represented not only by how we view ourselves, but also by how others view us. For this reason, it is important that teachers "help ELLs see their native languages and family cultures as resources that contribute to education rather than something to be overcome or cast aside" (National Council of Teachers of English, 2008, p. 19). The latter part of middle childhood and early adolescence are critical times when language acquisition can be positively or negatively influenced by factors related to culture and identity (Menyuk & Brisk, 2005). Collaboration between school and home, particularly around family discourse patterns and families' interests in their children's academic success, can mediate challenges ELLs face in managing more than one language and culture (Edwards, Paratore, & Roser, 2009).

WHAT THE RESEARCH SAYS ABOUT SUPPORTING ENGLISH LANGUAGE LEARNERS

There is a substantial research base on supporting ELLs. Findings from the research include the following (Cummins, 1981; Janzen, 2008; Lucas & Grinberg, 2008; Song, 2006; Yoon, 2008):

- Social language (BICS) and academic language (CALP) are different, and proficiency in academic language takes much longer to develop than proficiency in social language.

- L2 (English) develops most effectively when L1 (native language) is maintained.
- ELLs can successfully learn content and English simultaneously when provided with explicit, rigorous instruction.
- Language should be viewed positively as part of ELLs' culture and identity.

Albers, Kenyon, and Boals's (2009) study compared commonly used English language proficiency assessments that were created before and after No Child Left Behind (NCLB) legislation to determine which assessments were most useful for teaching ELLs. The researchers found moderate correlations between the assessments, but determined that post-NCLB assessments like WIDA's ACCESS for ELLs (explained earlier in this chapter) were more useful as they focused on academic language proficiency, not just verbal language proficiency like many pre-NCLB assessments. De Jong's (2002) research considered a two-way bilingual education program with Spanish and English speakers in an East Coast city elementary school. She found that all children's academic achievement improved, and most scores were well above national norms. Dudley-Marling's (2009) research on urban parents' perceptions of school-to-home literacy practices found that family routines, cultural values, and expectations were not met well by the one-way communication from school to home. Parents of African American and immigrant ESL students in two urban communities did not feel that their schools were responsive to their families' needs, nor did they feel like their schools were respectful of them, their children, or their communities, reinforcing the need for two-way communication between families and schools for ELLs' success in both venues. Echevarria, Short, and Powers' (2006) comparative study in large urban school districts measured students' academic literacy development over time using pre- and posttests of expository writing. The students who received classroom instruction in content and language using the SIOP model made greater gains in literacy achievement than did the comparison group. Finally, Wassell, Hawrylak, and LaVan (2010) explored how ELLs who recently graduated from an urban high school perceived their agency, or ability to access necessary resources for learning in urban classrooms. All 14 of the students were immigrants who attended high school in one of two urban districts close to the university where they were enrolled in an ESL bridge program at the time of the study. The researchers found that teachers either provided resources to support learning, such as one-on-one time with the teacher, or presented roadblocks to learning, such as providing watered-down curriculum that made ELLs fall further behind in their content learning. See Table 4.3.

Table 4.3 Research Studies on Supporting ELLs

Author(s)	Purpose	Findings	Implications	URL
Albers, Kenyon, & Boals (2009)	Researchers compared English language proficiency assessments that were created before and after No Child Left Behind to determine which were most effective for informing classroom instruction.	Results indicated that there were moderate correlations between pre- and post-NCLB assessments. Post-NCLB assessments focus more on academic language proficiency and align with standards, providing more utility for classroom instruction and interventions for ELLs.	WIDA's ELP standards and ACCESS for ELLs assessment provide valuable information teachers can use to teach academic content and language to ELLs.	http://aei .sagepub .com/ content/ 34/2/74.full .pdf+html
De Jong (2002)	The researcher studied the academic achievement of students in a two-way bilingual education program that enrolled 128 English speakers and 130 Spanish speakers at an elementary school located near a major metropolitan area on the East Coast.	Compared with national norms, both English and Spanish speakers scored above grade level in Spanish reading and mathematics and English mathematics. Spanish speakers were just below grade level in English reading, but they substantially outperformed other LEP students on state assessments.	An additive bilingual environment where L1 and L2 are used for instruction benefits English and Spanish speakers, and it is applicable to more content areas than just reading.	
Dudley-Marling (2009)	The researcher considered how 18 African American and	Parents did not feel that the one-way, school-to-home literacy initiatives	Schools should create spaces for urban parents to share their	

(Continued)

Table 4.3 (Continued)

Author(s)	Purpose	Findings	Implications	URL
	14 immigrant ESL parents perceived various school-to-home literacy initiatives.	valued their family routines, cultural values, or expectations.	concerns, needs, and values. Communication should be two-way between home and school.	
Echevarria, Short, & Powers (2006)	Researchers measured the literacy achievement of students in urban classrooms that integrated content and language instruction using the SIOP model.	The intervention group showed statistically significant gains over the control group in literacy achievement.	The SIOP model is an effective way to teach academic literacy skills, specifically writing. Teachers should explicitly teach academic language and the culture of the classroom (rules, routines, turn-taking, etc.).	
Wassell, Hawrylak, & LaVan (2010)	Researchers conducted a qualitative study of 14 ELLs who were recent urban high school graduates to determine how classrooms affected their agency, defined as their ability to access appropriate resources to have their learning needs met.	Resources that students effectively accessed were space, time, and caring. Roadblocks included poor instructional practices, lack of empathy, and a watered-down, redundant curriculum.	Teachers have the power to create classroom structures that allow ELLs to access their agency. Teachers should get to know their ELLs well; allow them time to speak more English during class, especially one-on-one with the teacher; and provide rigorous curricula with appropriate supports.	http://eus .sagepub .com/ content/ 42/5/599 .full .pdf+html

PRACTICE

In this section, practicing urban teachers **Karen Coyle Aylward** and **Brenda Murphy** describe how they support ELLs to improve achievement and learning. With more than 25 years of teaching experience between them, Karen teaches high school English language arts in Boston, Massachusetts, and Brenda serves as an elementary school ELL specialist in Portland, Maine, providing direct services to students and professional development for teachers. Their firsthand accounts illuminate the theory and research reviewed earlier in this chapter.

First and foremost, both teachers view ELLs as an asset in their classrooms. It is critical to hold positive views of your ELLs in order to work with them effectively.

Karen: While the strategies I teach my ELLs are very important, I think the beliefs that we hold about these learners are equally critical to our students' success. We convey our beliefs to students through our words, actions, and a thousand other subtle ways. What we need to convey to our ELLs is that their growing bilingualism is an asset. We need to show them that we do not see them as students with a deficit, but rather students with a rich range of cultural experiences who can teach us about language and the process of learning language.

Each year when my seniors write their college essays, I have a student who will say, "I don't want the college to know that I am still working on my English and that I only moved here a few years ago." Always, I respond by telling them how much colleges and society value the hard work they have put in to learn two languages and how much more mature they are because they can navigate two cultures. For some students, seeing their bilingualism as a strength is hard for them to do and is a long process that takes time and effort from me, them, and all of their teachers. It is important for all of us to remember that with support emotionally, socially, and instructionally, there is no limit to what our ELLs can achieve.

Brenda: I see my ELLs as an asset to my classroom and to my school. They are coming to school with a wealth of knowledge; it just might not be knowledge that is seen as being useful in school. The majority of my students are refugees. Some of them were born and raised in refugee camps. They are survivors. They have found a way to survive in a refugee camp, and their parents have managed to get their children out of an unsafe country to the United States. All of my students speak at least one other language besides English and many of them speak two or three other languages. Since the majority of my students are refugees, they have very strong survival skills. Just because ELLs don't speak English doesn't mean their lives aren't rich with other languages, cultures, and experiences. I try to honor what my students bring to the classroom because they come to school with many skills.

Often roles are reversed once families arrive in the United States. Parents become children, and children start taking care of their parents because the child is the one going to school, learning English, and learning about American culture. It is the child who discovers the unspoken cultural rules of living in the United States. Because many of my students' parents are isolated at home or are surrounded by their native language for the majority of the day, it takes them longer to gain English proficiency. They depend on their children to translate for them at the doctor, grocery store, and bank. That is why I say my students come to school with a wealth of knowledge: my ELLs know how to do things that many of their American counterparts won't learn how to do until they are in college. It is crucial that teachers of ELLs see all the wonderful things these students are bringing to the table.

I love working with ELLs because they have such a passion for learning. The students I work with have a number of reasons for wanting to learn English, but their desire to learn is a common thread that runs through them. I especially like working with ELLs because they are so diverse. Just because two children are from the same country, it doesn't mean they are going to be exactly the same. They could speak two different languages, practice different religions, or have different experiences that led them to the United States. I love learning about the languages and cultures of my students. Most important, I am so impressed that my students have gone through so much in their young lives and are still able to be open to all the new experiences in the United States. I feel lucky to be working with ELLs as they learn English and experience life in America.

Second, Karen and Brenda share how language learning is a developmental process that takes time and how teachers must respect the diversity of the ELL population in America's schools.

Karen: One important thing I have learned is that there are always more ELLs in my classroom than I realize when I first meet my classes in September.

There are ELLs who have a special code on my class list of LEP (limited English proficiency) or others who are coded as FLEP (former limited English proficiency). However, these often make up only one small part of the spectrum of ELLs in front of me. Because students' social language develops so much faster than their academic language, it can be hard to recognize an ELL through casual conversation. It takes time, observation, and close examination of student work to understand who your ELLs are and what each individual needs.

I often have students who were mainstreamed from a bilingual program five, seven, or nine years ago who speak fluently in conversation and appear to have no distinguishable accent. Yet I may find when those students are writing that there are gaps in their awareness of grammar and understanding of syntax. I may also have students who were born in the United States and have been speaking English most of their lives, but their family does not speak English at home and so they do not practice their English outside of the school day. For these students, I may notice that they struggle with academic language and they may have limited exposure to challenging vocabulary. It is always important for me to keep in mind that so many of my students (often more than half) struggle with the English language in some way and it is my job to support them and scaffold the content for them so that they can achieve at the same high levels as their native-speaking peers.

The thought of supporting so many ELLs in our classrooms can be overwhelming, but one key thing to remember is that good teaching for ELLs is good teaching for all students. When I prepare classroom materials, deliver instruction, or design assessments with the needs of my ELLs in mind, I am also helping my struggling readers, my special education students, my students who have attention or behavioral issues, and my high-achieving students because all students can benefit from these strategies and techniques.

Brenda: "Why is that student receiving ELL services?" is a common question for an ELL teacher. When a mainstream teacher hears a student speak English well, the teacher will often question the reason why a child gets ELL services. My response is, "They have their BICS but not their CALP." Many of my students become fluent in English quite quickly because they are surrounded by native speakers and they are in a multilingual school system. Four years ago I had Benson, from the Sudan, and Jesus, from the Dominican Republic, in my classroom. They were both beginning English speakers and they were best buddies. Since they didn't speak each other's native language, English became their common language. Those boys learned

English quickly because they spent all of their time together and they were highly motivated to learn. Benson and Jesus learned "playground" English. They could talk to each other and have conversations about the lunch, their classmates, or the games they were playing. These students had acquired their BICS but not their CALP. By teaching students content-specific academic language, teachers can help students acquire their CALP. The problem is it takes years to acquire your CALP.

There is a lot of pressure on students to learn academic English quickly and exit ELL programs. I always think of what would happen if I were dropped into the middle of the Sudan and required to attend a university there. I would first go into culture shock trying to figure out what the hidden cultural rules were. What are the rules for a woman my age? How am I supposed to act? What is and isn't culturally appropriate? While negotiating the new culture, I would also be learning how to communicate with people. I would learn Acholi or Arabic very quickly if there were no other English speakers for me to talk to and I had to communicate on my own. After getting a grasp on the oral language, I would now start to learn the academic language required of me in my university lessons. Thankfully, I can transfer my knowledge of being in a university and what is expected of me into my new situation. But I would still have to learn all new vocabulary words and concepts in a foreign language, all the while trying to not offend anyone with my limited knowledge of the Sudanese culture. I would be very proud of myself if it only took me five years to become fluent! It is key to keep in mind how difficult learning a new language and learning academic language is. We should have the same expectations for our students as we do for ourselves.

Karen and Brenda fully understand that they have students at many different levels of English proficiency, and they are committed to knowing who needs language support in the classroom and what support will be most effective for each student. Karen and Brenda next explain how they approach vocabulary instruction, concept development, and building background knowledge in their classrooms.

Karen: When I choose, create, or modify the materials I will use in my English language arts classroom, it is important for me to be aware of the vocabulary knowledge required for each reading or assignment. Whether we are reading *Hamlet* or *The Bluest Eye,* I must preview each chunk of reading and reflect on the key words that students will struggle with. One strategy I use is exposing students to the words from one part of a difficult text before we begin reading it. I might have them sort the words into categories with a group of their peers (e.g., positive vs. negative words, action vs. describing words). I could also define three or four key words for the day's reading and allow them time to create visuals or play charades. What is important is that I am acknowledging that there will be challenging vocabulary and I am setting them up for success on at least some of the key words.

When ELLs are learning new vocabulary, it is also important to keep in mind that most dictionaries are not helpful to them. Often dictionary definitions are too complex to give them any understanding of the word, and dictionaries provide them with no context for how to use the correct form of the word in conversation or writing (noun, verb, adjective, etc.). Therefore, I always provide students with working definitions that I think are accessible to them.

Another key part of preparing materials is recognizing the vast array of idioms that appear in our reading. Since idioms do not translate between languages, I try to avoid them in my own conversation as much as possible or at least provide explanations for students. For instance, when I use expressions like "don't beat around the bush" or "really scraping the bottom of the barrel," ELLs are left confused and futilely struggling to translate those phrases into their native languages. I may want students to get to work and stop "dragging their feet" and they are looking down at their shoes wondering what I am talking about! While I cannot teach ELLs every unknown word they will encounter or explain every idiom, it is important for me to be aware of the obstacles they will encounter and to try to create successful situations for them whenever possible.

Creating visuals for ELLs to refer to is also very helpful. When we are reading a novel, I often start with photographs of the setting or pictures of the characters from a movie version to help students visualize the text. Last year, before I read *Othello* with a class that contained many ELLs, I had students watch the movie *O* with Julia Stiles and Mekhi Phifer, a modern version of the text that follows the plot very closely. My purpose was to familiarize students with the plot and characters so that as we began reading students had enough background knowledge that we could focus our energy on interpreting Shakespeare's language itself. When reading *The Crucible* this year, I had to explain to my students that a "poppet" was what we might call a puppet today, and I brought a miniature Voodoo doll to class so that students could touch it and make this foreign concept more concrete. They probably wouldn't find "poppet" in a dictionary and may never have heard of a Voodoo doll. With that simple clarification, Act Two makes much more sense. I also try to create a classroom that is rich in visuals, with reference charts of key concepts and word walls of our key literary terms. All of these visuals help ELLs to connect concepts with language and provide them support as they are acquiring English.

Brenda: I always tell my students, "You can't write about video games or TV shows. Those are the two rules for your writing ideas." My students reply with groans and complaints. "Ms. Murphy! What are we supposed to write about if we can't write about TV or video games?" They were right. What were they going to write about? When my colleague and I established these "rules" in our writing workshop, I didn't predict that it would it become a big issue. What I quickly found out was that video games and TV shows were the main things that my students (1) were familiar with and (2) could write about. After weeks of reading students' writing that described Friday night's WWE wrestling match or all of the bad guys in the video game Vice City, I had had enough. Yes, I wanted my students to write about their true-life experiences. I just didn't feel like my students' TV guide summaries were the way to do it.

To help my ELLs acquire vocabulary and writing topics, we began to go on field trips. We went to a hockey game, the local seafood restaurant, the fish market, the fireboat, the pizza place, the public market, a gym, and so on. I went anywhere people said yes to 25 elementary school students. The amazing thing was that I never once had a person say, "No, you can't bring your boisterous third/fourth graders to my place of business." Instead, every single person said yes. At the seafood restaurant, the owner gave us a tour of the restaurant, including the kitchen. After our trip, the students wrote about what they saw and did. One student wrote, "Today we went to Avery's restaurant. It was really fun. Mr. Avery gave us lobster, shrimp, and scallops. I had never had it before. Now I know I don't like seafood." The words were inside my students; they just needed an experience to get them out. This is my take on the Language Experience Approach. But because my students had enough knowledge of written English, I didn't have them dictate their stories to me; I had them write together in pairs about our trips. I added the students' writing to photographs from our trips and then made them into books. My students loved these books because they had made them and they were about them.

Karen and Brenda's awareness of ELLs' language challenges allows them to teach vocabulary and model language that their students may emulate.

Teachers often use idioms, for example, when explaining concepts to the class, and Karen reminds us that attention must be paid to use of idiomatic phrases. Brenda provides enriching firsthand experiences through field trips to help her ELLs develop ideas for their writing. Also important is how to differentiate instruction for ELLs.

Karen: I use a reader's workshop approach in my classroom, and each student is always reading an independent reading book along with our whole-class text. Students can choose any book from my classroom library, from our school library, or on their own. This is a great opportunity for ELLs to choose a text that is comfortable for them at their independent reading level. They can choose topics that interest them, and they often choose characters and settings that represent their own cultures. Through independent reading, they get to practice their inference and analysis skills on a text that is more accessible to them, while the native speaker sitting next to them is practicing those same skills on a more challenging text that is more appropriate for the native speaker's reading level. What ties all of us together is our whole-class text where we all practice these skills on an instructional reading level (slightly above their comfort zone) with my support.

One way I support my ELLs and all of my students in our whole-class text is by modeling my own reading process and making my thinking transparent to students through think-alouds. I will take a chunk of text that is manageable for students. With Shakespeare this might be one soliloquy, and with *A Raisin in the Sun* this might be two to three pages of text. I will project the text on the overhead while all students have their own copy in front of them, and I will literally talk them through my thinking out loud as I read. I tell them the questions I ask myself, the conclusions I draw, the inferences I make, and I also model for them how I work through understanding a challenging word using context clues. By showing them the steps a good reader takes, I am giving them the tools to unlock meaning themselves. Then, I follow up by providing students with a similar manageable chunk of text and asking them to make their thinking visible as well by annotating or marking up the text with their thought process. The notes they take help me to assess their understanding, but they also help students when they need to go back and review. I can collect these annotations and, with a quick read through them, I can see who understands the text independently and who needs more support.

As students practice the reading skills that I model each day, I can choose to have them work independently, in pairs, or in small groups. Pair work and group work provide a great opportunity for ELLs to practice their language.

For a large part of the day, our students are acting as passive learners (listening and reading), and yet ELLs acquire more language and acquire it faster when they can be active learners and can produce language themselves (through speaking and writing). Pairs are especially useful because the ELL cannot choose to be a quiet listener. He or she must interact with a partner. I always make an effort to pair my ELLs with a classmate who is supportive and will make speaking a low-risk activity for the ELL. At times I may choose to pair them with someone who can provide clarification in their native language, and other times I purposely put them with a classmate who does not speak their native language to push them to use even more English. No matter how I choose to set up the groupings, it is key for ELLs to be pushed slightly out of their comfort zones with regard to producing language and to be given ample opportunities to speak in English.

In addition to differentiating instruction through reader's workshop, I also implement writer's workshop in my classroom. Students have writer's notebooks where they respond and work to build writing stamina. I also model revision techniques and give students opportunities to apply these strategies to their own writing. One of the key elements of writer's workshop that supports ELLs is the modeling of good writing. It is so important for me to provide students with models of strong writing and to discuss together why a piece is strong. When writing a critique of literature, I may choose to project one student's introduction on the overhead and do a mini-lesson on the elements that make this introduction strong. I want to make it clear to my ELLs what good writing looks like so that they know what they are reaching for with their own writing. When writing memoirs, we immerse ourselves in memoirs (excerpts from published novels, clips from films, and student examples) and critique their strengths and areas for improvement. As we prepare for our state reading tests or the SATs, I share with students several models of student work and ask them to grade them on a rubric like the testing companies will, and then we have a discussion about what grade they assigned and why. ELLs are often struggling to make the grammar right or to get the sentences out, and it is important for them to see student writing or my own writing that models a strong voice and more complex sentence structures. They need to see what the end product could be before they can be expected to create powerful writing themselves.

Brenda: Part of making students feel comfortable is allowing their native language to be spoken in the classroom. Yes, you want ELLs to practice English. But you also want them to feel like their home life is valued in school. Sometimes it is just easier to translate new information into the student's native language. It is times like these when I love having two students who speak the same language in the classroom. If a more experienced ELL student can translate for a newer student, it makes everything easier. The new student has a better handle on what we are talking about in class, and the more experienced student can feel a sense of pride in speaking both languages. And the student translating is using his knowledge to explain the new concept! Being knowledgeable of second language acquisition theories is a huge asset to mainstream teachers because it will help them understand what their ELLs are going through. I worked with a new ELL teacher who was unfamiliar with second language acquisition theories. She was discussing an ELL student of hers who didn't speak, when I mentioned that this student was in the silent period of her language development. This teacher had never heard of the silent period and didn't know that is why her student wasn't speaking. Knowing where your students are in learning English enables you to support them in their language development.

"How can I teach all of these children? They are all at different levels where some speak English and some don't. What am I going to do?" This thought used to cross my mind all the time. My response was always the same: "Meet them where they are." To do this, I have to use their background knowledge and go from there. To help my ELLs, I pay attention to what I'm saying and how I'm saying it. Am I talking too fast? Is there a simpler way for me to say this? Putting students in small groups or pairs is great because students can support each other and get more opportunities to speak than if they were in a large group.

When I first started teaching, I would give directions once (orally) and then have students return to their seats to do their work. Or at least that was the plan. Do you know what happened? Chaos. Students were wandering around the classroom, talking to each other, fooling around, or still sitting on the rug trying to figure out what they were supposed to do. That is when I learned how to give directions. I needed to say it orally and write it down, then have a student repeat the directions. I found that having the students explain things to each other was a wonderful way to check in. If a student couldn't explain what to do, then she didn't know what to do. I find that using the gradual release of responsibility model works really well. I teach and then model, next I have the students do a guided practice, and finally I have the students practice independently. This allows me to model what I want students to do, but it also lets me observe them in action.

Students learn from doing, but they also need to see what it is they are supposed to do. Think-alouds are also a wonderful tool for modeling reading strategies to students. While I am reading a story aloud, I show my students what I'm doing in my mind. When I model a think-aloud on inferencing, I say, "Wow! I wonder what is going to happen next. I don't understand why Sally doesn't look out the window to see the beach. It doesn't tell me why in the story, so I will have to use what I know about the story and read between the lines to make an inference about what is happening." (I would have taught my students what "read between the lines" means at the beginning of the lesson.) After the students watch me do a think-aloud, we do a think-aloud as a class, charting lines from the story and our inferences about what is happening. What I've learned from mistakes in the past is that any strategy I teach my students needs to be taught, modeled, and practiced a number of times before the students can use it independently.

Last month I found that my group of students didn't understand how to write the main idea and details of a story or article. To teach this skill, we would read a book together and talk about the main idea. And talk. And talk. My students had a great understanding of the book we read, but they weren't sure of how to convey that understanding in writing. As a classroom teacher, I used to feel guilty about "just talking" about a book. I used to have my students answer comprehension questions about the books they read. But as a reading and writing specialist, I've understood the power of discussing a text. Students get an opportunity to talk about what they've read and share their understandings with their peers. In their discussions they can deepen their understanding of a book, learn new vocabulary words, and formulate some writing ideas. I am also modeling what we do as adults. You never hear of a book group answering questions at the end of the chapter. People get together and talk about the book, to help them understand the book and get them excited about what they are reading.

By modeling their own thinking, Karen and Brenda afford their ELLs a window into how proficient readers, writers, and speakers of English use and analyze language. These teachers also suggest differentiation and routines to support ELLs. Finally, Karen shares how she assesses her ELLs to provide meaningful feedback on their learning, while Brenda reflects on the home-school connection.

Karen: While planning and instruction are key elements in supporting ELLs, giving regular assessments and providing targeted feedback is also crucial to helping ELLs make progress. Assessing the writing of ELLs on a test or in written work can be very tricky. As teachers, our first impulse is to want to correct everything, but this can be demoralizing for ELLs; it takes forever for the teacher; and honestly, it is not useful to the students either. It is more useful for me to give my students targeted feedback on the skill that I am actually assessing at that moment. For example, if they are taking a particular test because I want to assess their reading comprehension with a response to a passage from our whole class text, it would not be purposeful for me to grade them on their writing and grammar when I am really looking to see their thoughts and ideas. On a reading assessment, I may choose to grade them solely on their thoughts and reading skills and not grade them on their writing skills.

The same can sometimes be true for a writing assessment. My first priority when assessing writing is to give my ELLs feedback on their ideas and their thinking. They have struggled to create a meaningful response, and if I cover it in corrections in red ink, it can be very discouraging. However, there is a constant tension we teachers face between building a student's confidence and being honest about the weaknesses of his work. Therefore, when I am grading a student on a piece of writing, I typically choose to focus on one to two patterns of errors to point out. For instance, I may take an essay that is full of grammar and usage errors and just circle the places where the student has errors in subject-verb agreement. Then, I can conference with that student and purposefully teach him how to improve his subject-verb agreement. By focusing on one skill, I am giving the student a chance to be successful in this one area rather than bombarding him with twenty errors and five to ten grammar rules all at once. Yet, as in all areas of teaching, we need to differentiate based on the students in front of us. Some students will ask to come after school and have me explain all of their errors so that they can fix them all and turn in an error-free paper. In that case, I welcome the chance to teach those students more grammar while I present the grammatical corrections to other students in doses they can handle.

Brenda: It is okay to admit that you don't know a lot about Burundi or Somalia. See your ELLs as an opportunity to learn about a new country, language, and culture. Many parents or community leaders are happy to come into the school and teach a class on how to cook a traditional meal or read a story to students in their native language. What a great way for the student to see that their language and culture is valued in their new school! I have worked with educators who are afraid to call home because they don't know if their ELL parents speak English. We are lucky in our district to have translators who speak the major languages in our schools. If you don't have translators in your school, still reach out to your ELL parents. The majority of time there will be someone in the family or community who can help translate for the parents.

In addition, your ELL parents might be unsure of what the cultural norms are for parents in the United States. Many cultures allow teachers to have full responsibility of students when they are in school, and the parents might be unsure of how to be involved in school. It is so powerful to reach out to parents, even if they have limited English, and let them know what you are doing in school. The families I work with put a huge emphasis on the importance of school and succeeding in school. Teachers are highly valued, and education is seen as a way to achieve lifelong goals in the United States. Many of my parents have had limited or interrupted education because they are coming from war-torn countries. It is a great idea to let the parents know what you are doing in school and what your expectations are for their children. Don't assume that parents don't care because they haven't signed a homework paper; they might not know what is expected of them. I find that parent-teacher conferences and open houses are a great time to share your expectations and student work with parents. "I'm so thankful that you are teaching my child" is the response that I usually get at the end of my parent-teacher conferences with my ELL families.

By sharing how they approach ELLs in their classroom, Karen and Brenda illustrate for us what it means to be an urban teacher who supports ELLs. Both attend to content and skills while nurturing the social and cultural development of their students.

WRAP UP

This chapter was framed by the opening question, "How do urban teachers best support English language learners?" We explored second language acquisition theory, pointing out that despite recent politically driven rhetoric in education, knowledge and maintenance of the first language supports second language development. We explained stages of language development, the importance of comprehensible input, the difference between social and academic language proficiency, and how schools assess ELLs' language proficiency and determine appropriate program models for ELLs. In terms of instruction, content-based ESL approaches such as the SIOP model increase comprehensibility in content and language instruction. Teachers should also implement varied strategies for developing academic English and teaching vocabulary while bridging ELLs' home and school cultures and identities. The Practice section revealed how two urban practitioners approach ELLs with authentic and content-based language activities in their classrooms. Taken together, the theory, research, and practice provide urban teachers with some ideas to consider when supporting their ELLs. Perhaps the greatest message cutting across all sections of this chapter is that all teachers can make a difference with language learning by promoting bilingualism, biculturalism, and biliteracy.

Here we simply remind urban teachers that with some preparation and development of knowledge and skills, they can effectively meet the needs of their ELLs as well as their native-English-speaking students:

> Teachers will often find that in contributing to ELLs' language development (for example, providing models of good narratives, explaining how to write a lab report, modeling a good classroom presentation, giving instruction in reading word problems) they will also foster the development of the academic language of monolingual students in their classrooms. (Valdes, Bunch, Snow, & Lee, 2005, p. 157)

EXTENSION ACTIVITIES

Reflection

1. React to Karen Coyle Aylward's comment from the Practice section: "What we need to convey to our ELLs is that their growing bilingualism is an asset. We need to show them that we do not see them as students with a deficit, but rather students with a rich range of cultural experiences who can teach us about language and the process of learning language." What do you believe about ELLs? Bilingualism? Language acquisition and learning? How do your beliefs compare and contrast with Karen's?

2. Consider the varied experiences of ELLs who may be in your classroom someday. How will you approach meeting the needs of each individual while managing a room full of students? On what principles will you base your strategies?

Action

1. Ask to review your school district's plan for assessing, instructing, and transitioning ELLs into mainstream classrooms. With permission, observe an ELL assessment or complete one yourself with an individual

student. What are the student's strengths and areas for improvement? Then write an instructional plan based on your assessment.

SUGGESTED RESOURCES

Books and Articles

Cary, S. (2007). *Working with English language learners: Answers to teachers' top ten questions* (2nd ed.). Portsmouth, NH: Heinemann.

Echevarria, J., Vogt, M., & Short, D. (2007). *Making content comprehensible for English language learners: The SIOP model* (3rd ed.). Boston, MA: Allyn & Bacon.

Gibbons, P. (2002). *Scaffolding language, scaffolding learning: Teaching second language learners in the mainstream classroom.* Portsmouth, NH: Heinemann.

Lucas, T., Villegas, A. M., & Freedson-Gonzalez, M. (2008). Linguistically responsive teacher education: Preparing classroom teachers to teach English language learners. *Journal of Teacher Education, 59,* 361–373. doi:10.1177/0022487108322110

McIntyre, E., Kyle, D. W., Chen, C.-T., Kraemer, J., & Parr, J. (2009). *6 principles for teaching English language learners in all classrooms.* Thousand Oaks, CA: Corwin Press.

Murphy, A. F. (2009). Tracking the progress of English language learners. *Phi Delta Kappan, 91*(3), 25–31.

Optiz, M. F. (with Guccione, L. M.). (2009). *Comprehension and English language learners: 25 oral reading strategies that cross proficiency levels.* Portsmouth, NH: Heinemann.

Websites

The Academic Word List (www.victoria.ac.nz/lals/resources/academicwordlist)
Provides teachers with information on Coxhead's list of 570 academic words. A related website (**www.academicvocabularyexercises.com**) has online activities for learning words from the Academic Word List.

The Center for Research on Education, Diversity & Excellence (http://crede.berkeley.edu)
Focused on improving education for culturally and linguistically diverse students.

Common ELL Terms and Definitions (**www.air.org/focus-area/education/index.cfm?fa=view Content&content_id=872**)
Provides a glossary of terminology that refers to students described as ELLs as well as program models for these students.

The National Association for Bilingual Education (www.nabe.org)
The only professional organization devoted to bilingual learners and educators in the United States.

The National Clearinghouse for English Language Acquisition and Language Instruction Educational Programs (www.ncela.gwu.edu)
The federal government's website for research and resources in support of high-quality education for ELLs.

Stephen Krashen's website (http://sdkrashen.com)
Includes Krashen's full-text publications on language acquisition and literacy.

REFERENCES

Albers, C. A., Kenyon, D. M., & Boals, T. J. (2009). Measures for determining English language proficiency and the resulting implications for instructional provision and intervention. *Assessment for Effective Intervention, 34,* 74–85. doi:10.1177/1534508408314175

Bigelow, M., Ranney, S., & Dahlman, A. (2006). Keeping the language focus in content-based ESL instruction through proactive curriculum planning. *TESOL Canada Journal, 24*(1), 40–58.

Brisk, M. E., & Harrington, M. M. (2007). *Literacy and bilingualism: A handbook for ALL teachers* (2nd ed.). Mahwah, NJ: Lawrence Erlbaum.

Brown, C. L. (2004). Content-based ESL curriculum and academic language proficiency. *The Internet TESL Journal, X*(2). Retrieved from http://iteslj.org/

Clayton, C., Barnhardt, R., & Brisk, M. E. (2008). Language, culture, and identity. In M. E. Brisk (Ed.), *Language, culture, and community in teacher education* (pp. 21–45). New York, NY: Lawrence Erlbaum.

Collier, L. (2008). The importance of academic language for English language learners. *The Council Chronicle, 17*(3), 10–13.

Colombo, M., & Furbush, D. (2009). *Teaching English language learners: Content and language in middle and secondary mainstream classrooms.* Thousand Oaks, CA: Sage.

Coxhead, A. (2000). A new academic word list. *TESOL Quarterly, 34,* 213–238. doi:10.2307/3587951

Cummins, J. (1981). Empirical and theoretical underpinnings of bilingual education. *Journal of Education, 163*(1), 16–29.

Cummins, J. (2003). Reading and the bilingual student: Fact and friction. In G. G. Garcia (Ed.), *English learners: Reaching the highest level of English literacy* (pp. 2–33).

Newark, DE: International Reading Association.

De Jong, E. J. (2002). Effective bilingual education: From theory to academic achievement in a two-way bilingual program. *Bilingual Research Journal, 26*(1), 65–84.

Dailey, A. (2009). Success with ELLs: A decade of ESOL experience in about a thousand words. *English Journal, 99*(1), 127–129.

Dudley-Marling, C. (2009). Home-school literacy connections: The perceptions of African American and immigrant ESL parents in two urban communities. *Teachers College Record, 111,* 1713–1752.

Echevarria, J., Short, D., & Powers, K. (2006). School reform and standards-based education: A model for English language learners. *Journal of Educational Research, 99*(4), 195–210. doi:10.3200/JOER.99.4.195-211

Echevarria, J., Vogt, M., & Short, D. (2007). *Making content comprehensible for English language learners: The SIOP model* (3rd ed.). Boston, MA: Allyn & Bacon.

Edwards, P. A., Paratore, J. R., & Roser, N. L. (2009). Family literacy: Recognizing cultural significance. In L. M. Morrow, R. Rueda, & D. Lapp (Eds.), *Handbook of research on literacy and diversity* (pp. 77–96). New York, NY: Guilford Press.

Hudelson, S., Poynor, L., & Wolfe, P. (2003). Teaching bilingual and ESL children and adolescents. In J. Flood, D. Lapp, J. R. Squire, & J. M. Jensen (Eds.), *Handbook of research on teaching the English language arts* (2nd ed., pp. 421–434). Mahwah, NJ: Lawrence Erlbaum.

Janzen, J. (2008). Teaching English language learners in the content areas. *Review of Educational Research, 78,* 1010–1038. doi:10.3102/0034654308325580

Krashen, S. D. (1981). *Second language acquisition and second language learning.* Oxford, UK: Pergamon Press.

Krashen, S. D. (1985). *The input hypothesis: Issues and implications.* New York, NY: Longman.

Krashen, S. D., & Terrell, T. D. (1983). *The natural approach: Language acquisition in the classroom.* San Francisco, CA: Alemany Press.

Lantolf, J. P., & Thorne, S. L. (2007) Sociocultural theory and second language learning. In B. VanPatten & J. Williams (Eds.), *Theories in second language acquisition* (pp. 17–35). Mahwah, NJ: Lawrence Erlbaum.

Lucas, T., & Grinberg, J. (2008). Responding to the linguistic reality of mainstream classrooms: Preparing all teachers to teach English language learners. In M. Cochran-Smith, S. Feiman-Nemser, & D. J. McIntyre (Eds.) (with K. Demers), *Handbook of research on teacher education* (3rd ed., pp. 606–636). New York, NY: Routledge, Taylor & Francis.

Menyuk, P., & Brisk, M. E. (2005). *Language development and education: Children with varying language experiences.* New York, NY: Palgrave Macmillan.

Moll, L., & Gonzalez, N. (2003). Engaging life: A funds-of-knowledge approach to multicultural education. In J. Banks (Ed.), *Handbook of research on multicultural education* (2nd ed., pp. 699–715). San Francisco, CA: Jossey-Bass.

National Council of Teachers of English. (2008). English language learners: A policy brief produced by the National Council of Teachers of English. *The Council Chronicle, 17*(3), 15–22.

Ruiz, R. (1984). Orientations in language planning. *NABE Journal, 8*(2), 15–34.

Song, B. (2006). Content-based ESL instruction: Long-term effects and outcomes. *English for Specific Purposes, 25,* 420–437. doi:10.1016/j.esp.2005.09.002

Teachers of English to Speakers of Other Languages. (1996–2007). *PreK–12 English language proficiency standards framework.* Retrieved from http://www.tesol.org/s_tesol/sec=13323#levels

U.S. Department of Education. (2008). *Characteristics of the 100 largest public elementary and secondary school districts in the United States: 2005–06.* Retrieved from http://nces.ed.gov/pubs2008/100_largest_0506/tables/table_a12.asp

U.S. Department of Education. (2009). *The condition of education: Participation in education.* Retrieved from http://nces.ed.gov/programs/coe/2009/section1/index.asp

Vacca, R. T., & Vacca, J. L. (2005). *Content area reading: Literacy and learning across the curriculum* (8th ed.). Boston, MA: Pearson.

Valdes, G., Bunch, G., Snow, C., & Lee, C. (with Matos, L.). (2005). Enhancing the development of students' language(s). In L. Darling-Hammond & J. Bransford (Eds.) (with P. LePage, K. Hammerness, & H. Duffy), *Preparing teachers for a changing world: What teachers should learn and be able to do.* (pp. 126–168). San Francisco, CA: Jossey-Bass.

VanPatten, B., & Williams, J. (2007). Early theories in second language acquisition. In B. VanPatten & J. Williams (Eds.), *Theories in second language acquisition* (pp. 17–35). Mahwah, NJ: Lawrence Erlbaum.

Wassell, B. A., Hawrylak, M. F., & LaVan, S.-K. (2010). Examining the structures that impact English language learners' agency in urban high schools: Resources and roadblocks in the classroom. *Education and Urban Society, 42,* 599–619. doi:10.1177/0013124510375598

White, L. (2007). Linguistic theory, universal grammar, and second language acquisition. In B. VanPatten & J. Williams (Eds.), *Theories in second language acquisition* (pp. 37–55). Mahwah, NJ: Lawrence Erlbaum.

WIDA Consortium. (2007a). *English language proficiency (ELP) standards*. Retrieved from http://www.wida.us/standards/elp.aspx

WIDA Consortium. (2007b). *WIDA membership*. Retrieved from http://www.wida.us/membership/index.aspx

Yoon, B. (2008). Uninvited guests: The influence of teachers' roles and pedagogies on the positioning of English language learners in the regular classroom. *American Educational Research Journal, 45*, 495–522. doi:10.3102/0002831208316200

CONTRIBUTING AUTHORS

Karen Coyle Aylward has been teaching English language arts in the Boston Public Schools for 12 years and has also served as the ELA Content Teacher Leader for the past 6 years. She received a BA in secondary education and English from Boston College and an EdM from Harvard University in educational administration. In 2005 she earned National Board Certification, and she was named Boston Educator of the Year for 2009.

Brenda A. Murphy, who is featured in the chapter's opening vignette and in the Practice section, is an ELL specialist at Ocean Avenue School, in Portland, Maine. She earned an MA in teaching English to speakers of other languages from the School for International Training and an MS in education in literacy education from the University of Southern Maine. Brenda began her teaching career as a Peace Corps volunteer in Latvia and has taught EFL/ELL overseas and in the United States for the past 14 years.

CHAPTER 5

TAKING AN INQUIRY STANCE ON TEACHING

VIGNETTE: AN INQUIRY STANCE IN ACTION

Ms. Plemmons, a first-year teacher in Texas, teaches three junior English classes each day. She recently taught a lesson that she described as "an incredible flop." She had arranged for students to practice their multiple-choice state assessment while they'd had a substitute, and she wanted to review the answers with her students the following day (so as not to confirm their belief that it was busy work). She took time to make a PowerPoint slide-show with each answer choice and the book's justification for it being the best choice. With first period, she just went over the answer choices. Participation was minimal, and her students were bored, but they remained well behaved. She began to think, "I know I won't be as lucky with my other two English classes. I need to rethink this lesson." With second period, she re-read the stories from the assessment practice materials first and then went over the questions. Participation was better, but students were still bored. Then, Ms. Plemmons asked for advice and reflected on ways to encourage students' engagement. She decided to try partnering students for her final class, having them discuss the answer choice and why it was correct after they re-read the stories. She also spoke honestly to her third class: without a lot of participation, that day would be long and boring. She needed their help to make it work.

Despite her best efforts and intentions, Ms. Plemmons still felt that the lesson was not a great one. While the activity went a lot better with the third group, it was still a hard sell, and the students let her know it. However, her honesty with them and allowing them to take a break for small (on-task) conversation earned her appreciation and some participation. Though she did not figure out how to make multiple-choice state assessment reviews engaging, she did manage to improve her relationships with her students. Reflection helped guide her to make an unsuccessful lesson more successful. Ms. Plemmons says that reflection improves lessons, improves rapport with her classes, and helps her manage five unique class periods.

FOCUS QUESTIONS

- How does taking an inquiry stance on teaching support urban teachers' resilience and success?
- What effective teaching practices are associated with reflection and systematic inquiry?
- How can reflection and inquiry help teachers avoid the pull for "recipes" and "magical answers" and address perceived problems as opportunities for further study and problem solving?

As Ms. Plemmons's vignette reveals, urban teaching is likely to pose many "puzzles" of practice (Ballenger, 2009; Munby & Russell, 1990). Whether you approach these puzzles as overwhelming challenges or as opportunities to learn and develop may have a significant impact on your own success as well as that of your students. Are you an inquirer when it comes to teaching and learning? Are you inquisitive about your students and your teaching practice? Are you ready to challenge assumptions and the status quo? Do you see the challenges and puzzles of urban education as opportunities to be explored in order to change unproductive, inequitable, and unjust teaching and educational practices? In this chapter, we will explore **inquiry as stance** (Cochran-Smith & Lytle, 1993), a habit of mind in which the practitioner generates local knowledge in order to transform urban teaching, learning, and schooling.

"Puzzling moments" (Ballenger, 2009) are bound to be plentiful in the often highly complex and relatively unpredictable process of urban teaching. Reflection can lead to an inquiry stance in which our teaching practice changes and improves, fueled by continuous learning, the generation of new knowledge, and a cyclical return to reflection. The questions that come out of these moments may be some of the most exciting and challenging aspects of urban teaching, particularly because we have voice and personal investment in the inquiry process. In this chapter, we first review theories on reflection that serve as the foundation of an inquiry stance. Then we examine what it means to take an inquiry stance on teaching.

THEORETICAL FRAMEWORK
FOR REFLECTION AND INQUIRY

Critical Reflective Practice

As Raines and Shadiow (1995) point out, "the two words *reflection* and *practice* are a part of everyone's general vocabulary, so it is easy to reduce the complexities and challenges of the phrase to something like 'thinking about the doing'" (p. 271). Yet, for teachers, reflective practice is much more than simply thinking about what they have done, are doing, or will do. Often, teachers and others in education assume teachers are naturally reflective, but reflection is a process that must be learned, studied, and practiced over time. Reflective practice involves teachers taking a deliberate pause from their everyday activities; maintaining an open perspective; engaging in complex thinking processes; examining their beliefs, goals, and practices; developing new insights and understandings; and taking actions that improve students' learning (York-Barr, Sommers, Ghere, & Montie, 2001). The key here is that reflection cannot merely stop with the thinking; for a teacher to truly be a reflective practitioner, he or she must *do* something as a result of that thinking.

Critical reflective practice is not an easy process, however, as it requires asking ourselves difficult and penetrating questions about why we teach the way we do. What do we believe is best for our students and why? How might our own biases and assumptions about ourselves, our students, and our teaching cloud our ability to uncover the impact of our practice and make more informed decisions? Can we recognize when our reasoning shapes and influences our practice in inappropriate or unproductive ways? In what ways do we defer to habitual or instinctive modes that may not actually serve our students?

Why would a teacher, then, go to all this trouble to be a reflective practitioner? After all, "under the press of large class sizes, increasing extracurricular responsibilities, and vociferous calls for technical reform," reflection is often seen as extra "fluff" (Raines & Shadiow, 1995, p. 274). However, the goals and results of critical reflection are many: to help us make informed actions, to help us develop a rationale for practice, to ground us emotionally, to enliven and activate our classrooms, and to increase democratic trust in our students (Brookfield, 1995, pp. 22–25).

Critical reflection helps teachers make informed choices that can be explained to others and have a greater chance at achieving the desired result. This rationale enables teachers to know *why* they do what they do. Through critical reflection, teachers can avoid "self-laceration" (Brookfield, 1995), the blame that earnest, serious urban teachers may place on themselves if students aren't learning as much as the teachers would like. As Palmer (1998) eloquently writes, "Small wonder, then, that teaching tugs at the heart, opens the heart, and even breaks the heart—and the more one loves teaching, the more heartbreaking it can be. The courage to teach is the courage to keep one's heart open in those very moments when the heart is asked to hold more than it is able" (p. 11). Rather than taking on blame and suffering heartbreak, critical reflection helps teachers understand why learning is not taking place and allows them to keep their hearts open to possibilities for the future. Critical reflection, like inquiry, encourages teachers to make their thinking public, which can be a powerful catalyst for engaging with both colleagues and students.

Many scholars have conceptualized the idea of reflective practice. In particular, Dewey, Schön, and Brookfield offer varying but complementary ways to assume a reflective stance toward teaching and learning. Their ideas can be synthesized into the following categories, which are expounded below: reflective action; reflection in-, on-, and for-action; problem setting; and examination of multiple lenses.

Reflective Action Versus Routine Action

Philosopher and educator John Dewey (1933) defined reflection as "active, persistent, and careful consideration of any belief or supposed form of knowledge in the light of the grounds that support it and the further conclusions to which it leads" (p. 9). He contrasted reflective action with **routine action**, or the everyday process of stream-of-consciousness thinking and doing. Routine action is what people—or teachers—do to get a certain response; **reflective action**, however, is the *inquiry*-based process that focuses on the process, not the product.

For reflective action to occur, Dewey (1933) believed that teachers must possess three important characteristics: open-mindedness, responsibility, and wholeheartedness. Teachers who are open-minded, in the truest sense of Dewey's definition, will listen to and consider multiple sides of an issue and question their own beliefs, even if those beliefs are the ones they hold most dearly. Responsible teachers actively contemplate the consequences of their actions and apply new information to better solve problems. Wholehearted teachers are committed to being open-minded and responsible, and they demonstrate this commitment by attempting meaningful changes for their students and schools.

Reflection-in-Action, Reflection-on-Action, and Reflection-for-Action

Closely related to Dewey's distinction between reflective and routine action is Schön's (1983) theory of reflection-in-action and reflection-on-action. Unlike Dewey, who clearly foregrounds reflection-for-action as more important, Schön's first two categories of reflection are interdependent. **Reflection-in-action** is considered the spontaneous "thinking on our feet" in which we make decisions based on our intuition. We think about our practice as we engage in it, and we apply previous experience and understandings to inform our action. We make the immediate decision, for example, to speak to a sad-looking student after class, instead of calling him out in class, because we know he does not like to be the center of attention. In contrast, **reflection-on-action** occurs after practice as we explore why and how things occurred as they did. For example, using Ms. Plemmons in the opening vignette as an example, we may decide to alter the amount of test preparation material we teach based on our experiences with students from the prior year. This process often generates questions and ideas about our practice. For example, "How can I prepare my students adequately for standardized tests without sacrificing time for meaningful learning?" Dewey would agree that making sense of our experience as we draw on a repertoire is at the heart of critical reflection. According to Schön, reflection-on-action is a rigorous professional process involving acknowledgment of and reflection on uncertainty and complexity in one's practice, leading to "a legitimate form of professional knowing" (p. 69).

Several years after he first posited this theory, Schön (1987) added a third category: **reflection-for-action**, the culmination of reflection-in-action and reflection-on-action. After carefully evaluating problems spontaneously while they are occurring and then further analyzing potential solutions, teachers should then *take* action. It is important to note that one incident in a classroom can—and often should, depending on the import of the issue—lead to all three types of reflection.

Problem Setting Versus Problem Solving

Problem solving is something that teachers have been doing since they were students themselves. Indeed, many of us can recall specific mathematics lessons devoted solely to improving our problem-solving skills. Later, we learned the scientific method as a way to solve particularly challenging problems, and in urban schools problem solving involves similar strategies: "make sense of a challenging situation, identify areas of practice needing scrutiny, define goals for improvement, and pursue actions to accomplish them" (Yost, Sentner, & Forlenza-Bailey, 2000, p. 40).

However, Schön (1983) differentiates between problem solving and **problem setting**, and this distinction is an important one for new teachers in urban schools:

> In real-world practice, problems do not present themselves to the practitioner as given. They must be constructed from . . . situations which are puzzling, troubling, and uncertain. . . . Problem setting is a process in which, interactively, we name the things to which we will attend and frame the context in which we will attend to them. (p. 40)

Schön's argument is that teachers cannot solve a problem without first recognizing what that problem is, where it stems from, and what can be done, within the boundaries of their profession, to solve it. This is especially important for teachers in urban schools, who may be confronted with "problems" that are set by those outside the school or the education sector. For example, many policy-makers view multicultural education as a problem, and they believe that students' challenges will be solved if we return to a core knowledge curriculum that emphasizes traditional learning through traditional methods. However, if an urban teacher does not agree with their policies, it is her responsibility to set her own problems and solve the issues she truly views as problematic for her students, rather than solving artificially created problems that are imposed upon her.

Multiple Reflective Lenses

Teachers must realize that they are not alone in the classroom. Their practice is informed by their personal beliefs, their students, their colleagues, and society. Brookfield's (1995) notion of reflective practice encourages teachers to stand outside of themselves, uncover assumptions and false reasoning, and, therefore, come to a more focused understanding of their practice. He offers four different lenses through which we can better understand our practice: our autobiographies as teachers and learners, our students' views and perceptions, our colleagues' perceptions, and relevant theoretical literature. We can begin the reflective process by examining our own autobiographies and putting ourselves in the position of the "other." In doing so "we see our practice from the other side of the mirror, and we become viscerally connected to what our own students are experiencing" (p. 29). When we put ourselves in the position of our students, we are better able to recognize power dynamics in the classroom and to determine whether our intentions are actually being enacted in practice. Similarly, when we invite colleagues into our classrooms and engage in critical conversations with them, together we may explore and uncover hidden practices and determine new responses. Lastly, Brookfield urges us to use theoretical literature to help us "name" our practice, seeing the generic in what often feels idiosyncratic to ourselves and our context. Theory can also help us better understand the contradictions of urban teaching practice, such as policies that restrict children in the greatest need from resources that would benefit them.

Brookfield's (1995) work is particularly helpful for many teachers because it offers specific and practical strategies for engaging with each reflective lens. For example, he encourages the use of teaching logs, a weekly record of critical incidents that help to uncover our assumptions and blind spots. Events that elicit particularly strong emotion have the potential to reveal us. Another strategy, "survival advice memos," has teachers imagine leaving their position and write a memo to a successor. This memo has the potential to bring to the forefront both the knowledge and the assumptions the teacher deems crucial for success (p. 78).

Critical reflection is an important step in effective urban teaching. When we take the next step of posing questions and systematically collecting and analyzing data that result from reflection, we move into an inquiry orientation to teaching.

An Inquiry Orientation to Teaching

An **inquiry orientation** or **stance** can help keep us open to truly seeing and making sense of our students, our practice, our schools, and our community. This requires examining our biases, assumptions, and judgments—however well intentioned—and learning how they might affect our perceptions and actions. In her own inquiry into urban teaching, Ballenger (2009) discovered the following: "Research questions, I realized, weren't so much the ones I had encountered in graduate school, ones originating in theory; rather they were what I thought of as irritating or troublesome or funny—this was actually worthy of study, indeed in many cases these events were things we should feel compelled to study" (p. 5). When teachers are also researchers into their own practice, they are well positioned to develop understandings of and take meaningful action in response to the immediate needs and concerns within their practice, school, and community. In researching our educational practice, "we are not simply looking at what methods or strategies we use or should use; we are raising questions about the values we hold and about our own self-image. When this starts to happen, action research becomes for us an exploration of who we are and what we stand for" (Cochran-Smith & Lytle, 1999, p. 271).

Whether you are preparing to become an urban teacher or are already teaching in an urban school, you have undoubtedly read research and theory and studied promising practices for the classroom. Rather than being a recipient of research, seeing research as belonging in the external realm of scientific studies or viewing research as an "if I have time" activity, teacher inquiry/research is intended to be an integral part of teaching and schooling practices. Inquiry into teaching "involves teachers doing what they have to do anyway—paying careful attention to what is going on in their classrooms" (Hubbard & Power, 1999, p. xv). An inquiry orientation keeps us open to truly seeing and beginning to make sense of our urban practice by reflexively posing questions, systematically collecting and analyzing data, and generating and sharing new, contextualized knowledge.

The process of inquiry helps us reframe what we know and what we think we know about urban teaching. Cochran-Smith and Lytle (1993), who have developed the concept and coined the phrase **inquiry as stance**, promote the

> idea of teachers as deliberative intellectuals who constantly theorize inquiry as part of the practice itself and that the goal of teacher learning initiatives is the joint construction of local knowledge, the questioning of common assumptions, and thoughtful critique of the usefulness of research generated by others both inside and outside contexts of practice. (p. 2)

There are several ways one can build an inquiry stance, including teacher research, action research, and participatory action research. In the next section, we further explore the theoretical framework for an inquiry stance into urban teaching practice by looking at the common features of different forms of inquiry as well as each individual type of research itself.

Common Features and Types of Teacher Inquiry

The inquiry methods of teacher research, action research, and participatory action research share important common features, but each is open to various conceptual interpretations (Cochran-Smith & Donnell, 2006; Cochran-Smith & Lytle, 1999). Rather than being informed solely by outside research, the educator engaged in inquiry is both practitioner and researcher. Teachers most frequently, but also students, principals, parents, community organizers, and other stakeholders, may be involved in the research process. Of critical importance is community—including the community of stakeholders working together, promoting unity and communication, and sharing publicly with others. Key assumptions about who can "know" and what they know are also a common feature across inquiry research. One of the key tenets of inquiry research is the generation of knowledge that is developed within a local, immediate context. The practitioner himself, as well as others involved in the inquiry, is best positioned to know about that particular puzzle, child, practice, or situation. Indeed, the children, colleagues, and communities we work with become our research sites. Inquiry enables teachers, students, parents, and others to take an active role in forming, designing, and analyzing investigations into community, school, and classroom life. Inquiry research is also systematic; it is essential that the research is planned and well defined, occurs over time, and uses appropriate data sources. Additionally, we should make our inquiry research public. That is, our goal is not only to use this new knowledge to further support our practice and our students, but to share what we learn about urban teaching practice with others. When we use the context of practice to study practice itself, there is a blurring of boundaries (Cochran-Smith & Lytle, 1999) between research and practice. Research and practice are not mutually exclusive, but rather inform one another in a cyclical fashion. Parsons and Brown (2002) define the process as one of a systematic "adjustment of theory *to* practice and of theory *from* practice" (p. 3, emphasis added).

Just as students may experiment and collect data in the classroom, urban teachers should also conduct research to further their practice and share findings with others in the community.

Teacher research generally refers to the renewed interest in teacher inquiry that first emerged in the late 1980s (Cochran-Smith & Lytle, 1999; Lagemann, 2000). The role of teacher research continues to be part of practitioners' discussions about teacher learning, school reform, and the knowledge base for teaching. Educational stakeholders work in collaboration and use teacher research to better understand teaching and learning by posing questions and collecting data around critical, locally generated issues in teaching and learning. This process of inquiry has been conceptualized by Cochran-Smith and Lytle (1993, 1999) as the central task of teaching across the professional lifespan (Cochran-Smith & Donnell, 2006). Beyond reflection, teacher research involves teachers' systematically collecting data and documenting their practice and students' learning. The key tenets of teacher research are that it is situated in the teacher's context, usually the classroom; is focused on and honors the development of local knowledge within teaching practice; and results in "living educational theory" (Whitehead, 1989).

Action research is a systematic and cyclical way of deepening our understanding of how changes in our actions or practices can benefit a community, particularly with respect to social justice concerns. In the early 20th century, John Dewey (1938/1993) disputed the orthodoxy of scientific research methods as they did not include those directly involved in the practice of education. Dewey further highlighted the important component of reflection, coupled with experience, to equal learning. He worked toward developing theory that guided the practice of teaching and learning. Scholars have built upon his theoretical approach and developed the methodology of action research (Lewin, 1946). Corey (1953) defined action research as the process through which practitioners study their own practice to solve their personal practical problems. Whereas teacher research is most often carried out by classroom teachers, action research is understood to be more broadly conceived as research conducted by any educational stakeholders on any educational problem. Many of the efforts are focused on addressing curricular issues, challenging status quo school practices, and working for social change (Cochran-Smith & Donnell, 2006). Reason and Bradbury (1997) define action research as a process of "seeking to bring together action and reflection, theory and practice, in participation with others, in the pursuit of practical solutions to issues of pressing concern to people, and more generally the flourishing of individual persons and their communities" (p. 2). As with other forms of inquiry, action research consists of cycles of posing problems, systematically collecting data, reflecting, analyzing, taking data-driven action, and returning to a redefined problem and a new cycle. The key tenets of action research include finding socially just solutions to improve a classroom, school, or community and its performance; simultaneously addressing practical issues and contributing to the knowledge base; involving reflection and making explicit and challenging one's interpretations, biases, assumptions, and judgments about educational practice; and collaboratively conducting research.

Participatory action research (PAR) finds its roots in Paulo Freire's (2007) concept of **critical pedagogy**, an educational theory and orientation toward teaching and learning practices that are designed to enhance learners' critical consciousness concerning social justice issues. PAR focuses on social change within a community and seeks to actively involve key stakeholders in all aspects of the process. This is an important distinction from action research: PAR participants are coresearchers, sometimes with an outside researcher who assumes insider status for the duration of the study. The goal of PAR is often social and political transformation. Increasingly, urban middle and high school teachers are finding PAR to be an excellent way to engage students in all aspects of their educational process and to strengthen their commitment to their community and to democracy (Fletcher, 2004). Participatory action research's key tenets are that knowledge is based on social relationships; research should be conducted by and for the group or community; research addresses situations that are viewed as problematic; and research is focused on co-constructed inquiry, collaborative change, and action.

Students who actively participate in classroom research have an increased awareness of their community ties and their own power to enact change.

Applying Inquiry to Urban Teaching Practice

Although each form of inquiry has its own methodological orientation, all share a common set of research procedures. In this section, we outline the essential steps for designing and implementing your own inquiry research. This overview is meant to be a general guide for those interested in beginning the process. For more detailed information about conducting inquiry research, please see the Suggested Resources at the end of this chapter.

While these steps may seem linear in nature, remember that inquiry is a cyclical process in which each step continually informs and reshapes the process. Notice the cycle of reflecting, acting, evaluating, and returning to reflection embedded in the following procedures.

Developing and Refining Your Research Question

Remember that the most effective inquiry research is based on the questions, concerns, and problems you face daily. Though you can discuss your research questions with colleagues and students, it is ultimately your personal decision based on what you think needs changing in your classroom, and only you know that. It can be helpful to generate ideas for your research question by reflecting on and brainstorming the puzzles or wonderings you have associated with urban education and teaching. Return to the issues and ideas that frustrate, excite, confuse, bother, and interest you. Beginning broadly may generate the most meaningful ideas to choose from.

Generating a *what, how,* or *why* question will help you avoid posing a question that has a general yes or no answer (Hubbard & Power, 1999). More specific question stems include "What happens when . . ." or "What is going on with . . ." (Cochran-Smith & Lytle, 1993). For example, a teacher may wonder how to communicate more effectively with parents about the curriculum and ask, "What happens when I work with a community translator to send home a weekly newsletter to parents in the language they speak at home?" Or a teacher may be puzzled by the behavior of a tired, withdrawn student and ask, "What is going on with deShawn? What is contributing to his fatigue in class? How can I help him engage more in classroom life?" The critical point in both of these examples is that the teacher is not merely identifying a problem, but seeking a solution. See Figure 5.1.

Purpose

Once you have determined a question, you will need to be clear about the purpose of your inquiry. Why are you studying this question? What about it is important to you, to your students, to your school, and to your community?

Figure 5.1   Developing Your Research Question

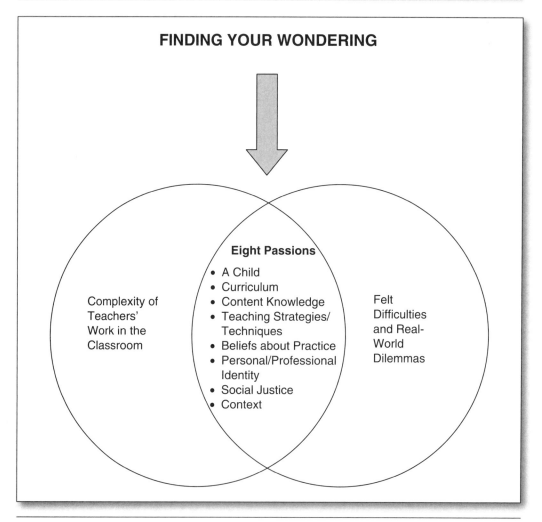

Clarifying the purpose and significance of your question will ensure that you are researching a question that is meaningful for you and others and will also keep you on track to solve one critical issue at a time. For example, in the instance of the withdrawn student explained above, the teacher's main purpose is to engage deShawn and determine why he is withdrawn. Keeping this central purpose in mind will prevent the teacher from diverging to other questions that, while valuable, may distract from this purpose. She may also wish for deShawn to bring in his homework more regularly or to write more effectively, but the main goal is to engage deShawn in classroom life, and this should not be neglected.

At this point, it is also valuable to explore the assumptions, biases, or prior judgments you may have about this issue or question. These may be difficult questions to answer, but they are necessary. In deShawn's situation above, it is important to consider *why* the teacher thinks he is tired and withdrawn. Is she comparing him to students from other cultures or to herself as a student? Does she believe he is not learning because of concerns at home, and if so, what evidence does she have for this? What assumptions about students does the teacher bring to her classroom that may influence her interactions with deShawn?

Looking to Others

There are two important ways in which the work of others can help on the inquiry path. One way to connect your work to others is by reading what has already been written about the general topic. Traditionally, a review of the literature is considered an important step in connecting theory and practice and in situating your inquiry in the larger framework of urban education. A literature review can include books, monographs, journal articles, popular press, or other types of writing that are related to your topic. This process can reveal other studies that have asked similar questions as well as effective practices associated with your inquiry. But perhaps most important, "what we read as we do research determines in part what we see in our classrooms and who we are as researchers" (Hubbard & Power, 1999, p. 161).

Another way to connect your work to others is by discussing your inquiry with colleagues and others in your educational community. Too often, individual teachers see their classrooms as cocoons and work in isolation with their students, either due to urban school culture or because they are afraid to ask for help. Inquiry research, and especially reflective practice, becomes more significant, more compelling, and more effective when shared with others. Let people know what you are doing, for there may be others with whom you can collaborate. Ask for feedback in the form of sharing stories, observing each other's classrooms, or co-constructing an action plan. Above all, seek support.

Data Collection

To find answers to your inquiry question, you will need to collect information, or data. Look to the nature of your question to decide what data will be most significant in exploring this issue. Think about the sources of data available to you. These may include, but are not limited to, observations, student work, video and audio tapes, a personal journal, photos, conferences notes, assessments, and records. In particular, many teachers focus on students through descriptive review. **Descriptive review** is a process by which a detailed and balanced description of the student and/or the student's work is developed in order to more fully understand the child's school experience (Himley & Carini, 2000). A similar group of protocols, often called Looking at Student Work, brings teachers together to reflect on important questions about teaching and learning by focusing on small samples of student work. As you make decisions about which process to use, ask yourself how each possible data source will help you answer your question. Multiple sources of data will allow you to engage with your question from different perspectives. For the teacher concerned with deShawn, helpful data might include observation notes on deShawn in various settings, like whole-group and small-group discussion, deShawn's class work, and notes from conferences with parents and colleagues.

Data Analysis

After you have collected data, you will need to determine how to analyze the data. In this process, you are reviewing the data you have collected and are making meaning relative to the question you have posed. There are three types of data analysis methodology: quantitative, qualitative, and mixed methods, which is a combination of the first two. **Quantitative analysis**, as the name implies, would be conducted if you have numerical data, such as test scores, checklists, or other data that can be quantified. Though educational researchers use sophisticated analytical paradigms and programs, you do not need to be a mathematician or a statistician to use quantitative analysis in your inquiry research. For example, deShawn's teacher could count the number of times he participates in whole-class and small-group discussion; she could do this before, during, and after an intervention that she has determined might help deShawn participate more, such as giving him a silent, private, prearranged signal before she is going to call on him. She could then compare her counts longitudinally, or over a particular period of time, and analyze the results using simple, descriptive statistics.

Qualitative analysis can be conducted using narrative data, such as notes, observations, or interviews and can involve looking for themes, patterns, and categories. This can be done through **coding**, a process by which you demarcate segments of the data and assign them terms that help to organize and categorize. For example, using notes that she took from observing deShawn in discussions over a period of four weeks, deShawn's social studies teacher might notice that he participated once in a discussion of the local mayoral election, twice during a debate on economic reform, and three times during a small-group activity about the United States' participation in foreign wars. The teacher is able to see a pattern of actions here, and she can code, or categorize, these events as "Current Events." She can then search her other data sources to verify her interpretation that deShawn is more engaged and participatory when discussing current events. Written memos can also be used to theorize answers to your questions as you go.

Sharing and Collaboration

Whether or not you write a formal report, sharing the knowledge you have generated with others is an integral part of the inquiry process. Sharing your findings with the participants in your study can be one of the most rewarding aspects of inquiry. Some teachers choose to discuss their study with colleagues in their courses or schools, while others form or engage in more formalized collaborative groups, such as small learning communities. Others make presentations at professional meetings or conferences, while still others write and publish papers online, in journals, or in books. (See the end of this chapter for sources of disseminating your inquiry.)

Reflection and the Evolution of Your Question

The recursive nature of inquiry often brings us to new questions. As you make sense of your initial question and reflect on your learning, consider how you can take action to improve urban education practice and continue to take charge of your own learning.

The cyclical process of engaging in inquiry is critically important to apply in urban teaching. The contexts and conditions of urban schooling pose multiple challenges daily and are often cited by urban teachers as a reason for leaving urban teaching in favor of suburban districts and/or leaving teaching altogether (Ingersoll, 2001). For example, urban school systems often rely on top-down change processes, stifling bureaucracies (see Chapter 7), and commercially produced curricula that promise quick fixes for struggling learners (see Chapter 6). Urban teachers who believe in their efficacy, trust their professional judgment, and use critical reflection and systematic inquiry can develop multiple solutions for their classroom- or school-level challenges that are particular to their urban context.

WHAT THE RESEARCH SAYS
ABOUT REFLECTION AND INQUIRY

Research on the process of inquiry and its foundation in critical reflection identifies several key ways in which urban education stakeholders benefit from and are supported by inquiry (Anderson, Herr, & Nihlen, 2007; Ballenger, 2009; Christensen, 2000; McIntyre, 2003; Nieto, 2005). The following are some of the many benefits of inquiry:

- It empowers and helps to promote change.
- It enables teachers to respond more critically to research, curricula, and policy.
- It shifts knowledge about teaching from sources outside to inside the classroom.
- It results in immediate benefits for students based on teacher learning.

It is especially exciting to note that, increasingly,

the body of published practitioner research reflects a distinct commitment to investigating issues of equity, engagement, and agency in classrooms and schools across the country. . . . In addition to compelling practitioner studies in their local sites, many educators in schools and universities have documented inquiry-based curricula that put students at the center of investigating topics of concern to them in their own lives and communities. (Cochran-Smith & Lytle, 2009, p. 34)

The five studies highlighted in Table 5.1 represent the ways in which researchers use reflection and inquiry in urban teaching practice. In one compelling example of teacher research, a group of beginning teachers of color in an urban school district researched their perceptions of gender equity, racial identity, and culturally relevant teaching (Burant, Gray, Ndaw, McKinney-Keys, & Allen, 2007). As a result of their subsequent changes in practices and deepened sense of community, they encouraged other urban teachers to engage in inquiry, noting that "teacher research could have a more prominent and important role to play in assuring that equity and justice are not buried beneath stacks of reproducible worksheets and standardized tests" (Burant et al., 2007, p. 18). Two teachers used action research to design and evaluate social skills education to promote resilience in sixth graders (Meyer & Farrell, 1998). They investigated a curriculum intervention program in an effort to reduce and prevent youth violence in a high-risk urban environment. Cochran-Smith and Lytle (1992) investigated the importance of teacher inquiry and reflection in urban schools to better understand and value cultural differences. Ravitch and

Wirth (2007) examined the action research study of a professional development program for teachers in an urban elementary school. Finally, Weiner (2002) investigated the importance of research in urban schools and the specific types of research that are found to benefit the schools in various ways.

Table 5.1 Research Studies on Reflection and Inquiry

Author(s)	Purpose	Findings	Implications	URL
Burant, Gray, Ndaw, McKinney-Keys, & Allen (2007)	Beginning teachers of color in an urban school district researched their perceptions of gender equity, racial identity, and culturally relevant teaching.	Teacher researchers found that each made substantive changes in his or her teaching practice as a result of their research. They also felt a stronger sense of community with one another, which resulted in renewing their commitment to social justice issues.	Teacher research may be able to contribute to addressing equity and justice issues in the classroom.	
Cochran-Smith & Lytle (1992)	Researchers drew from examples of two teacher research projects, one from a beginning teacher and one from an experienced teacher, to demonstrate how teacher inquiry benefits teachers with an opportunity to explore cultural diversity.	Researchers argued that teachers found conducting research to be a successful way to understand how both they and their students construct and reconstruct teaching and learning. When teachers from a variety of different categories (race, class, etc.) work together, a positive mix of perspectives may result. When both beginning and experienced teachers have chances to inquire about knowledge and differences, they become increasingly committed to both school and pedagogical reform.	Urban teachers can use research in working with other teachers and teacher educators to examine what they already know about race, class, and ethnicity; what they acknowledge when observing their own students; and the steps that can be taken regarding discrepancies.	http://jte .sagepub .com/content/ 43/2/104.full .pdf+html

(Continued)

Table 5.1 (Continued)

Author(s)	Purpose	Findings	Implications	URL
Meyer & Farrell (1998)	Two teachers designed and implemented a social curriculum in order to promote resilience in urban sixth graders.	Researchers found that the curriculum intervention program did, in fact, reduce and prevent youth violence in a high-risk urban environment.	Using inquiry research, teachers are able to investigate the efficacy of curricula they have designed or implemented.	
Ravitch & Wirth (2007)	Researchers evaluated an action research study of a professional development program for teachers in an urban elementary school. They examined the research process to explore the various implications for teachers engaging in school-based practitioner-driven research that is based on action research.	Researchers found that reciprocal empowerment existed during the research process. When teachers and school leaders collaborated, there was an identified positive effect of conducting action research in the urban school setting.	Knowledge of the importance of action research in urban school settings creates possibilities for the revisioning of educational policies, practices, and outcomes. Engaging in action research requires an ongoing investigation of one's identities, roles, and relationships and the possibilities for school change.	http://arj .sagepub .com/content/ 5/1/75.full .pdf+html

Author(s)	Purpose	Findings	Implications	URL
Weiner (2002)	The researcher investigated how urban teacher inquiry and teacher research have been impeded and how this research can improve urban schools.	Two types of research were found to be relevant in urban teacher education: research on who people are as raced, classed, and gendered and the way their social origins, thoughts, beliefs, and values configure their teaching; and investigation of the influences of schools' organizational characteristics on teachers and students. The development of a body of useful research has been hindered by the fact that few urban teachers are knowledgeable about the existing research.	Urban teachers can be educated regarding the existing urban research and the way in which this research can be expanded. This knowledge will aid them in addressing their existing research needs and possibly the goal of pursuing them.	http://jte .sagepub .com/content/ 53/3/254

PRACTICE

In this section, coauthor **Alyssa Hadley Dunn** shares her views about inquiry in urban classrooms. Drawing upon her teaching experiences in Boston, Massachusetts, and Atlanta, Georgia, she discusses how teachers can realistically and systematically incorporate inquiry into their pedagogy. In addition, **Sarah Hess**, a former Teach for America teacher and current graduate student, writes about the role of reflection in her teaching in Phoenix, Arizona. She specifically discusses the ways in which reflection supported her decision-making processes around reading instruction.

First, Alyssa describes her introduction to an inquiry stance and how she learned about its relationship to teaching practice.

Alyssa: As a senior in college, while participating in my student teaching practicum, I also had to enroll in what my university called an "Inquiry Seminar." This seminar was designed to teach student teachers how to engage in our own teacher research and reflection during our practicum experiences. At first, I was frustrated by this process, as many novice teachers are, because it seems like teacher research is something extra you have to add to your already overfilled plate. I could not figure out how, on top of grading papers, planning lessons, calling parents, and counseling students, I was going to undertake a research project. I valued the goal of teacher research—to learn more about how your students learn and how you can best teach them—but I also worried that I would be taking time away from what I really needed to do if I were to focus on my own research.

At the time, "research" was still something outside the classroom. It was something my professors did, it was something I read about, but it was not something I did *myself.* Even though my university stressed the link between theory and practice, I had not yet conceptualized how to make that link resonate with taking up an inquiry project.

Alyssa is careful to note that she struggled with being a teacher researcher, as many novice teachers do. She goes on to elaborate on how she resolved this inner struggle between thinking inquiry was something extra and valuing its goal of improving learning for all.

Alyssa: For me, this issue resolved itself once I settled on an inquiry topic. My cooperating teacher had been encouraging me to attempt Socratic Seminars with my tenth-grade English students, but as these seminars tend to do, mine failed miserably the first time I attempted it. Students were not used to taking such high level of responsibility for leading a discussion, and they needed time to learn the structure and value of such a seminar. I realized that I could use teacher research and an inquiry-based approach to problem solving on an issue that I was *already* having in the classroom. I didn't have to create a project in this sense; instead the project came to me when I realized that I needed to find out how students were learning and how they were envisioning their role in the Socratic Seminar process.

I designed a self- and group-evaluation survey that students completed after each Socratic Seminar, which I scheduled once a week for eight weeks.

These evaluations asked them to consider how they performed, how they could have performed better, and what they would do differently next time. They were also asked to rate their peers and write down what they had learned from each other. I then charted their results and compared how their participation changed—and hopefully increased—as they took more personal responsibility and reflected on their process.

In the end, I found that, for many students, being able to have a few moments after each seminar to think about what they did and how they could change gave them the impetus to *actually* change it the next time. Students began to speak up more, to engage their peers in critical reflection on the readings, and to find important evidence from the text to support their points—all of which were three major goals of the Socratic Seminars. Though my study was an informal one that may never be published or disseminated widely, it served its purpose in my classroom.

I think this is the key to using teacher research effectively: use it to illuminate a problem that you are already having. Then it does not become some extraneous add-on to your work, but becomes central to improving your work, and the problem is a genuine one rooted in experience.

Alyssa makes the important point that sometimes teachers have to renegotiate what they think of as research and how they solve problems in the classroom. Inquiry as stance does not "solve" problems immediately, but it addresses them systematically and often quite effectively. Next, Alyssa ponders the potential obstacles for teachers who attempt to use inquiry in their own classrooms.

Alyssa: Many school systems today, and urban schools in particular, are completely at odds with allowing teachers to be inquirers. In this era of high-stakes testing, accountability, and prescriptive curricula, teachers are supposed to have all the answers, because, after all, they are often given all the answers in prepackaged scripts and textbook manuals. For a teacher who wants students to question and wants to continue questioning herself, this is a difficult environment in which to work.

On the surface, many schools appear to have some basis of inquiry. For example, I was required to give my students biweekly benchmark assessments to "measure learning." Then I had to chart the number of items they got correct on the pretest and compare it what they got on the posttest. This looks an awful lot like teacher research in that I appear to be measuring what and how my students are learning. However, the goal is not to improve learning but to improve data collection; it is not to see how I can make changes in my curriculum, but how well I follow the state-mandated pacing guides. It does not measure at all how I am teaching or how students are learning, but rather how well students can remember the answers to 10 multiple-choice items over a two-week period. I know that many urban systems are moving toward—if they are not already strongly invested in—such measures, but novice and veteran teachers cannot be lulled into thinking that this number crunching is actually research. Teacher research, and especially action research and participatory action research, is dichotomous to this data-driven, numerical-infested way of measuring learning.

Many urban teachers will face such obstacles as Alyssa presents, including the desire to drive practice through hard data, which maintains the illusion that student and teacher success can be measured by filling in bubbles. In the face of such odds, Alyssa shares a concrete example of how she used inquiry in her own classroom.

Alyssa: The thing about good teaching is that it can thrive even in the most stifling of conditions. For example, I knew my students had to take the benchmark assessments or I could literally lose my job. My students are obviously smarter than the district gives them credit for because they saw right through the purposes of the benchmark tests. Some refused to take it, others memorized the answers from week to week, and there was nothing I could do about this. What a horrible predicament in which to put a teacher: I was supposed to force my students to complete an assignment that I knew did not have anything to do with what they needed to know.

After struggling with my own beliefs about such assessments, I took an inquiry approach to the benchmarks. Instead of making it a meaningless activity, in which the students felt further burdened and ignored by the system, I had students reflect on the assessments and offer ways to change it. After each posttest, we would examine the questions and figure out if they were "good" questions or "needs improvement" questions. Then they created alternative assessments that they felt *truly* measured their own learning. Interestingly, but not surprisingly, many students discussed how their learning could not be encapsulated in a multiple-choice item. They wrote essay questions and project guidelines, and what's more, they used their persuasive writing skills—which, again, I was required to teach for the high-stakes writing exam—to write letters to the district explaining why they felt benchmark tests were or were not actually measuring their learning. I had found a way to teach the standards without standardizing the curriculum or teaching to the test, and I had incorporated action research at the same time.

In the end, the district did not respond to our pleas or the students' letters. Benchmarks are still in existence, and they have moved beyond the English and math classrooms to all core subjects. My students were discouraged, but I tried to reassure them that the point was not only to get the tests changed. It was also to make them feel like they had a *right* to have their voices be heard, that they had a *right* to participate in their own learning. Their reflection on their own learning was equally important; instead of being passive consumers, they were analyzing what they wanted to know, what they needed to know, and the best way for them to learn it.

Though Alyssa's action research project did not have the results that her students wished, she explains that they were able to give voice to their concerns and participate actively in their own learning. She also describes how important reflection was for their process. Alyssa also tells about the value of reflection for her own practice.

Alyssa: If teachers want students to reflect on their learning, we have to be committed to reflecting on both our learning and our teaching. Reflection is something that comes naturally for me, and I am glad that it does because it allows me to take a step back from the hustle and bustle of the day and actually process what is happening and why. Reflection, for me, is about renewal; it enables me to think critically about my place in the classroom and about what I need to do to make my place more meaningful. It also helps me see that some things are out of my control and I cannot blame myself for everything. Reflection renews my spirit because it gives me the freedom to be emotionally engaged in my work.

Alyssa describes how reflection helps her and other teachers be more resilient.

Alyssa: Too often, teachers internalize their fears and problems. We are desperately afraid that someone will criticize us because this assignment didn't work, or this student failed, so we do not share our deepest fears and innermost thoughts with others. Teaching is such a public and exposing endeavor. Yes, teachers "complain" and "vent" all the time, in teachers' lounges over lunch, but the true problems a teacher is having may never be shared with anyone because of the concern that she is inadequate. I am reminded of Parker Palmer's (1998) discussion in *The Courage to Teach* that "teaching is a daily exercise in vulnerability" (p. 17). Reflection, I believe, can help one feel less vulnerable.

Individual reflection allows me to process what is going on in the classroom. I am able to figure out how I need to do things differently to make my classroom a better environment in which students and I can learn together. It forces me to think of new solutions that may not have been immediately apparent in the heat of the moment. Collaborative reflection, or reflection with others in a learning community, also helps keep me resilient because it shows me that I am not alone. All teachers have concerns and feel vulnerable, and together we are able to pose many questions to each other and help formulate potential solutions.

As part of my graduate program, I was able to lead a reflection seminar for preservice teachers. I felt it was so valuable that these new teachers begin reflecting in a group at the start of their careers. They learned so much from each other, and as a facilitator, I constantly felt renewed and hopeful as they developed action plans for how to improve their practice. If school systems or individual schools encouraged this type of group reflection, I believe teachers would not get burnt out as quickly.

Alyssa also believes that reflection can contribute to teachers' success.

Alyssa: As a first-year teacher, I tended to throw out some lessons that just "didn't work." For some reason or another, I believed students didn't learn what they needed to learn, so I just discarded the assignment. Looking back, I see this was such a waste of good material and of the possibility for reflection. When a lesson doesn't go as planned, or a particular student is having an issue that a teacher feels should be addressed, I think the tendency is just to say, "I can't do anything about it. It's out of my control. Let's move on." But the reality is that reflection can turn a not-so-good assignment into a great one. For example, a tradition in my classroom was to do a big paper and presentation on the Harlem Renaissance. Students researched a person or an event during this time and, either as a group or individually, presented their research in a creative way in a "Living History Museum." The first time, we spent weeks on this; we went to the library, we wrote drafts, and finally the big day came when other teachers and parents joined us for the presentations. However, some of the presentations were very disappointing to me. I thought I had given students plenty of time to prepare. I had also given them free rein with the method in which they conveyed their information. Yet I watched as one group after another presented a smattering of research on

PowerPoint slides. The graphics were more impressive than the content, and students seemed uncomfortable speaking to the group.

After this, I was tempted to throw out the project. It was too much work for such disappointment. Only when I stepped back and reflected on the assignment did I ask myself what *I* could have done better to make sure the results were what I wanted. How could I have changed the assignment and/or my instruction? Most important, though, I also asked the students what *they* thought. Many were also disappointed, and while they were willing to take some responsibility for the outcomes, they also shared some valuable insights into how the project could have been scaffolded differently to make them feel more confident. For example, many other teachers required students to do PowerPoints, so my open-ended rubric about "choose whatever mode of presentation you feel best coveys your information" was too open-ended. They had never learned that they could just as convincingly present their information in a skit, dance, dramatic reading, art gallery, or other creative format. The following semester, I offered these suggestions to students, and the results were much improved. The students also felt I had not given them enough opportunities to speak in front of the class before the "big day," so they were nervous. At first, I was bothered by this; I prided myself on allowing my students to be active learners. They had debates, small-group jigsaw activities, and dramatic readings of plays. But this was different, they said; in those instances, they had all learned the information from me already. Here, they were required to be "teachers," and this came with a certain responsibility that they feared. The following semester, I began asking students to "teach" the class much earlier in the semester, so they were fully prepared for the culminating presentation on the Harlem Renaissance. Without my reflection on this project and without asking my students to reflect and wonder aloud with me, I would have discarded a valuable assignment. Reflection, then, enabled both my students and me to be more successful.

Like Alyssa, Sarah has found reflection to be a powerful process in supporting teacher and student effectiveness and success, while resisting scripted teaching and "recipes." Here, Sarah explores how critical reflection supported problem solving and was needed to address challenges her students were facing with reading skills.

Sarah: As a fifth-grade teacher in Phoenix, Arizona, authentic assessment wasn't in my vocabulary. I had been placed in my classroom by a nonprofit organization that seeks college graduates with leadership experience, trains them in a condensed summer-long program, and places them in high-need, high-poverty schools. My training focused on learning theory, literacy development, and instructional planning and delivery, but also on diversity and teaching as leadership. I attended clinics on engaging reluctant families and workshops on building a culture of achievement in the classroom. We were encouraged to support, discuss, observe, and reflect on the teaching of others, and in turn I was observed daily, then weekly, until I (and my advisors) felt I was competent.

Both in my summer-long placement in Houston, Texas, and in my permanent placement in Phoenix, my students faced poverty, transience, language barriers, deportation, and fear. Some had parents in jail, 100% received free lunch, 97% were English language learners. I learned to tread carefully over the cultural friction that existed between my Mexican and Mexican American students and found creative ways to involve both students and parents in big, long-term goals. Resources as simple as books and photocopies were difficult to come by, but professional development on crucial topics like differentiation and inclusion abounded.

In Phoenix, I worked with a revolving group of 29 fifth graders ranging in reading ability from first- to eighth-grade levels. Many days I felt like I was drowning in practicalities—Jose stopped coming to school, Efren told me he couldn't do his math because he had to work with his dad, Blanca might actually have known more English than she wanted me to believe, and so on. The immediacy of an announcement from the office easily drowned out my creeping suspicion that something about my reading instruction was not quite right, and I pedaled on, for weeks, swallowing the thought that many of my students weren't getting all they could from that busy slice of morning reading time.

As Sarah honestly notes, many wonderings come from concerns or issues that resurface continually and prompt us to dig deeper. However, we may wonder just how much we can and should do about our creeping suspicions.

Sarah: As a first-year teacher, prescriptives from the central office, the school office, the team, or a well-meaning mentor seemed like law. When I was given a class set of reading texts and an explicit call for Friday reading quiz scores, it never occurred to me that I had any discretion. Our reading program followed a chapter-per-week format: Mondays were for vocabulary and prereading, Tuesdays we read the text aloud, Wednesdays we interpreted the text through a graphic organizer, Thursdays were reserved for comprehension questions, and on Fridays there was a standardized comprehension and vocabulary quiz on the material, the results of which were to be recorded onto a spreadsheet and submitted to the administration.

For the first part of the year, my students learned vocabulary, read aloud, dutifully penned sequence charts, and responded to first short-answer and then multiple-choice questions. My students' scores were fine, my reading block looked like reading blocks in the other fifth-grade classrooms, and my principal was happy. But one evening a few weeks into October, I found my way to an online teaching forum about reading in upper elementary classes, and I was captivated by the possibilities: there were so many ways different teachers had found to explore genres, demystify literary elements, and even investigate class-identified community problems through text sources as diverse as police reports, newspaper articles, and letters. These teachers were teaching the same comprehension strategies and allowing for the same—or better—reading practice that I was, but in creative, authentic ways.

Sarah's desire to learn more, to become the best teacher she can be, and to best serve her students prompted her to seek out additional resources—in this case, an online forum. She exhibits a willingness to maintain an open perspective toward and to engage in complex thinking processes about her teaching practice. Notice, in the next section, how she begins to focus her reflection and zero in on what she might do.

Sarah: I went back to school, suspecting that my reading block needed an overhaul but not yet convinced I could do it. I did start immediately to mentally catalogue the problems. My students were inconsistently and superficially engaged by the texts, but I could increase engagement with dressed-up vocabulary games and reader's theatre approaches to the narratives. For many of my students, the text was too easy or too difficult, but I could use structured social learning strategies to compensate for the vast differences in reading abilities. The narratives failed to reflect my students' racial, cultural, or linguistic norms, and they also tended to be superficial in contrast to the very grown-up problems and responsibilities my students faced at school and at home. In contrast to issues of identity and citizenship and the very grown-up barrier of poverty, a story about Sally and her dog who wants to play fetch just seemed silly.

I tried to make the readings more relatable to my students. Sometimes we changed the characters' Anglo American names to students' own Mexican, Mexican American, African American, and Native American first names. Sometimes we reset our stories in settings from students' own cultures: Sally is Agata, and her sister's sailboat birthday party is actually a quinceañera. Sometimes we consciously compared the differences between the characters and ourselves and then stepped back, seeking the underlying human story.

Each of these changes yielded short-term engagement with its novelty or with its frank assessment of difference, and each was a step in the right direction. Still, my list of concerns was tangling itself into several more substantial questions. I wondered whether reading aloud (whether as buddy reading, reader's theatre, or seesaw reading) benefited students the same way that independent reading would. My suspicion was that the texts were regularly read aloud because oral reading—which amounted to listening for most students most of the time—increased comprehension scores on the Friday quizzes, but what about the long-term impact?

As noted earlier in this chapter, both reflection and inquiry are cyclical processes. Often, one question or wondering opens up many more. Sarah is now both expanding and deepening her reflection into her students' work and her own teaching practice.

Sarah: When I taught strategies for independent reading, I did so haphazardly in those famous teachable moments that pop up throughout the school day. But shouldn't independent reading strategies be the focus of my reading lessons? Shouldn't my students experience the same challenge to construct their own meaning from the text on a regular basis that they experience on the state tests, if we're all reacting to the scores? On the other hand, if I taught independent reading strategies and gave my students time to work through the stories rather than guaranteeing that they could listen each week, would their Friday scores drop? How would I explain that?

Even more than my Monday-to-Thursday approach, I began to question the Friday assessment itself. Having a dedicated weekly assessment period during reading block mandated that my students were only spending 80% of their reading time on lessons and practice. On top of that, I wasn't convinced the Friday assessment scores were actually reflective of my students' understanding. In some ways, the quiz seemed designed to be tricky: rather than questioning overall story themes, quizzes would target things like the feelings of subcharacters as evidenced by words nested around dialogue—she spoke "hesitantly" or he "sniffled despite his bravado." My classroom of English language learners so easily missed the nuances that the questions seemed to target, and in some ways this was adaptive: wouldn't I rather they interpret unknown words through context and complete the reading rather than stumble through a dictionary in frustration once or twice a sentence?

I finally sat down, took out a notebook, and tried to sort these problems into two categories: problems that I could fix and problems that were out of my control. My list addressed the questions I'd been struggling with in concrete terms:

1. Engagement: Mandated readings are not relatable to students, partly because they are not multicultural. I can try to supplement with more appropriate literature.

2. Differentiation: Mandated readings are too hard for 30% of my class, too easy for another 30%. Guided reading groups could target needed skills for struggling readers and create enrichment for more advanced readers.

3. Oral reading: Reading aloud won't directly help my students' independent reading progress. I could read aloud with guided reading groups who aren't able to approach the text independently, but let students who are ready work on their own at times.

4. Assessment: Friday quizzes do not help inform my teaching or show student progress.

5. Objectives: My reading period objectives are vague. Basically, my students read stories and do activities—but to what end? If I don't know what I'm trying to accomplish, I won't get there. I need better objectives.

When I looked closely at these problems, there was only one thing I really couldn't change: the Friday assessments would have to go on, which meant my students would have to read the texts in this book. However, they didn't need to read only the texts in this book, and they didn't necessarily need to follow the Monday-to-Thursday schedule of prereading followed by vocabulary followed by oral reading and so on. By writing down exactly what I perceived as problems with my reading period, and vetting these problems for out-of-my-control elements, my next steps were immediately obvious: find solutions and try them out.

Some of my solutions were adaptations more than overhauls, but even the first set of changes felt like a huge relief to me. When I wrote everything down, it was easy to decide that helping students score well on an end-of-the-week assessment that might lack validity was less important than foundational reading skills that could yield long-term results. I looked to state standards and national reading guidelines, creating a "tool shed" bulletin board devoted to strategies that fluent readers use to help them understand what they're reading. With clear objectives and strategies to lead my class toward those objectives, a final necessity became my own end-of-the-week assessments to check that students were learning to apply reading strategies to new content. I was finally on my way to finding a place where I didn't have to openly defy the directives that had been passed down any more than I had to center all of my students' learning on them.

I had a goal that made sense, a means to that goal, the mindset that I needed to be flexible in my approach, and frequent enough feedback to recognize and correct situations in which students weren't making progress. Throughout the rest of the year, my own inquiry would lead to dozens of pedagogical changes and, ultimately, significant, measurable progress for my students.

What Alyssa and Sarah's examples from practice show us is that effective urban teachers operate from an inquiry stance. Both teachers identified their wonderings and acted appropriately to improve their practice and their students' learning.

WRAP UP

In this chapter, we examined the potential for urban teachers who assume an inquiry stance to face the complexity of urban teaching head-on and become resilient and successful in their teaching. We discussed various conceptualizations of reflection and teacher research, including the basic steps for conducting classroom-based inquiry to improve teaching and learning. We believe that urban teachers who are consistently setting problems rather than looking for quick fixes to solve their problems will develop into reflective, effective teachers of all children.

Urban educators live in "trying times" (Cochran-Smith & Lytle, 2009, p. 5); however, many are resisting the "deskilling" of teachers into scripted technicians delivering prepackaged curricula (Apple, 2000). Instead, they promote urban teachers as thoughtful, deliberative, individual professionals who regularly inquire into their practice. An inquiry stance empowers urban teachers to refuse to sit idly by while their interests and their students' interests are continuously underserved. Instead, teachers can partake in "a continual process of making current arrangements problematic; questioning the ways knowledge and practice are constructed, evaluated, and used; and assuming that part of the work of practitioners individually and collectively is to participate in educational and social change" (Cochran-Smith & Lytle, 2009, p. 121).

Fullan (2007) suggests that educational change becomes possible only when teachers reinvent practice through personal development and participation in communities where continuous learning is a fundamental part of practice. Change is the one thing we can be sure of as urban educators. Urban teaching requires us to develop strategies for effectively responding to change—strategies that will help us implement responses to new circumstances and problems. The practices of inquiry and critical reflection offer teachers multiple opportunities to reflect upon, learn about, and adjust their understandings of teaching (Olson, 2000) and to make meaningful and intellectual contributions to the professional knowledge base (Lytle & Cochran-Smith, 1990).

EXTENSION ACTIVITIES

Reflection

1. Is teacher research really research? What are the different perspectives on this question? Why do inquiry and teacher research matter for you personally and for the field of urban teaching? How might the generation of your own knowledge improve practice, increase the success of students, and address inequities and injustice in urban schools?

2. Practitioner inquiry has the potential to bridge theory and practice. Do you agree? Why or why not?

3. How might you use critical reflection and inquiry to foster resilience in urban teaching practice? Cite specific examples from the chapter to support your point.

Action

1. Select a "puzzling moment" from your own educational experience.

    a. How might that puzzle be posed as a practitioner inquiry question to be studied at your site?

    b. Is teacher research, action research, or participatory action research the most appropriate method? Why?

    c. Brainstorm a list of potential data to collect. Evidence might include, but is not limited to, questionnaires/surveys, student work, interviews, observation, tests and records, and personal journals.

    d. If possible, collect and analyze sample data to address your wondering. What have you learned that will inform your practice?

SUGGESTED RESOURCES

Books and Articles

Cochran-Smith, M., & Lytle, S. (1993). *Inside/outside: Teacher research and knowledge.* New York, NY: Teachers College Press.

Compton-Lilly, C. (2003). *Reading families: The literate lives of urban children.* New York, NY: Teachers College Press.

Dana, N. F., & Yendol-Hoppey, D. (2009). *The reflective educator's guide to classroom research: Learning to teach and teaching to learn through practitioner inquiry.* Thousand Oaks, CA: Corwin.

Hubbard, R. S., & Power, B. M. (1999). *Living the questions: A guide for teacher-researchers.* York, ME: Stenhouse.

Falk, B., & Blumenreich, M. (2005). *The power of questions: A guide to teacher and student research.* Portsmouth, NH: Heinemann.

Lytle, S. L., Portnoy, D., Waff, D., & Buckley, M. (2009). Teacher research in urban Philadelphia: Working within, against, and beyond the system. *Educational Action Research, 17,* 23–42. doi:10.1080/09650790802667428

Murrell, P. C., Jr. (2006). Toward social justice in urban education: A model of collaborative cultural inquiry. *Equity & Excellence in Education, 39,* 81–90. doi:10.1080/10665680500478890

Websites

Action Research Expeditions (http://arexpeditions.montana.edu/index.php)
Offers an online professional journal developed to support creative and critical dialogue with the action research community.

Networks: An On-line Journal for Teacher Research (http://journals.library.wisc.edu/index.php/networks/index)
A peer-reviewed journal that publishes reports of action research from teachers at all levels, kindergarten though postgraduate.

Teacher and Action Research (http://gse.gmu.edu/research/tr/tr_action)
Compiles a range of resources and materials on teacher and action research.

Teachers Network Leadership Institute: Teacher Research (www.teachersnetwork.org/tnli/research)
Houses teacher research projects and papers across a range of professional development areas in K–12 schools and classrooms.

REFERENCES

Anderson, G. L., Herr, K., & Nihlen, A. (2007). *Studying your own school: An educator's guide to qualitative practitioner research.* Thousand Oaks, CA: Corwin.

Apple, M. W. (2000). *Official knowledge: Democratic education in a conservative age* (2nd ed.). New York, NY: Routledge.

Ballenger, C. (2009). *Puzzling moments, teachable moments: Practicing teacher research in urban classrooms.* New York, NY: Teachers College Press.

Brookfield, S. D. (1995). *Becoming a critically reflective teacher.* San Francisco, CA: Jossey-Bass.

Burant, T. J., Gray, C., Ndaw, E., McKinney-Keys, V., & Allen, G. (2007). The rhythms of a teacher research group. *Multicultural Perspectives, 9*(1), 10–18.

Christensen, L. (2000). *Reading, writing, and rising up: Teaching about social justice and the power of the written word.* Milwaukee, WI: Rethinking Schools.

Cochran-Smith, M., & Donnell, K. (2006). Practitioner inquiry: Blurring the boundaries of research and practice. In G. Camilli, P. Elmore, & J. Green (Eds.), *Complementary methods for research in education* (2nd ed., pp. 503–511). Washington, DC: American Educational Research Association.

Cochran-Smith, M., & Lytle, S. L. (1992). Interrogating cultural diversity: Inquiry and action. *Journal of Teacher Education, 43,* 104–115. doi:10.1177/0022487192043002004

Cochran-Smith, M., & Lytle, S. L. (1993). *Inside/outside: Teacher research and knowledge.* New York, NY: Teachers College Press.

Cochran-Smith, M., & Lytle, S. L. (1999). Relationships of knowledge and practice: Teacher learning in communities. *Review of Research in Education, 24,* 249–306. doi:10.2307/1167272

Cochran-Smith, M., & Lytle, S. L. (2009). *Inquiry as stance: Practitioner research for the next generation.* New York. NY: Teachers College Press.

Corey, S. M. (1953). *Action research to improve school practices.* New York, NY: Teachers. College Press.

Dewey, J. (1933). *How we think. A restatement of the relation of reflective thinking to the educative process* (Rev. ed.). Boston: D. C. Heath.

Dewey, J. (1993). *Experience and education.* Indianapolis, IN: Kappa Delta Pi. (Original work published 1938)

Fletcher, A. (2004). *Meaningful school involvement: Guide to students as partners in school change* (2nd ed.). Olympia, WA: Freechild Project. Retrieved from http://www.soundout.org/MSIGuide.pdf

Freire, P. (2007). *Pedagogy of the oppressed.* New York, NY: Continuum.

Fullan, M. (2007). *The new meaning of educational change* (4th ed.). New York, NY: Teachers College Press.

Himley, M., & Carini, P. R. (Eds.). (2000). *From another angle: Children's strengths and school standards: The Prospect Center's descriptive review of the child.* New York, NY: Teachers College Press.

Hubbard, R. S., & Power, B. M. (1999). *Living the questions: A guide for teacher-researchers.* York, ME: Stenhouse.

Ingersoll, R. M. (2001). Teacher turnover and teacher shortages: An organizational analysis. *American Educational Research Journal, 38,* 499–534. doi:10.3102/00028312038003499

Lagemann, E. C. (2000). *An elusive science: The troubling history of education research.* Chicago, IL: University of Chicago Press.

Lewin, K. (1946). Action research and minority problems. *Journal of Social Issues, 2*(4), 34–46. doi:10.1111/j.1540-4560.1946.tb02295.x

Lytle, S. L., & Cochran-Smith, M. (1990). Learning from teacher research: A working typology. *Teachers College Record, 92*(1), 83–103.

McIntyre, A. (2003). Participatory action research and urban education: Reshaping the teacher preparation process. *Equity & Excellence in Education, 36,* 28–39. doi:10.1080/10665680303497

Meyer, A. L., & Farrell, A. D. (1998). Social skills training to promote resilience and reduce violence in African American middle school students. *Education and Treatment of Children, 21,* 461–488.

Munby, H., & Russell, T. (1990). Metaphor in the study of teachers' professional knowledge. *Theory Into Practice, 29,* 116–121. doi:10.1080/00405849009543441

Nieto, S. (Ed.). (2005). *Why we teach.* New York, NY: Teachers College Press.

Olson, M. R. (2000). Linking personal and professional knowledge of teaching practice through narrative inquiry. *Teacher Educator, 35*(4), 109–127. doi:10.1080/08878730009555241

Palmer, P. (1998). *The courage to teach: Exploring the inner landscape of a teacher's life.* San Francisco, CA: Jossey-Bass.

Parsons, R., & Brown, K. (2002). *Teacher as reflective practitioner and action researcher.* Belmont, CA: Wadsworth/Thomson Learning.

Raines, P., & Shadiow, L. (1995). Reflection and teaching: The challenge of thinking beyond the doing. *The Clearing House, 68,* 271–274.

Ravitch, S. M., & Wirth, K. (2007). Developing pedagogy of opportunity for students and their teachers: Navigations and negotiations in insider action research. *Action Research, 5,* 75–91. doi:10.1177/1476750307072878

Reason, P., & Bradbury, H. (1997). *The SAGE handbook of action research.* London, UK: Sage.

Schön, D. (1983). *The reflective practitioner: How practitioners think in action.* New York, NY: Basic Books.

Schön, D. (1987). *Educating the reflective practitioner.* San Francisco, CA: Jossey-Bass.

Weiner, L. (2002). Evidence and inquiry in teacher education: What's needed for urban schools. *Journal of Teacher Education, 53,* 254–261. doi:10.1177/0022487102053003010

Whitehead, J. (1989). Creating a living educational theory from questions of the kind, "How do I improve my practice?" *Cambridge Journal of Education, 19,* 41–52. doi:10.1080/0305764890190106

York-Barr, J., Sommers, W. A., Ghere, G. S., & Montie, J. K. (2001). *Reflective practice to improve schools: An action guide for educators.* Thousand Oaks, CA: Corwin.

Yost, D. S., Sentner, S. M., & Forlenza-Bailey, A. (2000). An examination of the construct of critical reflection: Implications for teacher education programming in the 21st century. *Journal of Teacher Education, 51,* 39–49. doi:10.1177/0022487100051100105

CONTRIBUTING AUTHORS

Alyssa Hadley Dunn received her bachelor's degree in secondary education and English from Boston College and her master's degree and doctorate in education from Emory University. Her experiences in this chapter are gleaned from classrooms in Boston, Massachusetts, and Atlanta, Georgia, where she taught high school English language arts.

Sarah McGee Hess is a former Teach for America teacher and current graduate student. Sarah taught fifth grade in Phoenix, Arizona. She is completing her master's degree in teaching in elementary education at Roger Williams University.

Katie Plemmons, who is featured in this chapter's opening vignette, is an English teacher at Del Valle High School, in Del Valle, Texas, a Title I school outside of Austin. She received her master's degree in teaching from Emory University and her bachelor's degree in English and theatre from the University of Southern California.

CHAPTER 6

TEACHING TO THE STANDARDS WITHOUT STANDARDIZING THE CURRICULUM

VIGNETTE: STANDARDS IN ACTION

Test Question 1. Which one of the words below is a noun?

Teacher

Eating

Kicked

Ms. Richardson is preparing her students to meet a first-grade standard—to be able to identify a noun. Realizing that some of her students may struggle to simply sound out the words in the test question listed above, let alone know which one is the noun, she has taught them the Noun Rap, a simple way of allowing kids to have fun while learning. The Noun Rap is a repeat to a beat the kids make with their hands and feet. Ms. Richardson begins.

"OK, boys and girls. Let's do the Noun Rap. Remember, you repeat after me!" The rap begins with Ms. Richardson's question, "What is a noun?" (Students repeat two times.) "It is a person, place, or thing!" (Students repeat two times.) Then the class creates one person, one place, and one thing to add into the song. They sing, "I am a student . . . I am a person . . . I am a noun. I am at school . . . which is a place . . . it is a noun. I have a dog . . . it is a thing . . . it is a noun!" They repeat the song from the beginning, asking "What is a noun?" Ms. Richardson and her students sing the Noun Rap multiple times a week and have fun popping new words into each section for a person, place, or thing. As an urban teacher, Ms. Richardson knows how to take content standards and make them meaningful for the students in her classroom.

FOCUS QUESTIONS

- How do urban teachers teach to the standards without standardizing the curriculum?
- What are standards and standards-based education, and how have they evolved over the past two decades?
- How can standards lead to standardization of curriculum?
- What does effective standards-based education look like in practice?

Since the dawn of the 21st century, urban teachers have faced more pressure than ever before to provide evidence that their students are learning, and the currency for evidence today is standardized test scores. Whereas years ago teachers were entrusted with teaching students without much related accountability for students' performance, in today's schools the expectation is that all students will meet or exceed proficiency standards on standardized assessments. Otherwise, teachers, students, and schools may face serious consequences, including loss of teaching positions, inability to graduate high school, and state takeover of schools, respectively.

The current focus on **accountability** arose from a positive movement to define what K–12 students should know or be able to do at each grade level, known as **standards**. As you will see in this chapter, standards can provide teachers with valuable direction in planning curriculum and instruction. However, standards can also lead to **standardization** when students are only exposed to content and skills that appear on standardized tests. Urban teachers across the nation are meeting the accountability challenge while still engaging their students in meaningful, creative learning opportunities. In the next section, we will discuss standards and standards-based education, explain the evolution of the standards approach to systemic school reform, reveal how curriculum became standardized as a result, and identify the ways teachers can teach to the standards without standardizing the curriculum.

THEORETICAL FRAMEWORK FOR STANDARDS-BASED TEACHING

Standards-Based Education Defined

If standards represent the content knowledge and skills students need to master at each grade level, **standards-based education** represents a framework for the cycle of teaching and learning that privileges the standards over other sources of potential teaching topics. The move toward standards-based education from traditional education represents a paradigm shift: "The focus is on what students learn rather than on what teachers teach" (Zagranski, Whigham, & Dardenne, 2008, p. 6). This paradigm is also known as **outcomes-based** versus **incomes-based education**.

Traditionally, schools selected a curriculum and related instructional strategies, implemented instruction, and then designed and implemented assessments. Assessment was not used to determine curriculum and instruction, and sometimes seemed like an afterthought. In standards-based education, schools identify the appropriate content standards, then design the assessment and establish performance levels *before* designing the curriculum and planning and implementing instruction. After this sequence, students are assessed to see how well they met the standards, which leads to either reteaching or beginning the cycle again. These contrasting frameworks are represented in Figures 6.1 and 6.2.

Wiggins and McTighe (2005) have conceptualized a similar approach to the cycle of teaching and learning, which they call **backward design**. They call activity-focused teaching and coverage-focused teaching the "twin sins" of typical instructional design (p. 3). Like the pattern described by Zagranski

Figure 6.1 Drivetrain Sequence of the Traditional School

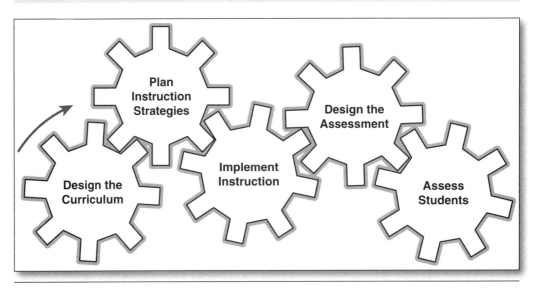

Source: Zagranski, Whigham, & Dardenne, 2008.

Figure 6.2 Drivetrain Sequence of the Standards-Based School

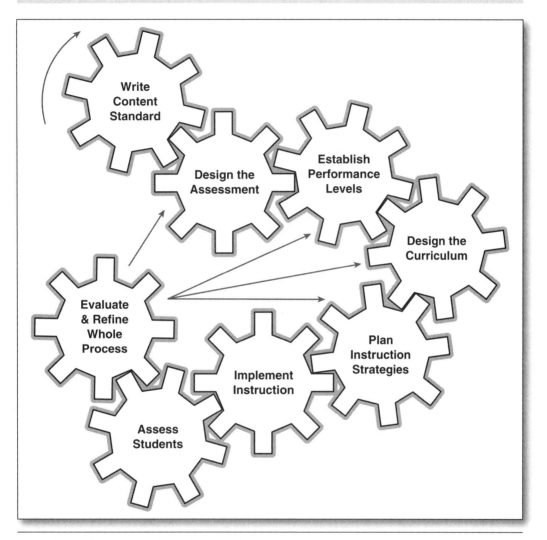

Source: Zagranski, Whigham, & Dardenne, 2008.

et al. (2008), these scholars ask teachers to identify the results they expect of students, determine the acceptable evidence, and then plan learning experiences. By considering the essential questions and understandings that will drive units and lessons and determining how students will show what they have learned before deciding on the appropriate instructional approaches, teachers avoid the "twin sins" and students "uncover" understandings.

Zagranski et al. (2008) argue that "in a standards-based system, this means teaching to the standards, using the data from assessment pieces to revise and adjust, and justifying that everything in the class is relevant learning" (p. 19). But what about those teachable moments that are sure to arise in any classroom? As these moments are often outside the parameters of the content standards, does this mean that they should be ignored? Absolutely not. Teachers and students are not robots that simply follow the standards-based curriculum sequence without any diversions. For example, on students' minds might be a current national event or a recent policy decision in the school district. We believe that it is perfectly acceptable for teachers to digress from the planned curriculum when students have authentic questions about things that matter to them. Teachers must always use their professional judgment about which teachable moments to capitalize on and which might be better left without elaboration.

The Evolution of Standards

The first content standards were developed by the National Council of Teachers of Mathematics in 1989, followed by other national organizations in the 1990s (Marzano & Haystead, 2008). These organizations provided broad standards stating what students should generally learn in a content area; the standards also represented each organization's theoretical commitments. For example, in 1996, the International Reading Association (IRA) and the National Council of Teachers of English (NCTE) released their standards for English language arts. The first standard reads as follows:

> Students read a wide range of print and nonprint texts to build an understanding of texts, of themselves, and of the cultures of the United States and the world; to acquire new information; to respond to the needs and demands of society and the workplace; and for personal fulfillment. Among these texts are fiction and nonfiction, classic and contemporary works. (p. 3)

This standard relates to students reading widely for information, for success in the workplace, and for individual pleasure. This standard is not written as an indicator of something measurable on a standardized assessment. It is important for content organizations to make these kinds of theoretical commitments as a means of grounding the beliefs and values of their members. Teachers can find it helpful to revisit these standards in addition to state standards as a reminder about the larger goals they are trying to achieve in their content area. (Links to all major content organizations' standards are listed in this chapter's Suggested Resources.)

In response to bipartisan support for statewide assessments (explained in the next section), states needed to create more specific standards with performance indicators and benchmarks that would be measured on such assessments. For example, the *Massachusetts English Language Arts Curriculum Framework* (Massachusetts Department of Education, 2001) includes the following standard for reading and literature in seventh grade (Standard 8):

Students will identify the basic facts and main ideas in a text and use them as the basis for interpretation.

- Use knowledge of genre characteristics to analyze a text.
- Interpret mood and tone, and give supporting evidence in a text.
- Identify evidence used to support an argument. (p. 37)

This standard has specific objectives that students must meet in order to be considered proficient in this standard as measured on a standardized assessment.

As noted in Chapter 4, there are also standards for teaching English language learners (ELLs). These standards for developing language proficiency can guide curriculum and instruction for ELLs in urban schools.

The Impact of No Child Left Behind

The standards-based education movement grew out of a real or perceived crisis in American education (depending on whom you ask) outlined in the 1983 report *A Nation at Risk: The Imperative for Educational Reform*. This report "painted a very dismal picture of American schooling" (Vinovskis, 2009, p. 16) and "helped launch the first wave of education reforms that focused on expanding requirements for high school graduation, establishing minimum competency tests, and providing merit pay for teachers" (p. 17). In the report, the National Commission on Excellence in Education (1983) argued, "The educational foundations of our society are presently being eroded by a rising tide of mediocrity that threatens our very future as a nation and a people" (para. 1). Since the release of the report, several presidential administrations have made educational policy a top priority, and yet equitable, quality education is still not readily accessible for many students across America.

For example, in 1989 President George H. W. Bush and the nation's governors held an education summit in Charlottesville, Virginia, and announced education goals called America 2000 (later signed into law by President Bill Clinton as the Goals 2000: Education America Act). The six goals to be achieved by the year 2000 included ensuring that American children started school ready to learn; increasing the high school graduation rate to 90%; requiring students show competency in English, mathematics, science, history, and geography in Grades 4, 8, and 12; securing first place in the world for American students in mathematics and science achievement; realizing universal literacy for every American adult in order to compete in the global economy and exercise rights of citizenship; and ensuring that every American school would be free of drugs and violence (Vinovskis, 2009, p. 27). Many of these goals were to be measured by voluntary state standards and districtwide report cards. Standards were viewed as means for solving the problem of "mediocrity" by increasing the rigor. Unfortunately, for many school communities the goals from 1989 remain unrealized today, more than 20 years since they were set and more than 10 years after the date when they were to be achieved.

Early in the 21st century, Goals 2000 developed into legislation known as the **No Child Left Behind Act of 2001 (NCLB)**. This reauthorization of the **Elementary and Secondary Education Act (ESEA)** required statewide annual testing in reading and mathematics in Grades 3–8 by the 2005–2006 school year. High school students were to be tested in reading, mathematics, and science at least once between Grades 10 and 12. States were to design their own assessments aligned with their state academic content standards. Though the standards movement had grown in the 1990s, NCLB solidified standards as the basis of curriculum, instruction, and assessment in American schools. In addition, states had to ensure that their students were making **adequate yearly progress** toward attaining proficiency standards as defined by the state within 12 years (2014). All public school teachers were to be **highly qualified** by 2005–2006. Though the definition of highly qualified varies by state, the primary requirement is a passing score on a teaching licensure exam. Finally, K–3 reading programs were to be adopted after they were purportedly proven effective by **scientifically based research,** and grant monies were made available for enhancing reading readiness for children in high-poverty areas (Early Reading First: Vinovskis, 2009, pp. 169–170).

NCLB has undoubtedly been controversial. Some have argued that adequate funding was not provided by the federal government for the states to meet the stipulations and that other subject areas receive less instructional time as a result of required testing in English and mathematics (Vinovskis,

2009). Urban schools have seen some improvements in student achievement on standardized assessments. For example, The Council of the Great City Schools, which represents 66 of America's largest school systems, has found that, on state assessments, math and reading achievement is improving and racially and economically identifiable achievement gaps appear to be narrowing in both subjects. However, urban school achievement is still below state averages in math and reading. The Council reports that, on the National Assessment of Educational Progress, large city and public school students made significant gains in math in Grades 4 and 8 and reading in Grade 4 (Uzzell, Simon, Horwitz, Hyslop, Lewis, & Casserly, 2010). It is encouraging that urban students are performing better on standardized assessments, but at what cost? Has valuable instructional time engaging in higher-level, meaningful, culturally responsive curriculum been lost to lower-level, skills-based reading and math tutoring? These questions will be further explored later in this chapter.

The number of standardized assessments that students must complete in order to pass a class or meet a state requirement continues to increase as federal policymakers demand a way to hold schools accountable for students' learning.

National Standards: The Common Core State Standards Initiative

At the time of this writing, debate swirls about President Barack Obama's commitment to reauthorizing ESEA, which is no longer referred to as the No Child Left Behind Act. The president intends to increase accountability by rewarding schools and teachers who accelerate student achievement, and he argues that it is a "moral imperative" to provide every child with a "world-class education." President Obama is also committed to holding students to higher standards so that they are "college and career ready" (U.S. Department of Education, 2010). Currently, states have the option to adopt the **Common Core State Standard**s in English language arts and mathematics, in Grades K–12, which President Obama and the Council of the Great City Schools support. At the time of this writing, 41 states and the District of Columbia have formally committed to these standards.

The initiative to develop national standards after decades of state-developed standards was led by the National Governors Association Center for Best Practices and the Council of Chief State School Officers. The initiative is described as a state-led effort to provide clear, rigorous, internationally benchmarked, evidence-based standards. The argument is that there will no longer be wide variation in what students are expected to learn from state to state: "Consistent standards will provide appropriate benchmarks for all students, regardless of where they live" (Common Core State Standards Initiative, 2010, para. 3). After years of policymakers of all political stripes maintaining that state and local control over education is most appropriate (Vinovskis, 2009), the shift in 2010 appears to have been to nationalizing standards.

The mathematics standards include foundational knowledge in Grades K–5, such as addition, subtraction, multiplication, division, decimals, fractions, and negative numbers; more advanced preparation for high school math in Grades 6–8, including geometry, algebra, probability, and statistics; and applications of mathematical thinking in real life and mathematical modeling in Grades 9–12, such as applying mathematical thinking in economics, public policy, and other situations. Here, we provide an example from the math standards in Grade 8. The Common Core State Standards defines a **standard** as "what students should understand and be able to do" (*Common Core State Standards for Mathematics*, n.d., p. 5). In this framework, the bolded statement and the numbered ones beneath it are all considered standards. These are a group of related standards, which the Common Core State Standards calls a **cluster**. The **domain**, or larger group of related standards, for the cluster below is geometry.

Understand congruence and similarity using physical models, transparencies, or geometry software.

1. Verify experimentally the properties of rotations, reflections, and translations:
   a. Lines are taken to lines, and line segments to line segments of the same length.

b. Angles are taken to angles of the same measure.

c. Parallel lines are taken to parallel lines.

2. Understand that a two-dimensional figure is congruent to another if the second can be obtained from the first by a sequence of rotations, reflections, and translations; given two congruent figures, describe a sequence that exhibits the congruence between them.

3. Describe the effect of dilations, translations, rotations, and reflections on two-dimensional figures using coordinates.

4. Understand that a two-dimensional figure is similar to another if the second can be obtained from the first by a sequence of rotations, reflections, translations, and dilations; given two similar two-dimensional figures, describe a sequence that exhibits the similarity between them.

5. Use informal arguments to establish facts about the angle sum and exterior angle of triangles, about the angles created when parallel lines are cut by a transversal, and the angle-angle criterion for similarity of triangles. *For example, arrange three copies of the same triangle so that the sum of the three angles appears to form a line, and give an argument in terms of transversals why this is so.*

What do we notice about these standards? They represent rigorous, abstract mathematical thinking, which underscores the point of creating the common standards in the first place—to increase the rigor in American schools. In addition, the bolded standard alerts the teacher to provide visuals of the geometry concepts, using actual models or ones represented on overhead transparencies or computer programs, which is helpful for all learners. However, they are written in academic language that may need to be explicitly taught to students or revised to student-friendly language before being written on the board as the day's content or language objectives (see Chapter 4 for more on the difference between content and language objectives). Another drawback to mention is that this cluster of standards contains a lot of content to "cover." It could take many lessons for all students to master this cluster, and there are many, many more standards for students to meet in eighth-grade mathematics. This is one of the major pressures on teachers—how to teach to all the standards so that students actually learn. Urban teachers Laura and Danielle talk about this in more detail in the Practice section of this chapter.

The English language arts standards include the areas of reading, writing, speaking and listening, language, and media and technology. The standards are broken down into three sections: Grades K–5, Grades 6–12 English language arts, and Grades 6–12 literacy in history/social studies, science, and technical subjects. Research and media technology skills are woven throughout the standards to represent how students must be able to gather and analyze data and read print and nonprint texts at multiple grade levels. Embedding media and technology throughout the standards is critical, as the definition of reading and literacy has expanded to what is now called **21st-century literacies**. NCTE (2008) argues that "technology has increased the intensity and complexity of literate environments" and that literacies today are "multiple, dynamic, and malleable" (para. 1). In its definition of 21st-century literacies, NCTE cites six things readers and writers need to be able to do:

- Develop proficiency with the tools of technology.
- Build relationships with others to pose and solve problems collaboratively and cross-culturally.
- Design and share information for global communities to meet a variety of purposes.
- Manage, analyze, and synthesize multiple streams of simultaneous information.
- Create, critique, analyze, and evaluate multi-media texts.
- Attend to the ethical responsibilities required by these complex environments (para. 1).

The Common Core State Standards recognize that literacy does not simply mean being able to read and write in the traditional sense (student sitting at a desk with a textbook and writing an essay on lined paper). *Literacy* has evolved into *literacies,* and schools will need to keep up with the multiple texts and forms of writing students will read and produce, such as students conducting research online and contributing to a wiki.

Though the Common Core State Standards website emphasizes that adopting the standards is not a move to nationalize education, along with adopting the standards, it encourages the development of textbooks, teaching materials, and assessments aligned with the standards. Of course curriculum should be developed that aligns with the standards. A major purpose of standards-based education is to use the standards as the basis for instructional decisions. At the same time, it also seems logical that if nearly all states are using the same standards, the same teaching materials and standardized tests would be adopted across the country. How these potential national standards, textbooks, and assessments influence urban teaching remains to be seen, but there is evidence that, as a result of increased accountability since NCLB, classroom teaching has already become more standardized and less individualized to meet students' needs, as explained later in the chapter.

The Standardization of Education

Standardization in education, known colloquially by teachers as "teaching to the test" or "the test prep method," occurs when teachers are handed prescribed curriculum materials that encourage "covering" the content and skills that will be tested without variation in delivery. However, this "test prep pedagogy," and providing all students with the same instruction each day across all schools in a district, is not what we consider to be equity in education, but rather reveals how standardized the teaching and learning process has become. What happens if many students in a class do not master the skill to be taught one day and the teacher is required to move on the next day? Is it acceptable to change course? How do standardized curricula relate to students' lives? How do these curricula inspire meaningful teaching and learning?

Standardization in education is best represented by **scripted lessons** and **pacing guides**. Scripted lessons are commercially produced lesson plans that give teachers a script to read word-for-word to students, then list what activities to do and how much time to spend on each one. These lessons, which have become very popular as a result of NCLB and Reading First grants that require schools to adopt scientifically based reading programs, have been described as "teacher-proof." Pacing guides are usually adopted at the district level and dictate which content should be taught on what days over the course of the school year. Used together, the scripted lessons map onto the pacing guides so that all teachers in all grades in all subjects across the district are teaching the same thing in the same order, often on the same day. Advocates say that scripted curricula are essential in urban schools to create continuity in a school context where many more teachers are underprepared, while critics say that the programs are too focused on basic skills and "reduce teachers to robots" (Oakes & Lipton, 2007, p. 455).

We draw on Weisberg, Sexton, Mulhern, and Kelling's (2009) concept of the "widget effect" to better understand the repercussions of standardization in education. We believe that "teachers are learners—thoughtful, individual professionals, not 'widgets'—interchangeable parts of equal effectiveness" (Donnell & Stairs, 2010, p. 193). Drawing on their knowledge, skills, and dispositions, urban teachers can resist feeling like robots or widgets in a standardized system of education. As Oakes and Lipton (2007) state, "There is simply no decent substitute for highly competent teachers and supportive colleagues who have flexibility to pursue the learning standards for their students in unique, creative, and situationally appropriate ways" (p. 454). The premise of this book is that urban teachers who adopt a positive view of themselves as professionals and their students as learners can make a difference in their students' learning and life chances. Teachers who follow scripted curricula and pacing guides 100% of the time may be providing an *equal* education to all their students, but they may not be providing an *equitable* education as a result of this brand of instruction.

Standardized testing and curricula often turn teachers into technicians and students into machines, but teachers can resist this "deskilling" of themselves and their students by remaining vigilant and committed.

Of course we firmly believe teachers should help students prepare for standardized tests—to teach them the language and format and kinds of questions they may expect to encounter. But we also strongly believe that the most effective urban teachers know how to negotiate the prescribed standards and curricula in ways that inspire real learning, as evidenced in the theory, research, and practice shared in the remainder of the chapter.

How Urban Teachers Teach to the Standards

In his book *Why Race and Culture Matter in Schools,* Howard (2010) profiles four urban schools, three in southern California and one in Chicago, that have closed the **achievement gap,** which is defined as "the discrepancy in educational outcomes between various student groups, namely, African American, Native American, certain Asian American, and Latino students on the low end of the performance scale, and primarily White and various Asian American students at the higher end" (p. 10). He purposefully separates Asian Americans into two groups because Japanese American, Korean American, and Chinese American students tend to perform significantly better than students of Filipino, Vietnamese, Cambodian, Laotian, Hmong, and Samoan descent. Based on his observations at these schools, he identified five common attributes: (1) visionary leadership, (2) teachers' effective practices, (3) intensive academic intervention, (4) the explicit acknowledgment of race, and (5) engagement of parents and the community (p. 134). Student work and data drove curricular and instruction decisions, which is typical of standards-based education. But the teachers at these schools did not simply teach to the test. They believed their students could learn; they provided rigorous, academic instruction; and they provided academic enrichment programs to help students catch up. One teacher in his study said, "We believe in acceleration, not remediation" (p. 137). A critical factor in the success of these schools was teacher collaboration. Teachers at all four schools had time scheduled every week to discuss teaching and learning.

Beginning urban teachers can learn much from these successful schools. Teachers can teach to the standards without "dumbing down" the curriculum. As mentioned above, teachers at these schools used evidence to make decisions about curriculum and instruction. We have had the experience of working in Boston schools where teachers have weekly common planning time and look at student work and standardized tests scores to collaboratively determine ways to improve teaching and learning opportunities. They do not simply take the pacing guide and scripted curriculum materials and follow the script, or take standardized test results and teach students only the material from questions they were unsuccessful in answering. If the school you are working in does not have collaborative opportunities to consider data and learn about effective pedagogy to support implementation of new teaching strategies, you may discuss the possibilities with your immediate supervisor or talk with other like-minded teachers to create your own group. Local college and university professors are typically very interested in supporting urban teachers long after they have left teacher education programs, and they can serve as a resource for you. There are many other teacher networks that can provide you with space to collaborate in meaningful ways in negotiating the pressures of standards-based teaching, such as the National Writing Project (www.nwp.org) and the Teacher Leaders Network (www .teacherleaders.org).

We would like to reiterate the importance of using knowledge of students and standards when planning curriculum and instruction. As Danielle and Laura illustrate so well in the Practice section of this chapter, urban teachers can be in control even when they are handed a set of commercial curriculum materials and district pacing guides. Using professional judgment is essential for effective urban teaching. Still most valuable to classroom teachers on a daily basis are the formative, authentic assessments they create and conduct to check for student understanding, such as classroom observations, journal responses, and individual conferences with students. Teachers cannot wait for the state standardized test results that may come after the students have moved onto the next grade. States have addressed this issue by doing intermittent standardized testing during the school year, which provides teachers with more data to drive instruction and provide results more quickly (for example, the Northwest Evaluation Association's Measures of Academic Progress, www .nwea.org). While these standardized tests can be helpful, they also take more time away from actual teaching and learning. Keeping excellent records of classroom assessment strategies serves teachers, students, administrators, and parents well.

Response to intervention (RtI) is one way many schools are addressing the varied learning needs of students through ongoing assessment, which in turn drives instruction. RtI is defined as "a systematic and data-based method for identifying, defining, and resolving students' academic and/or behavior difficulties" (Brown-Chidsey & Steege, 2010, p. 3). It refers to a process of gathering data about all students; providing quality, research-based classroom instruction; and identifying students who may need targeted interventions to progress in their learning. Interventions can take place in small groups in addition to regular classroom instruction, or the most intensive interventions may supplant regular classroom instruction. RtI is often conceptualized as a three-tier model. Tier 1 includes students who are well served by core classroom instruction, usually about 80% of students in a class; Tier 2 represents students who need small-group instruction, usually about 15% of students; and Tier 3 represents students who need intensive instruction and assessment, usually about 5% of students. The primary assumption of RtI is that schools should not wait for students to fail before they are assessed for special services; prevention and intervention are the keys to the model. The **Individuals with Disabilities Education Improvement Act (IDEA)** in 2004 encouraged the use of RtI methods for identifying students for special education services, which accounts for the growth of implementation across the nation (Brown-Chidsey & Steege, 2010). RtI can be helpful to urban teachers in that a concerted effort is made to assess, document, and support students' learning, which provides teachers with valuable information about students' strengths and needs. However, RtI also has the potential to standardize the curriculum even more when "research-based instruction" is translated to mean commercially produced curriculum packages that must be followed with fidelity.

Some urban teachers do not revise curriculum materials they've been given, but rather develop the curriculum along with their students and still meet the standards. Schultz (2008), who was also mentioned in Chapter 1, did just that with his students in Chicago. He shares his philosophy about standards-based teaching:

> Interpreting standards quite differently from others around me, I believed authentic learning—solving an actual problem—could actually meet standards by organically emerging out of the classroom curriculum. This approach would meet the objectives not for their own sake, but because the behaviors and outcomes outlined in the standards were necessary components in solving the problem. If the classroom curriculum was inverted so that students' pursuits led them to the outcome of meeting standards, the class members' ideas could be at the forefront, rather than what someone else expected them to know or understand at a particular time. Guided by a facilitating teacher, this experiential approach encourages each student's growth and nurtures individual development. (p. 12)

Schultz's approach to teaching, known as **problem-based learning**, is currently gaining momentum around the country. Schools are recognizing that students will more likely succeed in school and life and pass state assessments if they engage in complex thinking and higher-order tasks on a regular basis. In problem-based learning, students employ the habits of inquiry to learn content material, providing a rich alternative to reductionist, test-centered pedagogy.

WHAT THE RESEARCH SAYS
ABOUT STANDARDS-BASED TEACHING

The research on standards-based teaching in urban schools suggests the following (Darling-Hammond, 2010; Haney, 2000; Oakes, 2005; Pardo, 2006; Stiefel, Schwartz, & Chellman, 2007; Sunderman, Tracey, Kim, & Orfield, 2004):

- Curriculum has narrowed to only tested subjects, leaving many other content areas and skills ignored.
- Tracking students by ability continues and has been exacerbated by classes that teach to the test.
- Grade retention and dropout rates have increased as a means of manipulating schools' performance reports.
- Teachers have effectively negotiated the demands of standards-based teaching and improved standardized test scores without compromising rich curriculum and instruction.

Here we share some examples of effective research on standards-based teaching. Fisher's (2004) study at a large urban high school arose from one student's concern over the elimination of the sustained silent reading (SSR) period. Recognizing the importance of meeting the accountability demands of high-stakes testing in reading, and that providing students time to read and ensuring they do is important for success, Fisher spent two years conducting action research at the school, which saved the SSR program and dramatically improved the voluntary reading rate of the urban teenagers. Fusarelli (2004) assessed the potential positive and negative effects of NCLB on various elements of urban schools. This study found that underlying structural inequities must be addressed to truly reduce the achievement gap. Pardo's (2006) research on three beginning urban elementary teachers' teaching writing revealed that the accountability context can cause less experienced teachers to acquiesce to the school's demands for teaching to improve test scores, but that with more experience and better preparation, teachers can use their professional judgment in determining how to best teach writing. Smith et al. (2002) conducted a case study of a successful urban elementary school that implements a dual-language immersion program (content taught in English and Spanish to all students) where the community "will not allow highly motivated, well prepared bilingual teachers to become mere test preparation technicians" and high test scores are regarded as "icing on the cake. (Or, as a fourth-grade student suggested, 'the salsa on the tostada')" (p. 16). Stiefel et al. (2007) analyzed the impact of

NCLB's requirement that schools report racial subgroups and the implications that this has on urban schools. They found that, compared with smaller suburban or rural schools, large urban schools were held accountable disproportionately for subgroups' test performance. See Table 6.1.

Table 6.1 Research Studies on Standards-Based Teaching

Author(s)	Purpose	Findings	Implications	URL
Fisher (2004)	The researcher observed students during sustained silent reading (SSR) and surveyed teachers on indicators of SSR's success over two years.	As a result of a student-initiated and schoolwide commitment, the 20-minute SSR period improved the number of high school students reading daily during school time from less than 40% in the first year to 88% the second year.	It is possible to provide independent, free-choice reading time alongside initiatives to meet state accountability targets. Students' voices are critical when considering schoolwide initiatives. Systematic data collection and analysis provide information to make informed curricular decisions on schoolwide initiatives.	
Fusarelli (2004)	The researcher aimed to determine the potential positive and negative effects of NCLB on various issues in schooling, such as diversity, multiculturalism, and equity.	NCLB will most likely fail in bringing about the desired shrink in the achievement gap because of insufficient funds and a definition of the achievement gap that is overly simplistic. Funding will be the largest	The promise of NCLB to reduce the achievement gap will likely remain unfulfilled due to insufficient funding. The negative effects of NCLB will impact urban schools, and both education and	http://epx .sagepub .com/ content/ 18/1/71 .full .pdf+html

(Continued)

Table 6.1 (Continued)

Author(s)	Purpose	Findings	Implications	URL
		challenge as few states both mandate and fund intervention programs for students struggling to meet the standards.	reform needs are high for educators in these urban schools.	
Pardo (2006)	The researcher conducted a yearlong qualitative study of three urban teachers about implementation of their schools' writing curriculum.	Beginning urban teachers learned to teach writing by drawing on a variety of knowledge sources; writing instruction was heavily influenced by policy and school contexts; learning to teach writing was about managing conflicting aspects of individual teaching contexts. The teachers with more classroom experience were better able to meet the demands of the high-stakes testing environment than the first-year teacher.	Becoming informed about the current policy environment can help new teachers navigate conflicting policies. Examining the complexities of classroom contexts and standardized forms of writing during teacher preparation can help beginning teachers understand purposes and goals of writing.	http://jte .sagepub .com/ content/ 57/4/378 .full .pdf+html
Smith, Arnot-Hopffer, Carmichael, Murphy, Valle, Gonzalez, & Poveda (2002)	Researchers studied the long-term success of a dual-immersion bilingual school where 100% of third-grade students met or exceeded state standards in English reading while receiving 70% of instruction in Spanish.	Raising the status of the minority language, deep interactions between teachers and students, and strong connections with families were crucial for student success on standardized tests and meeting the bilingual/biliteracy mission of the school.	Test scores can increase when the community understands the difference between real learning and preparing children to take tests.	

Author(s)	Purpose	Findings	Implications	URL
Stiefel, Schwartz, & Chellman (2007)	Researchers analyzed the possible impact of the NCLB legislation's requisite for racial subgroup reporting in consideration of urban elementary and middle schools' substantial racial segregation.	The schools examined in this study were highly segregated, and over half of the schools in the study were too homogenous to report test scores for any ethnic or racial subgroup. The racial achievement gap was found to be greatest among the segregated schools. Urban schools were found to be more likely to be accountable for smaller subgroups.	With strict adherence to adequate yearly progress, racial gaps will not be closed through subgroup reporting. Further research needs to be conducted to determine efficacious means to lessen the achievement gap.	http://epx .sagepub .com/ content/ 21/3/527 .full .pdf+html

PRACTICE

In this section, practicing urban teachers **Laura Rosenfield** and **Danielle Richardson** describe their beliefs and assumptions about standards-based education and how they approach their teaching without standardizing the curriculum. Laura is a high school history teacher in Boston, Massachusetts, and Danielle is a first-grade teacher in Knoxville, Tennessee.

Laura and Danielle explain what they expected teaching to be like based on their teacher education experiences and the reality of standards-based education. They both experienced a disconnect.

Laura: When I was in graduate school, I designed a weeklong lesson on Adam Smith [Scottish philosopher and economist]. Later on, in a professional development course, I created a weeklong mock trial unit on women's suffrage. I also put together a two-week unit on the Holocaust that included stories and articles that would help students slowly build an understanding of the events and, equally important, of how something so unimaginable could come to pass. All of these efforts were infused with my graduate school idealism: the lessons went into great depth on a single topic, I tapped into prior knowledge, I used differentiated means of instruction, and I tried to find ways to help students take ownership of their learning. Today, seven years into my teaching career, I haven't used any of these lesson plans. Adam Smith takes up one slide of a lecture on the Industrial Revolution. I teach the Holocaust in one day.

My course, U.S. History II: 1877 to Present, follows a pacing guide based on city and state standards. The department, the school, and the city are getting ready to begin administering the MCAS—our state test, passage of which is required for graduation—in U.S. history in two years. (The exam has been used to test other subjects for a number of years, but is only now being applied to history.) Moreover, we administer a citywide final exam that determines 20% of the students' final grade, so even in advance of the MCAS we have to be sure to adhere to the pacing guide. Clearly these tests are on my mind while I plan and pace lessons, and I can't help but wonder how my students would fare on the MCAS if they had to take it this year.

Danielle: I have had many eye-opening experiences as to how the education program operates versus how it is now in the "real" classroom. In school [teacher preparation programs], we as future educators are encouraged to discover, research, and think outside the box in our future classrooms. We are taught and tested on enthusiastic and creative ways to address all of our students' needs and learning styles. However, in the past five years, it is amazing what of those things have almost been taken away. Too often we hear colleagues saying they are no longer allowed to be teachers, but are robots to the system.

Laura and Danielle share their beliefs and assumptions about standards-based education and high-stakes assessments. Both show that the issue is much more complex than being "for" or "against" standards.

Laura: One might think that I am opposed to the way that standards and testing have shaped my teaching, but in reality my opinion is much more complex. I have come to appreciate that there is value in providing high school students with a broad overview of the entire sweep of history. As much as I often find it disappointing to give such short shrift to topics that are both interesting and important, I also realize that every additional day spent providing more depth on, say, the suffrage movement or the Holocaust means one less day spent on giving students a basic understanding of other major historical events that have shaped our country. In light of the statistics about how many of our students cannot place major events even in the correct century, it is difficult to argue with the idea that a key part of my job is to give students a basic understanding of the timeline of history and a cultural literacy of names and places. This core knowledge, however superficial it may seem, is one essential tool—the other being a set of basic skills—that equips students to further their learning both in school and independently.

In addition, I've come to the conclusion that pacing guides need not supplant all other learning opportunities, and there are some strategies that I use to ensure that students go beyond the base curriculum. For example, I use the required material as a vehicle to teach and reinforce core skills. As a result, not only is there consistency in my class because of the repeated skills practice, but the students have an opportunity to learn and apply those skills in the context of the content they are learning.

Danielle: When people talk about the standardized curriculum in schools today, I have very mixed emotions and feelings toward the idea. Standardizing the curriculum does have both its positive and negative points. I have been able to experience teaching both in a program where the curriculum was standardized as well as where, at one point in time, it was not. As a new teacher without a mandated curriculum, I felt very overwhelmed and scattered when I planned out lessons. I was to rely on a bluebook of standards, a book provided by the state that lists the standards expected to be covered in each grade level and subject and to what extent. This gave me little foundation for curriculum as a new teacher. I did have other teachers to help me, but I was always feeling as if I was going to miss something. Many times I got caught up on the skills that the students struggled with and spent more time than originally planned, leaving less time for other skills.

I personally liked the guide given to me that told me when and what to do to reach all of the standards mandated for my grade level; however, I did not initially realize I was basically being given a script to teach my class daily. The reading basal is scripted word by word for all areas of literature, reading, writing, and phonics. Other content areas' curricula are not nearly this scripted. Rather than telling you what to say, they provide the options with the teacher's edition if needed on teacher prompts, and so on. They do give a scheduled guideline, which is expected to be followed and very helpful. There is a team of people who are aligning all other content areas with the reading basal, which is great for the kids and allows more teachable moments throughout the unit, having one content area feeding off of another. For example, in reading and writing we may be talking and focusing on the story of the Little Red Hen, in math we may be talking about things being equal or fair, in social studies we may be talking about sharing and helping others, and in science we may be talking about how plants such as wheat grow and can become bread.

However, I felt like my voice as the teacher had in a way been silenced with this new curriculum. In some ways, this was helpful and needed, and in others very hard to adapt to. First, not all students learn the same way, and second, what about the ideas I had used previously with my students that brought about so many wonderful student-centered lessons? Many questions ran through my head. This new curriculum was fast-paced, had multiple levels of testing, used vocabulary many of my students were unfamiliar with, addressed only three levels of learning (approaching, on, and beyond—what about the in-between?), and seemed to be, in a way, robotic.

Laura and Danielle explain what their teaching looks like now that they have mandated pacing guides and scripted curricula. What's evident is that both teachers still use what they know about their students and infuse creativity into their lessons.

Laura: A week in my class might look like this: On Monday I present a lecture on the Great Depression, and then I model taking notes from the textbook. That way, the students are introduced to the material—that is, we cover the names and events that the pacing guide requires—but also have a chance to learn and practice techniques for accessing the information: reading comprehension, distilling out the key information, and putting that information down in a form that the students can easily understand and access later. On Tuesday I present another lecture, and then the students pair up to synthesize the material, say, by analyzing political cartoons. On Wednesday I might use a Socratic Seminar to have students delve into a primary source. This helps them solidify their knowledge of the basic content, it adds a layer of richness, and it gives them an opportunity to practice a skill: academic discussion. On Thursday I give them time to study, which I like to do since most of my students do not study at home for tests. I often provide instruction on different study techniques as part of that time. On Friday I give a test to evaluate what the students have learned but also to help them practice their writing and test taking.

I remember once telling a friend that I had to cut either Kent State or My Lai when teaching Vietnam. She shared my confusion and my shock that there was no time to cover both of these critical events of that time period. Now I feel more comfortable with that kind of choice. I know it is impossible to cover all of history in detail and unrealistic to expect that students will retain all of the details that I might be able to teach. Even so, I have found some ways around that problem. This year I divided the class into groups and assigned each group a different standard from the unit on the Cold War. Each group researched one event in the Cold War and then presented it to the rest of the class. In this way, students had an opportunity to get familiar with all the basic facts and events while engaging in more depth with one of them. This may not be appropriate for all units or all classes, but it is another technique to strike a balance between covering the material and providing opportunities for more in-depth learning and skills development.

In this way, I have been able to strike what I feel is a reasonable balance between factual content, basic skills development, and opportunities for students to strike out on their own. My goal now is to introduce students to the broad sweep of history, teach them the key facts and knowledge that they need in order to continue to learn about history, and give them the tools to learn later what I can't teach today. Equally important, I hope to share my excitement for history so that students *want* to learn more. My favorite moments are when I hear from other teachers that a student has chosen to write an English research paper on Alice Paul [American suffragist leader] or chosen *MAUS* [a graphic novel about a Holocaust survivor] as independent reading. I love it when students run to me to tell me about a movie that has come out that relates to something we have studied together. Standards—at least the ones that I am expected to adhere to—have not eliminated these moments.

In the past, I sometimes tried to squeeze a huge wealth of resources into my classes. One day I would start class by playing "Brother, Can You Spare a Dime." Another day I would present Eleanor Roosevelt's letters about lynching, or show Shirley Temple clips, or listen to FDR's inaugural address, or read a poem by Langston Hughes called "Ballad of Roosevelt." I realize now that all this content, however rich, did not necessarily add up to the most effective teaching. I love all those primary sources, but students need to understand what the Great Depression was, what the responses to it were, and what its lasting impact on history was. Now I choose one of those sources every year, share it with the students, and base an exercise on it. This year I used the songs "We're in the Money" and "Brother, Can You

Spare a Dime," and I had students "go back in time" to write in their "diary" about how they felt about the songs. Now I don't feel like I am handing out too many papers a day or doing too many activities. I use these resources to enhance the standards.

Danielle: Over the past few years since adopting the mandated curriculum, I have begun to adapt my teaching, and although I do still struggle with many of the questions above, I have found many good points as well. I do have a pacing guide to follow; however, I now use the resources that are still readily available and were used prior to this program. For example, many students struggle with some of the vocabulary in the basal, especially in a school such as mine where experiences are limited. I have a passion for vocabulary and word work and have created daily activities beyond the basal to incorporate multiple learning strategies. I have a weekly schedule with my vocabulary words. I send home the next week's words on Friday. On Monday I point and say, and they repeat the words over and over in multiple arrangements. On Tuesday I write and they write the words on a large note card that will be taped to their desk/table as a resource for the week. Then they each practice writing the words at least five times. In centers on Tuesday, they also make their own individual note cards for each word of the week. On Wednesday they do a vocabulary hunt through our basal book story and locate where they found the words. On Thursday we do "Draw My Word," where we as a class put a picture to the words we can; by mid-year, I may allow them to create their own pictures and share with the class. Fridays are test days, but they are also fun days if the class has earned good work points through the week. On Fridays we may put shaving cream on desks and play a game where students spell words, we may play vocabulary bingo, we might write the words on the playground with chalk, we might make up a funny class story to publish with the vocabulary, we may play around the word wall. They love the opportunity for a "Fun Friday Activity" to review the week's words. This is also a great time for teacher observation to see if they have retained prior words as well.

I continue to use a variety of creative writing strategies and just find myself expanding on the basic writing process that is used. I started using my critical literacy and classroom library for supplemental read-alouds, having a Reading Book Club in my room that allows children to check out books to take home, and using a reward system for a free teacher read-aloud outside during our free time. (An incentive they love: listening to a story. How inspiring!) I have also incorporated extra centers beyond those mandated by the curriculum for the "in-between" learners. I do continue to use the levels and the groups that are provided in the curriculum materials, but I also incorporate peer groups and groups who work with my assistant to reach all levels in each area. For example, we always do a "Shapes Around Our World" walk where we take a digital camera around the school and students take pictures of shapes and patterns they see. We write class books on different subjects. I find anything they can use at home to practice what they are learning and apply it either in the lesson or at a center, such as pennies, noodles, beans, buttons, and household items they may have to practice counting. For our vocabulary words, my students not only do write-and-repeat drills, but they create visual pictures and art representing their words to share with the class. For science, there is usually some easy experiment that can give the students a visual of what they are learning. I just feel if students not only hear a lesson, but can see, create, or be a part of it, they grasp so much more than just that basic level of understanding.

Laura and Danielle have both found positive ways to teach to the standards without standardizing the curriculum. They are realistic about the demands of testing on their students, and they do their best to take what is positive from the standards, mandated curricula, and pacing guides to make teaching and learning effective and enjoyable.

Laura: A colleague tells me that I should be subversive and ignore the pacing guide. This, I think, is not a good approach. It means students will be unprepared for the exams on which their performance will be judged, and it is unclear to me that the educational outcome will be any better. Instead, I think teachers should demand more input into the standards that they are expected to use, and should work to ensure that those standards have the right balance of factual information and skills and, equally important, that the curriculum provides opportunities for teachers and students to learn and develop that knowledge in ways that cross disciplines and allow room for creativity. I have begun to work with the English teachers in my school to explore ways that we can better coordinate the material that they teach with the history standards. A curriculum that allows students to read the books that they already need—for example, *The Great Gatsby* or *Night*—in parallel with learning the historical contexts in which they are set can only be a good thing.

In my large urban high school, teachers and students face a host of challenges: absenteeism, language and literacy differences, discipline, and problems outside the school over which we have little or no control but that profoundly impact student readiness and performance. I want students to graduate, and to do so not only with the bare minimum of knowledge and skills to enable them to succeed in their further education, but with the ability to be knowledgeable and engaged citizens.

Teachers *can* find creative ways of ensuring that students can get a grounding in basic skills and have opportunities to put their analytical and creative talents to use, all while meeting the demands of a rigorous pacing guide. We may look forward to the day when standards are more well-rounded, when they are more clearly part of a coordinated interdisciplinary curriculum, and when teachers have more input into their development, but in the meantime we can take comfort in the knowledge that we can provide all the elements of a complete education even while meeting the standards that are handed to us.

Danielle: Through this whole process, I have had and still have many mixed thoughts and feelings toward a standardized curriculum. I will always and forever believe that not one of us learns the same way. We all have our individual strengths and weaknesses. A high-level verbal learner may be a terrible written test taker or vice versa. Some of my top students are the worst test takers because standardized tests do not give them the chance to apply what they know in any other way than how the test approaches it. Standardized testing does not allow for a variety of critical, analytical, creative, or self-discovery approaches in any sort of combination best suited for the students to apply what they have learned. However, the mandated curriculum has had a positive effect on other academic areas. The science and social studies curricula have now been aligned with the basal program, and that has been fun for the students as well as positive for the teacher. When the students are learning plant vocabulary, reading a story about plants, and learning the parts of a plant, it just expands on the learning process of that whole unit and we are able to focus on the subject with a lot more depth.

Laura and Danielle's honest reflections about how they approach standards-based education and mandated curricula and pacing guides reveal how they negotiate the complexity of teaching to the standards without standardizing the curriculum in urban schools today.

WRAP UP

In this chapter we have focused on the rise of standards-based education and some of the benefits and concerns about teaching with standards in urban schools. We defined standards-based education; described the evolution of standards, No Child Left Behind, the Common Core State Standards, and the subsequent standardization of education; and shared concepts and strategies for urban teachers to employ when teaching to the standards.

We conclude this chapter with Darling-Hammond's (2010) musings about the next steps in the accountability movement:

> Reform rhetoric notwithstanding, the key question for students—especially the least advantaged—is whether investments in better teaching, curriculum, and schooling will follow the press for new standards, or whether standards built upon a foundation of continued inequality in education will simply certify student failure with greater certainty and reduce access to future education and employment. A related question, a half-century after *Brown v. Board of Education*, is what will it take to secure a constitutional right to equal educational opportunity for all the nation's children? (p. 98)

We, too, wonder whether national standards will lead toward more equity in educational opportunities. We know that no matter what new mandates and prescriptive curricula may be enacted, effective urban teachers will always work hard to meet their students' needs above all else.

EXTENSION ACTIVITIES

Reflection

1. Locate the content standards for your subject and grade level. (This may depend on whether your state has its own standards or has adopted the Common Core State Standards.) Then, look at a textbook that is used in a local school as well as sample standardized test items. How well do the standards, curriculum materials, and assessments align? What is included? Excluded? What do you think about the standards, textbook, and test items?

Action

1. Rewrite a scripted lesson plan for your subject and grade level so that it is appropriate for your classroom. What did you change and why?

2. Identify a controversial curriculum issue in your school or district. What is your stance on the controversy? What theory, research, and practice support your stance? Write a persuasive speech that you might give at a school board meeting about this issue.

SUGGESTED RESOURCES

Books and Articles

Kohn, A. (2010, August 25). Turning children into data: A skeptic's guide to assessment programs. *Education Week*. Retrieved from http://www.alfiekohn.org/teaching/edweek/data.htm

Schultz, B. D. (2008). *Spectacular things happen along the way: Lessons from an urban classroom*. New York, NY: Teachers College Press.

Sleeter, C. E. (2005). *Un-standardizing the curriculum: Multicultural teaching in the standards-based classrooms*. New York, NY: Teachers College Press.

Websites

Common Core State Standards: www.corestandards.org

The following professional organizations offer recommended content area standards:

National Council of Teachers of English: www.ncte.org

National Council of Teachers of Mathematics: www.nctm.org

National Science Teachers Association: www.nsta.org

National Council for the Social Studies: www.socialstudies.org

American Council on the Teaching of Foreign Languages: www.actfl.org

Teachers of English to Speakers of Other Languages: www.tesol.org

REFERENCES

Brown-Chidsey, R., & Steege, M. W. (2010). *Response to intervention: Principles and strategies for effective practice* (2nd ed.). New York, NY: Guilford Press.

Common Core State Standards Initiative. (2010). *About the standards.* Retrieved from http://www.corestandards.org/about-the-standards

Common core state standards for mathematics. (n.d.). Retrieved from http://www.corestandards.org/assets/CCSSI_Math%20Standards.pdf

Darling-Hammond, L. (2010). *The flat world and education: How America's commitment to equity will determine our future.* New York, NY: Teachers College Press.

Donnell, K. A., & Stairs, A. J. (2010). Conclusion: Developing synergy between learning and practice. In A. J. Stairs & K. A. Donnell (Eds.), *Research on urban teacher learning: Examining contextual factors over time* (pp. 191–197). Charlotte, NC: Information Age.

Fisher, D. (2004). Setting the "opportunity to read" standard: Resuscitating the SSR program in an urban high school. *Journal of Adolescent and Adult Literacy, 48,* 138–150. doi:10.1598/JAAL.48.2.5

Fusarelli, L. D. (2004). The potential impact of the No Child Left Behind Act on the equity and diversity in American education. *Educational Policy, 18,* 71–94. doi:10.1177/0895904803260025

Haney, W. (2000). The myth of the Texas miracle in education. *Education Policy Analysis Archives, 8*(41). Retrieved from http://epaa.asu.edu/ojs

Howard, T. C. (2010). *Why race and culture matter in schools: Closing the achievement gap in America's classrooms.* New York, NY: Teachers College Press.

International Reading Association & National Council of Teachers of English. (1996). *Standards for the English language arts.* Retrieved from http://www.ncte.org/library/NCTEFiles/Resources/Books/Sample/StandardsDoc.pdf

Marzano, R. J., & Haystead, M. W. (2008). *Making standards useful in the classroom.* Alexandria, VA: Association for Supervision and Curriculum Development.

Massachusetts Department of Education. (2001). *Massachusetts English language arts curriculum framework.* Malden, MA: Author. Retrieved from http://www.doe.mass.edu/frameworks/ela/0601.pdf

National Commission on Excellence in Education. (1983). *A nation at risk: The imperative for educational reform.* Retrieved from http://www2.ed.gov/pubs/NatAtRisk/risk.html

National Council of Teachers of English. (2008). *The NCTE definition of 21st-century literacies.* Retrieved from http://www.ncte.org/positions/statements/21stcentdefinition

Oakes, J. (2005). *Keeping track: How schools structure inequality* (2nd ed.). New Haven, CT: Yale University Press.

Oakes, J., & Lipton, M. (2007). *Teaching to change the world* (3rd ed.). Boston, MA: McGraw-Hill.

Pardo, L. S. (2006). The role of context in learning to teach writing: What teacher educators need to know to support beginning urban teachers. *Journal of Teacher Education, 57,* 378–394. doi:10.1177/0022487106291563

Schultz, B. D. (2008). *Spectacular things happen along the way: Lessons from an urban classroom*. New York, NY: Teachers College Press.

Smith, P. H., Arnot-Hopffer, E., Carmichael, C. M., Murphy, E., Valle, A., Gonzalez, N., & Poveda, A. (2002). Raise a child, not a test score: Perspectives on bilingual education at Davis Bilingual Magnet School. *Bilingual Research Journal, 26*(1), 1–19.

Stiefel, L., Schwartz, A. E., & Chellman, C. C. (2007). So many children left behind: Segregation and the impact of subgroup reporting in No Child Left Behind on the racial test score gap. *Educational Policy, 21*, 527–550. doi:10.1177/0895904806289207

Sunderman, G., Tracey, C. A., Kim, J., & Orfield, G. (2004). *Listening to teachers: Classroom realities and No Child Left Behind*. Cambridge, MA: Civil Rights Project at Harvard University.

U.S. Department of Education, Office of Planning, Evaluation and Policy Development. (2010). *ESEA reauthorization: A blueprint for reform*. Retrieved from http://www2.ed.gov/policy/elsec/leg/blueprint/index.html

Uzzell, R., Simon, C., Horwitz, A., Hyslop, A., Lewis, S., & Casserly, M. (2010). *Beating the odds: Analysis of student performance on state assessments and NAEP*. Washington, DC: Council of the Great City Schools. Retrieved from http://www.cgcs.org/Pubs/BT9.pdf

Vinovskis, M. A. (2009). *From A Nation at Risk to No Child Left Behind: National education goals and the creating of federal education policy*. New York, NY: Teachers College Press.

Weisberg, D., Sexton, S., Mulhern, J., & Kelling, D. (2009). *The widget effect: Our national failure to acknowledge and act on differences in teacher effectiveness*. Brooklyn, NY: New Teacher Project.

Wiggins, G., & McTighe, J. (2005). *Understanding by design* (Expanded 2nd ed.). Alexandria, VA: Association for Supervision and Curriculum Development.

Zagranski, R., Whigham, W. T., & Dardenne, P. L. (2008). *Understanding standards-based education: A practical guide for teachers and administrators*. Thousand Oaks, CA: Corwin.

CONTRIBUTING AUTHORS

Laura Rosenfield is a high school history teacher in the Boston Public Schools. Prior to that, she taught at the middle school level in Malden, Massachusetts. She is certified by the National Board for Professional Teaching Standards, and she received her master's degree in education from Tufts University and her bachelor's degree in American Studies from Barnard College.

Danielle Richardson, whose vignette also opens this chapter, is a first-grade teacher in the Knoxville (Tennessee) Public Schools. She earned a master's degree in education, specifically focused in the area of urban multicultural studies, at the University of Tennessee and a bachelor's degree in healthcare administration at East Tennessee State University. She has taught for five years at the inner-city school where she completed her yearlong internship and is currently working with a pilot program incorporating inclusion into her classroom.

CHAPTER 7

WORKING WITHIN AND AROUND URBAN SCHOOL BUREAUCRACY

VIGNETTE: WORKING WITH BUREAUCRACY IN ACTION

Tom was practicing his recitation of short a words, like cap, tat, and hat. Was this a kindergarten or first-grade classroom? Actually, it was happening in a sixth-grade, self-contained English as a second language (ESL) classroom. However, Tom did not speak English as his second language. He was, in fact, a "newcomer"—a student who is new to the country and who has never been in an American school before. Tom was 12 years old, from Africa, spoke English, but had never attended school anywhere. Ms. Garcia was his first teacher, and this was his first experience in a classroom setting.

Technically, Tom should have been placed in a newcomer classroom, which is a classroom of multiage students. This type of classroom would better meet the needs of a newcomer because the instruction would be individualized, at a primary level, and would teach not just academics, but also social behavior and adjustment to school life. Ms. Garcia knew the ESL classroom was not the correct placement for this child, so she spoke to people in the system—her principal, the director of ESL, and the assistant superintendent. She was told the school did not have the money or space for a newcomer classroom. "You will have to teach him," they all told her. The school system had made this decision for them both. That's when a teacher has to be confident in what and how she teaches and do the best she can for her students. Ms. Garcia knew she had to work within the bureaucratic system.

FOCUS QUESTIONS

- How do urban teachers work within and around the bureaucracy of urban schools?
- How do the bureaucratic systems of urban schools and districts influence teaching and learning?
- Why is it important to understand the ways in which urban school bureaucracies work?
- In what ways can teachers proactively work within and around bureaucratic concerns?

When thinking about urban schools, media-driven images may influence your view with problematic, unfair, and often inaccurate connotations. Typically, we perceive urban schools as excessively large, dysfunctional, run-down institutions continually in need of significant reform. Such "savage inequalities" (Kozol, 1991) mark the difference between urban and nonurban community schools. In fact,

> "urban" has become a euphemism for schools with exclusively or predominantly poor students of color populations (especially Black and Latino) and connote schools that are characterized by underfunding, racial and economic segregation, inefficient administration, poor infrastructure, demoralized teaching faculty, poor equipment, resources, and facilities, overcrowded classrooms, outmoded and largely ineffective pedagogical approaches, student on student and student on teacher violence, chronic classroom management problems, dilapidated and/or dangerous neighborhoods, uninvolved and uncaring parents, etc. (Wright & Alenuma, 2007, p. 212)

While this view is quite common, it is not the only way to understand urban schools.

A **bureaucracy** is a specific form of organization defined by complexity, division of labor, hierarchical coordination and control, strict chain of command, and legal authority. A bureaucracy combines all of the organizational structures, procedures, systems, and regulations designed to manage activity. In its ideal form, it is impersonal, rational, and based on rules (Encyclopædia Britannica, 2011). Here the trouble begins: how can an organization designed to serve children and their families be based on impersonal relationships in its idealized form?

The contexts in which teachers both acquire and use knowledge affect their teaching practice. The school bureaucracy is one of these contexts. In order to teach well, teachers need to adapt their practice in response to the context in which they teach. Many of the constraining conditions (Feiman-Nemser, 2001) found in school bureaucracies do not support teacher learning and practice. Particularly in urban settings, where the constraints of classroom life are often directly regulated by larger political and societal contexts, it is essential that teachers understand and adapt to the contexts and the social conditions of schooling.

In this chapter, we will look at the characteristics of urban school bureaucracies and the ways in which teachers work within and around them. We will consider an alternate ecological model to traditional conceptions of school bureaucracies, proactive versus reactive teacher orientations, and overt and covert responses to bureaucracy. A presentation of relevant research helps us focus on key issues. The chapter concludes with the voices of two teachers as they describe the ways in which they work within and around bureaucracy.

THEORETICAL FRAMEWORK FOR UNDERSTANDING URBAN SCHOOL BUREAUCRACIES

Bureaucratic Ossification and Political Responsiveness Models

As you are learning in this book, there are many ways to think about and understand urban education. The same holds true for the bureaucratic nature of urban schools and the ways in which teachers work within and sometimes around these bureaucracies. Chubb and Moe (1990) have argued that there are two divergent ways to look at urban school bureaucracies. One is through the **bureaucratic ossification model.** Like supple tissue hardening into bone, school systems become rigid, isolated, and inefficient through layers and layers of rules, regulations, mandates, and red tape. Ossification is often the result of the size and scope, fragmentation, and underfunding of many urban school districts. Implied in this model is the idea that schools are isolated from and unresponsive to their urban communities. Schools become immune to families, neighborhoods, and their local context (Hess & Leal, 2003). For example, some schools, resulting from rules addressing safety issues, lock the school as soon as the students' day has ended, underutilizing a community building that has potential to support the surrounding neighborhood.

The **political responsiveness model** highlights the political vulnerability of urban school systems. This model comprises two distinct orientations: one in which administrators in urban bureaucracies respond to powerful and influential interest groups, such as teacher unions, and another that highlights administrators' responses to the pressure, demands, and expectations from local community constituents, such as business and political entities. By aligning themselves with some groups and excluding others, the administration becomes more insular and can respond only to select, politicized issues. Consider, for example, the recent trend in which urban charter schools are "backed" by large, local businesses that exert significant control over curricula and student outcomes. In this model, ideological and political barriers and disagreements discourage meaningful communication and change. As a result, urban districts and schools are buffeted about by external pressures, which have often led, ironically, to ossification (Hess & Leal, 2003). It is important to note that *neither* the ossification nor the responsiveness model creates positive working and learning conditions for teachers and students.

Bureaucratic Characteristics

Urban schools are run by bureaucracies, often referred to as "the central office," which share many unfortunate and debilitating characteristics. These include, but are not limited to, the following:

- massive numbers of schools, employees, and students
- transient superintendents and others in leadership positions
- highly centralized administration
- politicized school boards
- excessive regulations and paperwork, often referred to as "red tape"
- regulations that standardize educational practices
- susceptibility to fraud, waste, and corruption
- inadequate funding and resources
- lack of administrative accountability that places rigid accountability systems on schools and teachers
- low sense of urgency

From the above list, we will elaborate on three important concepts: centralization, fraud and waste, and standards and accountability. Each is a critical aspect of urban schools, and each highlights a different aspect of bureaucracy that teachers must learn to work within or around.

Centralization

Centralization occurs when the administrative authority is held completely by a small, central body, rather than in the local schools and their communities. All resources, such as personnel, finances, information, and technology, are controlled by the central administration. The central office decides the content of curricula, controls the budget, is responsible for employment and the building of educational facilities, determines discipline policies, and more. The centralization of all decision making in these massive, impersonal school districts is seen as archaic, unproductive, and overpowering, and is a direct result of ossification. Haberman (2003), for example, has argued that "the growth and maintenance of 120 failed urban school districts miseducating diverse children in poverty for over half a century is a predictable, explainable phenomenon, not a series of accidental, unfortunate, chance events" (para. 1). According to Haberman and others, school district central offices should not be allowed to ossify as monolithic bureaucracies that impede teachers' and administrators' work at the school level. In response, decentralization of urban school districts is viewed as one critical step in the overall process of systemic change (Segal, 2004). **Decentralization** occurs when decision making is passed down to individual schools and their communities. In areas where school systems have decentralized and schools themselves have become smaller, teacher and student achievement and satisfaction have improved (see, e.g., Raywid, 1996; Sergiovanni, 1996).

An adjunct to centralization in urban school administration is the controversial role of teachers' unions. As an urban teacher, you will need to think carefully about your choices regarding union participation. The two largest teachers' unions are the **National Education Association (NEA)** and **American Federation of Teachers (AFT)**. The NEA was originally designed to be a "professional" teacher organization, while the AFT has always been a labor union; the two groups often compete to obtain and organize their members. State and local chapters of these two unions or other small unions are often active in collective bargaining contracts and grievances. Unions are often criticized for obstructing educational reform and protecting underperforming teachers. Critics make the argument that unions, in the process of collective bargaining, create restrictions that impede school administration from making change and progress. On the other hand, advocates cite the teachers' union contract as an important framework for school improvements. They argue that teachers, along with administration, should work together to promote change.

With an increasing national focus on teacher quality, the news is filled with stories about teachers' unions. In the context of this (frequently negative) press, Weiner (1999) argues that

> for most city teachers—and parents, too—it's hard to imagine that teachers unions can be dynamic, democratic, and progressive. But they can be! The union should be your voice, exposing the system's problems, and organizing parents and citizens to join with the teachers to improve conditions. Unfortunately, urban teacher unions have become bureaucratic themselves, and in the largest cities, the union leadership is removed from the concerns of the teachers. (pp. 47–48)

The city of Cincinnati is an example of a promising exception to Weiner's (1999) assertion. For decades, the Cincinnati AFT has pioneered teacher quality initiatives in collaboration with school administration. Their uncomplicated peer evaluation and career programs are well established and well respected by all stakeholders.

Whether "downtown" in the school administration or in your union, you will undoubtedly be faced with the outcomes of centralization. We urge you, as does Weiner (2006), to develop your voice and to work to develop relationships with students, colleagues, families, and community that diminish the effects of a concentrated center that is removed from your daily teaching practice.

Fraud and Waste

Segal (2004) concludes that the root of the political tug of war within cities is systematic fraud, waste, and abuse in urban school systems. These systems are almost completely immune to city governments' urban improvement reforms. In the case of the so-called Texas miracle, student standardized test scores soared, and in the city of Houston, compared with double digits in many cities, a "miraculous" 1.5% of students were reported as dropping out of school. Principals were given handsome bonuses if their schools' test scores improved. An audit revealed that the higher scores were the result of high schools retaining more students in the ninth grade so they would not take the 10th-grade exam, placing more students in special education programs so their test scores would not count in schools' overall grades, and redefining dropouts out of existence and manipulating the way in which scores were computed (Haney, 2000). Students, teachers, and families are the losers in this situation. In another common example of waste and fraud, some principals resort to paying workers "under the table" to fix leaking toilets and broken chairs because submitting a work order through appropriate channels could take years (Segal, 2004). In many urban schools across the country, controls of fraud and waste at the school district level have failed. Segal argues,

> These controls actually eroded oversight, discouraged focus on performance, and required illicit behavior to work through red tape. The result is the worst of both worlds: Crooks who want to bilk the system can do so because the top has little handle on what is going down below, but employees who want to improve learning must sometimes break the rules. (p. xxiii)

Later in this chapter we will discuss the ways in which urban educators bend or break bureaucratic rules openly or discreetly. If teachers are to be held accountable for student achievement, they must be given control over the ways in which they deliver education. Top-down controls resulting from ossification must be adjusted to allow decision-making authority to move down to principals and teachers.

Standards and Accountability

The standards and accountability movement, a currently popular urban school reform strategy (Weiner, 2000), provides an example of the importance of an entire system supporting teachers' efforts in classrooms. In Chapter 6, you learned about the ways in which teachers use standards without standardizing the curriculum. **Accountability** refers to the idea of holding schools, teachers, and students responsible for results in student achievement and continuous improvement. Student success, as measured by standardized testing, is rewarded and failure is punished. Accountability measures have been enacted in federal law since the mid-1990s and are a major emphasis of the No Child Left Behind Act. Accountability, it is argued,

> is a widely appealing principle. It seems unlikely to operate in practice, however, unless educators come to internalize it as part of how they go about their work. This internalization seems most likely if a diverse body of stakeholders plays an active and at least partly informal role of oversight and if educators believe that they are receiving the kind of support that will enable them to succeed. Accountability, then, is less a mechanical process that can be imposed on unwilling subjects than a frame of mind to be shared by practitioners and by an attentive and involved set of stakeholders. (Stone, 1998, p. 17)

However, it is also argued that accountability is much more than just a "frame of mind." Strict, punitive measures placed on administrators and schools also define how accountability is operationalized. If test scores go up, teachers get merit pay bonuses. If test scores go down, the principal and half of the teachers in the school lose their jobs.

Furthermore, accountability, like other reforms such as charter schools and school choice, is linked to education's economic function (Rice & Roellke, 2003). School reforms designed to promote accountability and raise standards are assumed to lead to greater economic productivity in society. Here we see the work of "political responsiveness" at play. Many urban teachers struggle with the mandates and laws regarding standards and accountability. You will read about their experiences in the Practice section later in this chapter.

Ecological Models

Successful teaching requires recognition of the conditions of urban school bureaucracies and an understanding of how they influence teaching practice. It is true that urban education has struggled, historically and today, with inefficient and dehumanizing bureaucracies, a lack of funding and appropriate staffing, wave upon wave of new reforms and initiatives, gaps in school achievement and completion rates, and acute problems in the recruitment and retention of teachers for urban schools. As we discussed in the previous section, these are real and daunting concerns. As one beginning teacher commented while teaching in an urban school, "You feel the weight of society on your shoulders" (Donnell, 2004, p. 283).

However, an alternative paradigm from which to understand the success of many urban schools is an **ecological approach** (Bronfenbrenner, 1995; Comer, 1980; Weiner, 2000; Wideen, Mayer-Smith, & Moon, 1998). This approach views school life and classroom teaching as occurring within interconnected webs of settings and institutions that transcend classroom and school borders. Schooling is considered to be embedded in, and therefore influenced by, socially and culturally organized environments. Ecological systems, more than isolated factors such as outdated textbooks or school violence, affect schooling. Systems (such as the students, the classroom, the family, the school, the community, and the society) are nested within one other and have a cascading influence upon each other.

With regard to urban schools, an ecological view acknowledges that urban policy, structure, and customs are integrally related to what happens in urban classrooms. Urban schools function within an ecological web of social entities,

Urban teachers in centralized districts may feel overwhelmed, both physically and emotionally, by the amount of work that is necessary to keep pace in an urban school environment.

beginning with children in classrooms and extending out to schools, districts, and communities. These complex, layered contexts influence each other in bidirectional ways. Urban schools are embedded in a much larger context, one that requires multiple sectors of the community acting in concert. The teacher, students and their families, the school, or even the school district alone cannot bring about meaningful change in urban schools. But together they can create highly successful schools that ensure achievement for all students and that function as a service to the community.

Some educational thinkers have stressed that ecological, systemic change in urban schools requires economic, political, and social systems to be transformed along with urban schools and school systems (Anyon, 1997; Hill, Campbell, & Harvey, 2000). Stone (1998) argues that meeting the needs of urban schools, and therefore of urban teachers, is a civic, political process. As such, civic capacity, or the mobilization of an array of stakeholders in support of urban education, is a critical condition for change. Rather than focusing solely on teachers, Hill et al. adapted the African proverb "It takes a whole village to raise a child" to state, "It takes a whole city to educate a child."

In their history of the cultural reforms and community partnerships at a Boston high school, Gonsalves and Leonard (2007) focus on the importance of relationships within the ecology of the school and community setting. In particular, they note that the role of the "exosystem," the business community, higher education, government, and community organizations, is most effective when in relationship with people within the school. When these partners work directly with school constituents, they can "act as a web of connections that provide support for student, teachers, and school leaders" (p. 138). They argue that Dorchester High School serves as an example that "educational reforms are more successful when these networks are strong and firmly rooted within the school community" (p. 138).

With students at the center of an ecological web, optimal outcomes occur when there are strong and meaningful interconnections within and between each setting and among all stakeholders. Advocating for opportunities to have meaningful face-to-face relationships with students, parents, and administrators can make significant improvements in the quality of urban teaching and in the lives of urban students.

Characteristics of Proactive Urban Teachers

As a teacher working in an urban school, you may find yourself challenged or frustrated by the aspects of bureaucracy we have discussed. Advocating for change often takes more than just determination. Researchers have identified personal qualities or characteristics that are seen as supporting successful urban teaching, which involves working within and around school bureaucracies (Giroux & McLaren, 1986; Haberman, 1995; Ladson-Billings, 2000; Stanford, 2001):

- an ethic of personal accountability and risk taking
- resiliency
- persistence
- moral and political responsiveness

Teachers are encouraged to take a critical view of schooling, reflecting and acting on the institutional policies and practices that connect schools and society (Beyer, 2001; Cochran-Smith, 1991; Nieto, 2000). (See Chapter 5 for further discussion on the role of reflection.) Many researchers argue that in urban settings, where institutional hierarchy and bureaucracy combine with societal inequities, teachers are needed who understand the political nature of schools and who are adept at identifying inequalities in their own schools and classrooms, skilled in reconstructing the school and classroom culture to make it inclusive of all children, and committed to serving as change agents (Villegas & Lucas, 2002, p. xviii).

Donnell (2007) found that beginning urban teachers fell along a continuum of proactivity and reactivity in their approach to addressing the concerns of urban teaching. She conducted a research study that included a focus on how urban teachers deal with bureaucracy and their local context. We share some of the findings and comments from study participants in the rest of this section to illuminate the tensions that real urban teachers experience with bureaucratic structures.

Table 7.1 The Proactive/Reactive Continuum

Proactive	Reactive
Seek challenges and take risks	Avoid challenges and risks
High, realistic expectations	Low, unrealistic expectations
Clear priorities, conscious decisions	Ambivalence, fear of decisiveness
Seek out and use multiple resources	Unable/unwilling to seek out resources

Table 7.1 presents the anchors of the proactive/reactive continuum. Proactive teachers seek out challenges and are willing to take risks, while reactive teachers are more likely to avoid both challenges and risks. Proactive teachers develop high but realistic expectations of themselves and others. They accept problems but work actively to address them. In addition, proactive teachers are more likely than their reactive counterparts to make clear priorities and conscious decisions, and to seek out and use resources in their teaching and learning. Proactive teachers are much more likely to successfully adjust to the demands and constraints of urban teaching. One beginning teacher in the study explained, "I'm very proactive. I got myself elected to be on school council. And as part of school council, I was able to [have an impact] because we had the availability to interview vice-principal candidates [and] principal candidates" (Donnell, 2004, p. 152). For some teachers, rather than discouraging

them, their anger over the bureaucratic conditions propels them to proactively address these issues with their students. Urban teacher Mayva (pseudonym) shared the following:

> I haven't been discouraged. I mean like all the negativity has encouraged me. I mean if everyone just runs away because the system is messed up then the children just lose out, and it's not right for them. You know, we just have this whole population of people who have no options. I have been annoyed, really pissed off, angry, you know, wanting to yell and scream at everyone, but not my students. That's another thing I've realized, like when I first started I used to look at the students and say, "Why are you acting this way, why are you doing this?" . . . Then I started to realize how I was responding to the environment I was in, like the administration and other teachers around me. I began to understand what the students felt like more. They dealt with this situation the entire year. I mean they can see and hear and feel what is going on around them. (Donnell, 2004, p. 167)

Mayva continued to grow through risk taking in her teaching. The math program at her school did not seem to be meeting the needs of her students nor the expectations of the standardized testing required of the pupils. Mayva deviated from the mandated curriculum knowing that she risked criticism from her principal. Daisy, her experienced colleague and confidant, noticed.

> Daisy said to me, "You are the Rookie of the Year." "Why am I Rookie of the Year?" And she said, "Because you figured out how to pull this &%*! quicker than anyone else." She said, "You did it. You figured out that, you know what, I can't just teach them this flowery [math program] and expect that when they get it on the test, they can multiply fractions. It's not going to work." And I guess I wasn't afraid to do it, to make the changes. (Donnell, 2004, p. 168)

In taking the risk of deviating from the mandated curriculum, Mayva was able to better adapt her teaching in response to the needs of her pupils. This move required a willingness to "figure out" the system that was supported by Mayva's proactive stance.

Overt and Covert Challenges to Bureaucracy

Teachers who question the status quo tend to have highly proactive orientations and strong commitments to urban education. They are willing and able to challenge the system overtly; that is, their actions are open and intentional, and nothing is hidden. For example, Marta (pseudonym) had attained a high level of comfort with her teaching identity and ownership of her teaching practice. She was determined to resist pressure to conform and framed questions that pursued *why* decisions were made. Marta recounted a faculty meeting in which she questioned the seemingly immutable quality of school rules:

> And I think [it's important] being flexible. I feel like sometimes that as first year teachers you come in and you are like, "Ok, protocol says I have to do this, this, and this. No chewing gum. No doing this." I don't know maybe it's just me though, because even when [the faculty] were coming up with the rules I was mostly the one saying, "Well, why? I mean, what's the big deal if like. . . ." They can't dye their hair. And I was the one who was more, "Well, why not? I mean, why can't they dye their hair?" It seems like every time I'm like, "Why?" So there were a lot of things that I didn't agree with. But as a staff we can't go against one another. But we had to come up with ways of then explaining to each other why? Why? What's wrong with certain rules? Or what's the problem? And then we adjusted them. And I mean, with the kids I'm flexible. You know? I feel like different kids have different needs. And you approach them in different ways. And one rule can't fit everybody. (Donnell, 2004, p. 215)

Marta had developed the ability to think deeply, broadly, and flexibly about educational decisions and how these decisions impacted and influenced teacher and pupil learning. She questioned policies and expectations that were considered givens. Her learning and her teaching practice were responsive to the specific context and mindful of the larger landscapes that shaped this context. She was able to work within the bureaucracy of her school in an overt fashion.

At times, teachers experience challenging situations in which they are not comfortable overtly responding to their school bureaucracy. In these instances teachers may act covertly; that is, they don't openly challenge the bureaucracy but are willing to act in more subversive ways. For example, Dunn (2010) writes about her experience as an urban teacher struggling to work within the system that promoted teaching to the test. As explained in Chapter 5, instead of merely complying with county mandates to give 10-question multiple-choice benchmark tests every three weeks, she used the tests in "strategy sessions" where she taught students to critique materials, develop test-taking skills, and question whose knowledge was of most worth.

Weiner (1999) outlines three critical steps she has personally taken in determining when meeting students' needs may require skirting bureaucratic regulations, rules, or mandates. First, she says she "examined the problem from the students', parents', and administration's point of view. I assumed that all three parties were doing what they thought best" (p. 23). Next, she thought about her own values about education and analyzed whose point of view was most consistent with her own, questioning "the purposes of schooling and my moral responsibilities as a teacher" (p. 23). Finally, she would ask a respected colleague how and why he or she handled this type of situation, asking, "Was this strategy really fair to the students?" and "Would I be able to defend this method if an administrator questioned its use?" (p. 23). As Weiner notes, in most schools there are few opportunities for all involved to talk together about rules, procedures, strategies, and practices. As a classroom teacher you will likely need to take the initiative, speak with stakeholders, strategize, and decide the level of risk relative to gain that you are comfortable with. Ultimately, it's about doing what you think is in the best interest of your students, whether overtly or covertly.

As any participant in social movements knows, there is strength in numbers. Teachers who work together are more likely to successfully challenge the bureaucracy in urban schools.

WHAT THE RESEARCH SAYS ABOUT BUREAUCRACY

Much of the research on urban school bureaucracy focuses on systemic issues such as policy reform. More research is needed on the ways in which bureaucracies impact teacher practice and learning, as well as the ways in which teachers can themselves mediate and manage the resulting issues. Weiner (1993) has called for research that seeks to understand how "the bureaucratic and hierarchical organizations that characterize urban school systems influence instruction and teacher-student relationships" (p. 79). The five studies discussed in this section offer a representation of current research and further insight into how issues associated with urban bureaucracies impact teachers' practice.

Christman, Cohen, and Macpherson (1997) conducted ethnographic research in urban Philadelphia high schools, identifying three tasks that are essential for engaging students in urban high schools in their learning: building community, generating knowledge about change, and reinventing curricular instruction and assessment. Grossman, Thompson, and Valencia (2002) conducted a longitudinal study in two urban districts engaged in reform that focused on teacher learning. They sought to determine the influence of contextual factors in, and decisions made by, the district on teachers' learning. The districts served as teacher educators through the meaningful and intentional tasks, resources, learning environments, and assessments they implemented, confirming that bureaucracies can, in fact, support teacher learning. In a classic study of urban teacher effectiveness, Haberman (1995) aimed to predict the success of urban educators who faced, among other challenges, counterproductive bureaucracies. He found that with specific supports, such as organizational skills and training in systems and policies, teachers were successful at managing bureaucratic demands. Ingersoll (2001) analyzed statistical data to determine the causes of teacher turnover. He found that many teachers cite aspects of bureaucracy, such as lack of administrative support, in their decision to leave urban teaching. Pitts (2007) investigated the role of ethnic representation among school personnel on urban school bureaucracies. He found that teacher representation, but not administrative representation, is related to better organizational performance. Ethnic representation among teachers, therefore, has greatest significance at the "street level" rather than at the more bureaucratic administrative level. See Table 7.2.

Table 7.2   Research Studies on Bureaucracy

Author(s)	Purpose	Findings	Implications	URL
Christman, Cohen, & Macpherson (1997)	Researchers conducted an ethnographic study on how to engage urban students in their learning.	Three tasks were found necessary for engaging students enrolled in urban schools in their education: building community, generating knowledge about change, and reinventing curricular instruction and assessment. Those teachers previously devoted to reform found both clarity and understanding in the three tasks.	The understanding and research regarding ways in which urban teachers work for reform in their schools both strengthens the drive to continue this work and calls for additional reform.	http://uex .sagepub .com/ content/ 32/1/146.full .pdf+html
Grossman, Thompson, & Valencia (2002)	Researchers worked with two reform-active districts to determine the influence of contextual factors in, and decisions made by, the district on teachers' learning.	The districts served as teacher educators, through the meaningful and intentional tasks, resources, learning environments, and assessments they implemented. For example, the assessment tools offered by the district supported teachers in learning about teaching while at the same time learning about student progress. These tasks helped teachers look at their teaching in new ways.	District structures, whether intentional or not, can either support or deflect opportunities for continued learning within a subject area, while the strength of the lenses provided by curriculum policies, in particular, helps determine the depth and breadth of what teachers learn. Beginning teachers should expect their district policies and curricular and instructional guidance to help shape their learning about teaching in productive ways.	

Author(s)	Purpose	Findings	Implications	URL
Haberman (1995)	The researcher sought to predict the success of urban teachers, including the ability to address the "care and feeding of the bureaucracy."	In large urban school systems, successful teachers require the skills and knowledge to cope effectively with bureaucratic issues. The ability to adjust and cope with bureaucratic demands, not only with organizational skills but also with the knowledge of how to fulfill the minimum requirements of the bureaucracy and protect oneself from burnout, is essential.	Teachers can learn organizational skills and knowledge, but they also need support in developing the ability to contend with and effectively manage the demands and potential stress of bureaucratic issues. This support can come in the form of specific training and information regarding policies, protocols, and systems.	
Ingersoll (2001)	The researcher analyzed statistical data to determine the causes of teacher turnover.	Many urban teachers who leave the field cited working conditions, particularly the lack of administrative support and lack of teacher influence over decision making.	Teachers are more likely to stay with urban teaching if the working conditions in their schools include the involvement of their administration and the participation of teachers in the functioning of the school.	
Pitts (2007)	The researcher looked at the role of ethnic representation among school personnel on urban school bureaucracies.	Ethnic representativeness in school bureaucracies resulted in gains in organizational outcomes, although students of color benefited more than White students. Furthermore, representativeness among teachers had an impact on "street level" concerns, but less so on the administrative bureaucracy.	Students of color benefit from proportional representation among administrators and especially teachers. Teachers of color may help to improve dropout rates and standardized test scores for underrepresented students.	http://aas .sagepub .com/ content/ 39/4/497 .short

PRACTICE

In this section, practicing teachers **Tracey Kareemo** and **Jim Conti** describe how working within a bureaucracy has impacted their teaching practice. Tracey is a veteran fourth-grade teacher near Providence, Rhode Island, and Jim is a former sixth-grade teacher in Chicago, Illinois. Their firsthand accounts illuminate the theory and research reviewed earlier in this chapter. Responding to bureaucracy is a sensitive topic for those working within the system and wanting to stay in the system, however broken.

For Tracey, standardized testing has been an important touch point. For Jim, the rigidity of the bureaucracy has been challenging.

Tracey: When I first started teaching 14 years ago, standardized tests had little rhyme or reason. We never knew what was going to be on them, so success was like trying to hit a moving target. Failure was frequent and discouraging because once you saw the test you realized how much you had not taught. Any success was near impossible to replicate because the same teacher never had great consistency and the test was different every year.

Over the past few years, the GLEs (grade-level expectations) were implemented. A few New England states got together and created clear expectations of what a student should master at each grade level. After that process was done for Grades 1–8, the states hired a testing company to create a test for each grade that only had questions on it that were applicable to that grade's GLEs. At last: a description of my responsibilities and a way to assess my teaching and my students' learning. Finally, we were only being tested on what I was responsible to teach!

However, forgotten in this new equation was the urban school student. Often half of my class is significantly below grade level for a variety of reasons. Yet that same student is still required to test on grade level. This seems like a setup for failure.

Now that the district has a clear vision of what my fourth-grade students need to know and apply on the test, the central office has made some changes. These changes include pacing guides and schedules that tell us the pace at which we must cover the material. This requires more of me than there are hours in a day, let alone hours in a school day! I now must post a schedule on my door so administration knows what I am doing and for how long I am supposed to be doing it. Missing from this schedule, however, is time for feeding the student who is hungry, for behavior disruptions (big and small), for addressing habitual absences, for over-tired students, for frequent trips to the nurse and visits from the nurse (for head lice checks), for visits from family services, for in-school counseling, for ramp-up time and go-over-it-again time, for covering for another teacher, for going to the bathroom, and, of course, for the teachable moment.

Jim: The greatest challenge of bureaucracy is the rigidity with which it looks at our work. I had more days than I can count where my students and I would get caught up in a lateral conversation that didn't perfectly align with any of the standards. I find it hard to quantify my conversations with students regarding their futures or the injustices in our societies, but many of these conversations did not fall within the boundaries of "testing material."

Fortunately, I was blessed with administrators who understood the value behind these conversations. Were they to walk in to my classroom while something like this was happening, my administrators were more likely to join in than redirect back to the lesson plan that I had typed out on my desk. I realize that I was lucky in this, and that many teachers aren't as fortunate. At the same time—and this may be inviting trouble—I have sometimes wished for more rigorous supervision. As a beginning teacher, more structure and guidance would have been helpful in crafting my practice. The flexibility of my position and administration was great, really allowing me the room for creativity that I had hoped for as a beginning teacher, but with endless options came the challenge of deciding what and how to teach. I was just beginning; I certainly didn't believe in my own ability to craft curriculum and decide what my students needed to know.

Tracey reflects on the covert and overt ways in which she makes decisions and carries them out in her practice.

Tracey: The goal is to teach each student. To do that in an urban school, you have to know best teaching practices, your curriculum, your district's policies, the special education laws. You need to know and work with your support staff. You need to keep impeccable records, know your students and their families. If that also means you guide parents "off the record" to better the child, you do it. For example, I have encouraged parents to put in writing a request for their child to be tested or to be removed from a service that is no longer helping. The best overt challenge I have seen is the way in which one of our amazing special education teachers takes a stand for her population of students. At our school, when a student passes the state test, the student and a parent are invited to a free pasta dinner. This teacher boycotts the pasta dinner because her students will never be able to attend. She is still rallying for "percentage of improvement" gets you to the dinner. The good news is her effort is working! Our principal is working with her to change the criteria for next year's dinner.

In light of these issues and challenges, adhering to an ethic of personal responsibility and resiliency is important to both Tracey and Jim.

Tracey: For me, continuing to use research-based teaching practices (some provided by the teachers' union, some by my district, and some at the university) has been a liberating gift. It has provided me with the confidence to veer from the "prescription" of the strict pacing guides. I strongly believe that, at my grade level, learning to read is important, but having a love of reading and an intrinsic motivation to come to school is crucial!

I believe our administration has provided a core curriculum that is very good and provides an abundance of teaching opportunities for our grades. However, you have to know when, where, and how much to use it. Workbooks and short, often dry, reading books tend to suck the life out of students (and teachers). I regularly assess my students at their level and develop them from there at an accelerated pace. I use cooperative learning groups and centers to foster responsibility for their own learning (something I've found urban students really benefit from). In the centers, you'll find colorful hands-on support material. Unfortunately, only a small portion is on the prescription list provided by our administration. So I spend thousands of dollars every year on supplies for my room. My union provides $270 per year in reimbursements with receipts. (Don't tell my husband; he thinks it's $270 per trimester!)

Jim: I am still beginning and struggling through the challenges of being a teacher. I have to admit that I am still learning to teach. Tracey describes what I would love to see in my classroom every day. It has happened a few times, sure, but not consistently. I'm working on it.

A bit more personally, I find it necessary to first be critical of my own classroom and then use that to effect change in the larger school community. As a newcomer, my feedback about the school and the way things are done here can sometimes be taken sourly, being viewed as uninformed. Admittedly, this is mostly true. I find being honest about what is happening for me to be important. I look at my classroom and identify the challenges I face. I then look at the school and see if those same issues exist more globally. Often, they do. In this way, I am able to present "my" problem to the staff and then guide the conversation to a more global scale so as to address school policy. No, this is not universally effective nor does it always go well, but, as a new teacher, it is my way of being able to state what is on my mind, to stand up for what I believe in, and to make my school better for my students.

When asked whether they are able to maintain a positive approach and a sense of resiliency, Tracey and Jim responded in this way:

Tracey: Absolutely! I take my responsibilities for educating my students very seriously. If they are on level, I should advance them even more. If they are below level, I must ramp them up. If not me, then who? I teach fourth grade, and the window for their success is closing. Failure is not an option because several times a year one test or another is telling them they are unsuccessful. I monitor progress with every student on a weekly, if not daily, basis. When they succeed, I celebrate their progress with them. When they slow down or stop, I give them new tools or the pep talk they may need to turn it around. Think about it . . . at 10 years old it is easy to feel like a failure when you flunk the standardized test. They need to see how much they really improved so the continued learning becomes a doable thing for them. I just ignore our district saying that the improvements students made were not enough to be on level. They only see a number. I see a love for school, decreased absences, confidence, reading without being told, smiles, and "thank yous" from parents saying that their children finally love school.

Jim: Yes, I am certainly positive and engaged in the classroom, but it is hard. I'll say it again: I'm new. I still don't fully understand how to teach, what methods to implement with which students, and how best to convey the importance of education. I have supportive administrators and coworkers, but only to a point. They can't teach for me. I'm the one who needs to do that part. Teaching is hard, and trying to teach in a system that constantly feels like it is working against you is even harder.

That said, I wholeheartedly agree with Tracey that there are few experiences greater than those you share with students. In my first year, Ralph was, far and away, my most challenging student. Just about every conflict or challenge that could arise did arise. Toward the end of the year, I came back to my desk after a prep to find a small Jedi warrior figurine sitting atop a sticky note that said, "From Ralph." That figurine and sticky note will forever sit on my desk regardless of where I am.

WRAP UP

In this chapter we have shared how negotiating bureaucracy is part of any urban teacher's job. We discussed models and characteristics of bureaucracy as well as ways that teachers overtly or covertly challenge bureaucracy.

Unfortunately, the current political and economic climate has continued to be indifferent to the needs of historically underserved children. Whether society does, in fact, have the will to support community structures that would actually make effective urban schooling possible is an important question (Haberman, 2003). Hess (1999), for example, argues that as long as urban school systems rotate policy, continually replacing old policies and reform strategies with new ones with little effect, schools will continue to demonstrate symbolic rather than actual activity and change. Without flexibility, ossification persists. Real change will need to address the pervasive perspective in our society that connects children's low socioeconomic status with weak academic achievement. (See Chapter 1 for more information on this deficit perspective.) As an educational community, we sometimes contribute to this situation by "locating problems and solutions in individual performance" (Weiner, 1993, p. 82). As a result, urban students, their families, and their teachers

> are caught in a classic double bind: the problems of their communities affect both the quality of schools and young people's ability to benefit from schooling. The larger economic system constrains the future of their communities and their communities' capacity to support decent schools. (Hill et al., 2000, p. 5)

Ultimately, it is unfair and unrealistic to put pressure solely on school districts to create change (Hill et al., 2000). This approach continues to ignore the underexamined aspects of urban areas' political and economic isolation and exploitation (Anyon, 1997; Hill et al., 2000). Only by recognizing the influence of the sociopolitical context and working in concert with other agencies and constituents will school districts, and therefore teachers, be able to do their work effectively. More important than securing one particular part of the system is securing key elements across all parts of the system. For example, Hill et al. argue that the long list of current "name brand" reform proposals—such as decentralizing, large-scale retraining of teachers, imposing standards, and establishing vouchers—are all valid contributions. However, they must be part of a hybrid strategy. Hill and colleagues' research, based on case studies of six large city reform initiatives, calls for "break[ing] the hermetic seal" (p. ix) between school districts and other community assets. Three key elements, they argue, must be part of any urban education reform: strong incentives for good school performance, major investments in the capacities of teachers and schools, and freedom of action that allows school personnel to change how they work with students. Current reform proposals might be more effective if they were joined together with an emphasis on these prerequisites. In the meantime, urban teachers must work within and around bureaucracy to provide the best learning opportunities for their students.

EXTENSION ACTIVITIES

Reflection

1. To address some of the bureaucratic issues in a school, you must first consider your own level of proactivity, your ability to reflect, your willingness to seek the advice of allies, and your resourcefulness. Write a short analytic piece depicting a time in your life when you acted in a proactive manner to solve a problem that initially seemed out of your hands. What did you reflect on? Did you seek allies? If so, who and why? How was the issue eventually resolved? What does this process tell you about yourself and your potential to be a proactive teacher who can work with and around urban school bureaucracy?

2. Search an urban school district's website for policies and procedures that would have an impact on teachers' work (e.g., a faculty handbook, a teacher's contract). Select two or three policies, and explain how you might work with and around them in your teaching.

Action

1. Choose one aspect of the bureaucracy in your school or district that frustrates, discourages, or angers you and about which you feel a sense of urgency. Brainstorm a list of people that are allies with whom you can discuss this issue. Don't forget to include people in the community and in local businesses, if appropriate. Then, list four or five proactive responses or solutions that might help you address this issue. Try not to focus on potential obstacles or reasons why you think it won't work.

2. Conduct an interview with a current urban teacher. Design your interview questions around the ways in which this teacher tries to work within and around bureaucracy. What questions can you develop that address the teacher's proactivity or reactivity? What has the teacher's perspective taught you about managing educational bureaucracy?

SUGGESTED RESOURCES

Books and Articles

Frutcher, N. (2007). *Urban schools, public will: Making education work for all our children.* New York, NY: Teachers College Press.

Gatto, J. (2003). *The underground history of American education.* New York: Oxford Village Press.

Grossman, P. L., Thompson, C., & Valencia, S. W. (2002). Focusing the concerns of new teachers: The district as teacher educator. In M. Knapp, M. McLaughlin, J. Marsh, & A. Hightower (Eds.), *School districts and instructional renewal: Opening the conversation* (pp. 129–142). New York, NY: Teachers College Press.

Weiner, L. (1993). *Preparing teachers for urban schools: Lessons from thirty years of school reform.* New York, NY: Teachers College Press.

Websites

The Council of the Great City Schools (www.cgcs.org)
A national organization exclusively representing the needs of urban public schools since 1956. The website includes many resources, including a link to the Council's newsletter, *Urban Educator.*

"Why is there so much school bureaucracy and what can we do about it?" (http://newtalk .org/2008/11/why-is-there-so-much-school-bu.php)
A forum in which panelists discuss a range of issues associated with school bureaucracies.

REFERENCES

Anyon, J. (1997). *Ghetto schooling: A political economy of urban school reform.* New York, NY: Teachers College Press.

Beyer, L. E. (2001). The value of critical perspectives in teacher education. *Journal of Teacher Education, 52,* 151–163. doi:10.1177/0022487101052002006

Bronfenbrenner, U. (1995). Developmental ecology through space and time: A future perspective. In P. Moen, G. H. Elder, & K. Lüscher (Eds.), *Examining lives in context: Perspectives on the ecology of human development* (pp. 619–647). Washington, DC: American Psychological Association.

Christman, J., Cohen, J., & Macpherson, P. (1997). Growing smaller: Three tasks in restructuring urban high schools. *Urban Education, 32,* 146–165. doi:10.1177/0042085997032001008

Chubb, J., & Moe, T. (1990). *Politics, markets, and America's schools.* Washington, DC: Brookings Institution.

Cochran-Smith, M. (1991). Learning to teach against the grain. *Harvard Educational Review, 61,* 279–310.

Comer, J. (1980). *School power.* New York, NY: Free Press.

Donnell, K. (2004). *Learning to teach in an urban setting: The struggle to develop transformative practice* (Unpublished doctoral dissertation). Boston College, Chestnut Hill, MA.

Donnell, K. (2007). Getting to we: Developing a transformative teaching practice. *Urban Education, 42,* 223–249. doi:10.1177/0042085907300541

Dunn, A. H. (2010). "We know you're Black at heart": A self-study of a White, urban high school teacher. In A. J. Stairs & K. A. Donnell (Eds.), *Research on urban teacher learning: Examining contextual factors over time* (pp. 29–40). Charlotte, NC: Information Age.

Encyclopædia Britannica. (2011). *Bureaucracy.* Retrieved from http://www.britannica.com/EBchecked/topic/84999/bureaucracy

Feiman-Nemser, S. (2001). From preparation to practice: Designing a continuum to strengthen and sustain teaching. *Teachers College Record, 103,* 1013–1055. doi:10.1111/0161-4681.00141

Giroux, H. A., & McLaren, P. (1986). Teacher education and the politics of engagement: The case for democratic schooling. *Harvard Educational Review, 56,* 213–238.

Gonsalves, L., & Leonard, J. (2007). *New hope for urban high schools: Cultural reform, moral leadership, and community partnership.* Westport, CT: Praeger.

Grossman, P. L., Thompson, C., & Valencia, S. W. (2002). Focusing the concerns of new teachers: The district as teacher educator. In M. Knapp, M. McLaughlin, J. Marsh, & A. Hightower (Eds.), *School districts and instructional renewal: Opening the conversation* (pp. 129–142). New York, NY: Teachers College Press.

Haberman, M. (1995). Selecting "star" teachers for children and youth in urban poverty. *Phi Delta Kappan, 76*(10), 77–81.

Haberman, M. (2003). *Who benefits from failing urban school districts? An essay on equity and justice for diverse children in urban poverty.* Retrieved from http://www.habermanfoundation.org/Articles/Default.aspx?id=06

Haney, W. (2000). The myth of the Texas miracle in education. *Education Policy Analysis Archives, 8*(41). Retrieved from http://epaa.asu.edu/ojs

Hess, F. (1999). *Spinning wheels: The politics of urban school reform.* Washington, DC: Brookings Institution Press.

Hess, F., & Leal, D. L. (2003). Technocracies, bureaucracies, or responsive polities? Urban school systems and the politics of school violence prevention. *Social Science Quarterly, 84,* 527–542. doi:10.1111/1540-6237.8403003

Hill, P., Campbell, C., & Harvey, J. (2000). *It takes a city: Getting serious about urban school reform.* Washington, DC: Brookings Institution Press.

Ingersoll, R. (2001). *Teacher turnover, teacher shortages, and the organization of schools.* Seattle, WA: Center for the Study of Teaching and Policy.

Kozol, J. (1991). *Savage inequalities: Children in America's schools.* New York, NY: Harper & Row.

Ladson-Billings, G. (2000). Fighting for our lives: Preparing teachers to teach African American students. *Journal of Teacher Education, 51,* 206–214. doi:10.1177/0022487100051003008

Nieto, S. (2000). Placing equity front and center: Some thoughts on transforming teacher education for a new century. *Journal of Teacher Education, 51,* 180–187. doi:10.1177/0022487100051003004

Pitts, D. (2007). Representative bureaucracy, ethnicity, and public schools: Examining the link between representation and performance. *Administration and Society, 39,* 497–526. doi:10.1177/0095399707303129

Raywid, M. A. (1996). *Taking stock: The movement to create mini-schools, schools-within-schools, and separate small schools.* New York, NY: ERIC Clearinghouse on Urban Education. (ERIC Document Reproduction Service No. ED396045)

Rice, J., & Roellke, C. (2003). Urban school finance: Increased standards and accountability in uncertain economic times. *School Business Affairs, 69*(5), 30–33.

Segal, L. (2004). *Battling corruption in America's public schools*. Boston, MA: Northeastern University Press.

Sergiovanni, T. J. (1996). *Leadership for the schoolhouse: How is it different? Why is it important?* San Francisco, CA: Jossey-Bass.

Stanford, B. H. (2001). Reflections of resilient, persevering urban teachers. *Teacher Education Quarterly, 28*, 75–87.

Stone, C. (1998). *Changing urban education*. Lawrence: University of Kansas Press.

Villegas, A. M., & Lucas, T. (2002). *Educating culturally responsive teachers*. Albany: State University of New York Press.

Weiner, L. (1993). *Preparing teachers for urban schools: Lessons from thirty years of school reform*. New York, NY: Teachers College Press.

Weiner, L. (1999). *Urban teaching: The essentials*. New York, NY: Teachers College Press.

Weiner, L. (2000). Evidence and inquiry in teacher education: What's needed for urban schools. *Journal of Teacher Education, 53*, 254–261. doi:10.1177/0022487102053003010

Weiner, L. (2006). *Urban teaching: The essentials* (Rev. ed.). New York, NY: Teachers College Press.

Wideen, M., Mayer-Smith, J., & Moon, B. (1998). A critical analysis of the research on learning to teach: Making the case for an ecological perspective on inquiry. *Review of Educational Research, 68*, 130–178. doi:10.2307/1170752

Wright, H. K., & Alenuma, S. (2007). Race, urban schools, and educational reform: The context, utility, pros, and cons of the magnet example. In J. L. Kincheloe & k. hayes (Eds.), *City kids: Understanding, appreciating, and teaching them* (pp. 211–221). New York, NY: Peter Lang.

CONTRIBUTING AUTHORS

Tracey Kareemo has been teaching for 14 years and is currently a fourth-grade teacher in Pawtucket, Rhode Island. She is a mentor for new teachers and is on the building literacy team. She is also an American Federation of Teachers trainer for reading and behavior management.

Jim Conti taught sixth grade for two years on Chicago's West Side. He also served at a small Catholic middle school and was part of an alternative certification program. Currently, Jim does recruiting work for the same program he attended, supporting new teachers as they begin in the classroom.

Lisa Garcia, whose vignette opens this chapter, has worked as a teacher in regular education, special education, and English as a second language for 16 years. She has taught Grades K–8 in both Arizona and Rhode Island. She is currently a special education teacher in Pawtucket, Rhode Island.

CHAPTER 8

PROMOTING SOCIAL JUSTICE AND EQUITY IN URBAN TEACHING

VIGNETTE: SOCIAL JUSTICE IN ACTION

"Trash!" "Bad words!" "Cigarette butts!" "Someone tied up the swing!" The children's voices are clear and eager. Ms. Planert's first graders are in the middle of a thematic unit on the topic of community. After a visit to their local beloved playground, the children are recording the vandalism they have seen. Having discussed local "helpers" in the community, the class decides whom they might write to for support in cleaning up and reclaiming the playground. Eventually, the children work in teams to envision, draw, and write about their ideal community playground, complete with equitable access, resources, and "laws."

With the collaboration of her cooperating teacher and the special education teacher, Ms. Planert, a student teacher, has transformed a traditional social studies unit into an action research, service-learning project with her young students. The children, all six and seven years old, explore the actual playground by foot, but they explore complex social justice issues with their minds and hearts.

FOCUS QUESTIONS

- What is the role of social justice and equity in urban teaching?
- What does it mean to develop socially just and equitable teaching practice in urban classrooms?
- Why are issues of power, morality, equity, voice, identity, and action essential in shaping urban teaching practice?

Effective urban teaching requires teachers to be responsive to the daily realities of pupils' lives inside and outside of the classroom. Ms. Planert's work with first graders is an excellent example of doing just that. Critique of the standard social and educational systems that have historically underserved urban pupils is equally important. This demanding way of teaching necessitates

> one eye firmly fixed on the students—Who are they? What are their hopes, dreams, and aspirations? Their passions and commitments? What skills, abilities, and capacities does each one bring to the classroom?—and the other eye looking unblinkingly at the concentric circles of context— historical flow, cultural surround, economic reality. In doing so, [teachers begin] to enact more socially just, humanizing practice. (Ayers, 1998, xvii)

In this chapter we will explore elements of teaching for social justice that will help you determine your own orientation, beliefs, and goals related to socially just teaching practice.

THEORETICAL FRAMEWORK FOR SOCIAL JUSTICE AND EQUITY

Given the unjust and inequitable conditions in which urban children learn and live, increasing numbers of urban educators, researchers, and teacher educators view teaching for social justice and social change as a moral imperative. Teaching for social justice can be conceptualized as having three different parts (Chubbuck, 2010). The first and least controversial part encompasses curricula, teaching practices, and teachers' beliefs associated with improving "the learning opportunities (and, by implication, life opportunities) of each individual student, including those who belong to groups typically underserved in the current educational context" (p. 198). The second part "includes the transformation of educational structures or policies that diminish students' learning opportunities" (p. 198). The third and most controversial part involves teachers in understanding and, ultimately, challenging and dismantling any structures that perpetuate injustice and inequity at the societal level. Each of these levels involves both individual elements (e.g., beliefs, dispositions, decision making) and structural elements (e.g., bureaucratic traditions, diverse demographics, underresourced communities). (See Chapters 1 and 7, respectively.) Chubbuck argues that "both individual and structural factors affect the level of justice, in fact feeding off each other, and thus both need attention" (p. 198).

Given the unjust and inequitable conditions in which some urban children learn and live, increasing numbers of urban educators, researchers, and teacher

educators view teaching for social justice and social change as a moral imperative. Villegas and Lucas (2002) present a continuum from conceptions of teacher
as technician to conceptions of teacher as agent of social change (see Figure 8.1).

Figure 8.1 Villegas and Lucas's (2002) Continuum

Teachers as technicians ⟶⟶	*Teachers as agents of change*
View of schools:	*View of schools:*
Schools are neutral settings that function separately from the struggle for power in society and are not affected by this struggle. They provide all students with an equal opportunity to prove their merit.	Schools are intricately connected to society. Typically, they reproduce existing social inequalities by privileging the culture and interests of the dominant group. However, they have the potential to serve as sites for social transformation.
View of teaching and teachers:	*View of teaching and teachers:*
Teaching is principally a technical activity that involves the application of clearly defined instructional procedures or methods. Standard school practices are accepted uncritically. There is no need for teachers to develop a personal vision. The role of teachers is to impart to students the knowledge and skills that are packaged in the school curriculum. Teachers should strive to be "objective" in their words and deeds.	Teaching involves much more than applying instructional methods. It is essentially a political and ethical activity. Teachers are participants in a larger struggle to promote equity in society. They *must* develop a personal vision of why they are teachers and what is important in education and in the larger society. As agents of change, they assume responsibility for identifying and interrupting inequitable school practices. Their actions are never neutral; they either support or challenge the existing social order.

Source: Villegas, A. M., & Lucas, T. (2002). *Educating culturally responsive teachers*. Albany: State University
of New York Press.

Villegas and Lucas (2002) argue that, through self-exploration, starting in
teacher education programs and continuing through their careers, beginning
teachers must locate themselves along this continuum. In the following sections
we will look at five theoretical frameworks, with both individual and structural
elements, for teaching for social justice: interrupting oppression, teaching as a
political act, teachers as change agents, pedagogy as praxis, and teaching
against the grain.

Interrupting Oppression

Understanding, challenging, and interrupting **oppression,** the exercise of power or authority in an unjust manner, in its many forms, is integral to promoting social justice through our teaching. Hardiman and Jackson (1997) outline the defining features of oppression:

1. Oppression is *pervasive*. Social inequality is systematically integrated into social institutions as well as individual consciousness.

2. Oppression is *restrictive*. It imposes structural and material constraints that determine an individual's life chances and sense of possibility.

3. Oppression is *hierarchical*. Dominant or privileged groups receive advantages, often unacknowledged, over disempowered groups.

4. Oppression is *complex* and involves the multiple and cross-cutting social group memberships of one's identity. The constellations of our identities fluctuate, and they impact our experience. Oppression has consequences for everyone.

5. Oppression is *internalized*. Oppressive beliefs are internalized by those in both advantaged and disadvantaged positions. We are socialized to accept many aspects of oppression as "normal."

6. Oppression takes the form of many *different "isms."* Racism, classism, sexism, ableism, and other "isms" are part of the multiple manifestations of oppression.

We encounter oppression in our work as urban teachers in many forms, some overt and obvious—such as the disproportionate number of Black boys in special education programs—and others more subtle or invisible—such as the privileges heterosexual students and teachers enjoy in comparison to their gay, lesbian, bisexual, and transgendered counterparts. For example, when thinking about the students we serve, one component of interrupting oppression involves "looking more broadly and carefully at the causes of the behaviors [teachers] see, to develop multiple perspectives, and to make a commitment to working with their pupils, regardless of parental participation (or lack thereof)" (Ladson-Billings, 1994, p. 133). We have heard some teachers and administrators bemoan a lack of parental involvement in urban schools. Teachers who interrupt oppression realize that parents may be working multiple jobs or have commitments that keep them from attending school events, and these teachers find or create alternative opportunities to involve and engage parents in respectful, creative, and flexible ways.

The unjust, inequitable, and demeaning conditions of children's schooling experiences often anger beginning teachers and heighten their understanding of oppression as a moral issue. A sense of being "too angry to leave" urban teaching can act as an impetus to deepen teachers' commitments to urban education and socially just teaching (Quartz & TEP Research Group, 2003). A social justice orientation supports teachers' rejection of purely technical teaching. When the students and families in our schools face oppression and education is inextricably bound to issues of power and authority, teaching is seen as inherently political.

Teachers who interrupt oppression realize that inequities exist both inside and outside the school doors, and they are willing to work together and with families to challenge the status quo.

Teaching as a Political Act

Murrell (2000) has argued that "teachers' work is not simply a matter of acquiring the appropriate skills, techniques, and expertise, but also includes

being politically reflective and ideologically interpretive" (p. 31). Many educators have come to the conclusion that there is no neutrality in teaching; all
teaching is based on some set of core values and beliefs. You may be aware of
opposing views and opinions in educational theories that result from very different foundational beliefs. Education also functions within systems of power
and privilege. Politicizing teaching practice involves recognizing and challenging the ways in which power, inequity, and social injustice function in urban
schooling. What does it mean to regard education and schooling as inherently
related to issues of power, equity, access to knowledge, and privilege, and to
decide how to act within this perspective? This requires the difficult work of
uncovering implicit assumptions and beliefs about education, challenging the
status quo, and deciding what action to take within the specific context of
practice. Thinking about teaching in this way, especially for the first time, can
be both exhilarating and confusing.

   Teachers who take this critical view of schooling reflect and act on the institutional policies and practices that connect schools and society. Many educators argue that in urban settings, where institutional hierarchy and bureaucracy
combine with societal inequities, teachers are needed who

> understand the political nature of schools and teaching and who are adept
> at identifying inequalities in their own schools and classrooms, skilled in
> reconstructing the school and classroom culture in order to make it inclu-
> sive of all children, and committed to serving as change agents. (Villegas
> & Lucas, 2002, p. xviii)

   Brian Schultz (2008), a former fifth-grade teacher in Chicago who was mentioned earlier in this book, helped his students take on the seemingly impossible
task of convincing the community and educational bureaucracy to build a new
school. Although they did not achieve the goal, through astounding political
and academic challenges and successes, "spectacular things" did happen along
the way. As it did with Brian Schultz, understanding teaching in urban schools
as a political act compels many educators to take the next step, that of taking
action and creating change.

Teachers as Change Agents

   According to Fullan (1993), a champion of educational change, "Teaching
at its core is a moral profession. Scratch a good teacher and you will find a

moral purpose" (p. 7). The challenges of teaching for social justice, of interrupting oppression in our schools, of examining teaching as a political act, are built out of our sense of purpose and our beliefs about education. Fullan (1993, 2001) encourages us to *act* on our view as a moral imperative, to actively create opportunities to make a difference. In order to fulfill our moral purpose and engage in just teaching practices, we must become change agents, teachers who develop the skills and strategies necessary to accomplish their moral goals (Fullan, 1993). Fullan describes four core capacities that support our ability to effect change in schools: personal vision-building, inquiry, mastery, and collaboration. Developing a personal vision entails continually examining and reexamining our reasons for teaching and further developing and enriching those reasons. One beginning teacher framed her developing personal vision this way:

> I am able to say that the reason I'm teaching this class of kids or [am] there every day is because I care about the students. And I want them to reach their fullest potential. . . . And I can always believe that that's right. Like those are very fundamental truths, I think, to teaching any classroom of kids. And so as long as I can really apply that to what I'm doing then I can know that at least that much is right. (Donnell, 2004, p. 251)

It can be particularly helpful to normalize this personal process by making it public and exploring our personal vision with others (Chubbuck, 2010). As we discussed in Chapter 5, inquiry, the second capacity, engages us in continuous learning and provides us with the ideas, data, perspectives, and insights necessary to make meaningful changes in our practice and in the conditions that affect our practice. Developing mastery, the third capacity, helps us create change "both in relation to specific innovations and as a personal habit" (Fullan, 1993, p. 14). Finally, collaboration with others allows us to enhance our ability to effect change on both small- and large-scale efforts. We know one first-year urban teacher who began her school year having made a commitment to engage her middle school students as citizens and help them understand and critique their rights. She was determined to help them "discover themselves in the community" and to give them the tools they needed to succeed now and in the future. Becoming an active agent of change, empowering ourselves and our students, can be supported by the active relationship between theory and practice known as praxis.

Pedagogy as Praxis

Paolo Freire (1998), critical educator and renowned Brazilian author, encourages teachers to develop a particular type of awareness called critical consciousness. Critical consciousness enables us to recognize the connections between our individual experiences and the social contexts in which they reside. When we develop critical consciousness, we have moved toward praxis. Pedagogy as praxis involves a cycle of considering theory, applying the theory in our teaching, and assessing and reflecting on the process. Pedagogy as praxis views teaching as a mutual exchange of learning between teacher and pupils. This transformative approach to teaching contrasts sharply to a **transmission** or **banking orientation** to teaching in which "knowledge is a gift bestowed by those who consider themselves knowledgeable upon those whom they consider to know nothing" (Freire, 1970, p. 10). A Freirian orientation emphasizes learning about and utilizing how and what pupils are actually learning, which contrasts with an orientation in which the teacher presumes to know how pupil learning should proceed. In this sense, the teacher learns from the pupils as she teaches. The pupils learn from the teacher as they also teach. The dichotomy of the teacher-pupil relationship dissolves and a dialogic, more synthesized, less oppressive approach to teaching and learning takes its place. The teacher is not the authority and pupils are not subordinated. Rather, teacher and pupils productively and respectfully challenge one another.

This type of practice can be understood as **humanizing pedagogy** (Bartolome, 1994; Freire, 1970), particularly for urban children who often live and learn in oppressive and dehumanizing conditions. Freire (1998) argues that if teachers choose this democratic pedagogical approach and are able to connect theory with their practice, "which they constantly subject to critical analysis, they live the difficult but possible and pleasurable experience of speaking to and with learners" (p. 65). A move away from the idea that technical, decontextualized "best practices" are appropriate for all situations can help teachers move toward more meaningful and powerful learning experiences for themselves and their pupils. The prevailing ideologies that currently inform teaching lean heavily toward teaching as a technical activity. For example, what happens when teaching is viewed as imparting knowledge as in the banking model? Teacher education programs emphasize content preparation, not pedagogical or cultural/linguistic diversity. In contrast, what happens when teaching is viewed as a political act? Students are humanized, and schools become sites for improving students' life chances.

Teachers and students who learn from each other, sharing knowledge and experiences in a joyful way, are truly engaged in pedagogy as praxis.

Teaching Against the Grain

Becoming a change agent, interrupting oppression, politicizing teaching, moving between theory and practice—these are tall orders for all urban teachers, regardless of years of experience. Support from colleagues can be extremely helpful. Cochran-Smith (1991, 2001) developed the concept of **teaching against the grain**, a process of learning to reform teaching alongside experienced teachers who are also struggling to be agents of change. Education is essentially "someone teaching something to some student somewhere" (Irvine, 2003, p. 48)—and if the someone, the student, and/or the somewhere changes, the situation requires a different conceptualization. Recognition that teaching occurs in particular temporal and situational contexts is an important first step in teaching against the grain.

Cochran-Smith (1991) analyzes two approaches to teaching against the grain: critical dissonance and collaborative resonance, each based on different underlying assumptions. Beginning teachers can learn to teach against the grain through critical dissonance, or "incongruity based on a critical perspective" (p. 281). Dissonance or incongruity occurs between what a teacher is learning or has learned about schooling in teacher preparation at the university and what a teacher is learning in the school where he is teaching. However, Cochran-Smith notes that teacher education "programs that aim to create critical dissonance are intended to be transformative, to help students broaden their vision and develop analytical skills needed to interrogate and reinvent their own perspectives. Unfortunately, these programs have had limited success" (p. 282). Critical dissonance often results in a "setup" in which school-based practitioners are criticized by their higher education counterparts and beginning teachers are caught between the two, unable to reconcile the differences. Beginning teachers may learn constructivist methods and collaborative management strategies in their preparation programs, but then are told to "control" and "discipline" their students and adopt zero-tolerance policies in their schools. Consider the teachers in Chapter 6: they experienced critical dissonance when what they learned in teacher education (i.e., weeklong units on the Holocaust and suffrage) were directly contradicted with scripted curricula and pacing guides.

A different approach to teaching against the grain is to develop collaborative resonance, or "intensification based on the co-labor of learning communities." In this approach, links are developed and strengthened between university and school-based practices. As a result, students and teachers alike critique the cultures of teaching and schooling, research their own practices, articulate their own expertise and call into question the policies and language of schooling that are taken for granted. (Cochran-Smith, 1991, p. 283)

This is a conceptually different approach to learning to teach for social justice in that theory and practice are linked through reflection and inquiry. (Please refer to Chapter 5 for more on reflection and inquiry.) Cochran-Smith (1991) argues that this process is more effective when beginners and experienced teachers collaborate together, power is shared, and knowledge is socially constructed. For example, in a Boston-based program called Urban Immersion, teachers at Brighton High School, along with student teachers and faculty from Boston College, used collaborative inquiry to focus on improving student achievement (Stairs, 2010).

More recently, Cochran-Smith (2001) has cautioned that the current school practices related to standardization, prescriptive teaching, and standardized testing may actually reward "new teachers who are willing to work completely *with the grain*," and she concludes that

> we are at a crossroads in this country concerning the role of the college/ university in teacher education and the role of teacher education in society. We are chillingly close in some states to "learning to teach by numbers" at a time when more than ever we need teachers able and willing to teach against the (new) grain of standardized practices that treat teachers as interchangeable parts and—worse—reinscribe societal inequities. (p. 4)

We believe that urban teachers will be successful at enacting social justice and equity in their teaching by resisting the pressure to work with the grain.

WHAT THE RESEARCH SAYS ABOUT SOCIAL JUSTICE AND EQUITY

Despite being a relatively new and small body of literature, the research on learning to teach for social justice offers important insights into urban teaching (Esposito & Swain, 2009; Gay, 1993; Gutstein, 2003; North, 2006; Sleeter, 1996; Weiner, 2000). Findings include the following:

- Learning to teach for social justice involves rigorous and, frequently, painful individual self-reflection and examination requiring time and support.
- Developing a just teaching practice requires examining how societal structures—educational, political, economic, social—have shaped teachers' and students' experiences.
- Socially just teaching practices build on the cultural knowledge, norms, and communicative practices of students. (See also Chapters 1 and 3.)
- Teaching for social justice entails collaborative engagement with communities and recognition of the importance of partnerships.
- Students benefit from curricula that provide opportunities to consider the present and the future in ways they may not have imagined for themselves.

Four studies included in Table 8.1 illustrate the research in this area. Each study highlights the role of socially just pedagogy and/or curriculum in supporting equity and change for students and their communities. Agarwal, Epstein, Oppenheim, Oyler, and Sonu (2010) explored the ways in which beginning teachers enacted social justice pedagogy in their urban classrooms and found that small but meaningful steps can contribute to socially just practice. Chubbuck and Zembylas (2008) conducted a case study of a White novice teacher at an urban school and identified her **critical emotional praxis**, a praxis formed by the emotional resistance of teachers to the unjust elements of individuals' pedagogy. Gutstein (2003), a practitioner researcher, followed his students for two years to study teaching and learning mathematics for social justice in an urban, Latino classroom and the role of a National Council of Teachers of Mathematics (NCTM) standards-based curriculum. Quartz and the TEP Research Group (2003) propose strategies to curb urban teacher attrition. Included in these strategies is working toward becoming a change agent.

Table 8.1   Research Studies on Social Justice and Equity

Author(s)	Purpose	Findings	Implications	URL
Agarwal, Epstein, Oppenheim, Oyler, & Sonu (2010)	Researchers explored the ways in which beginning teachers enacted social justice pedagogy in their urban classrooms.	Beginning teachers needed opportunities to explore social reconstructionist curricula and to receive support in reflective thinking skills with experienced teachers committed to teaching for social justice.	While some degree of struggle to enact just teaching practice may be inevitable and should be elucidated, recognition of small but meaningful concrete steps in self-reflection, curriculum development, and context-specific decision making can support learning to teach for social justice.	http://jte .sagepub .com/ content/ 61/3/237 .full.pdf+ html
Chubbuck & Zembylas (2008)	Researchers explored the intersection between emotions, teaching, and social justice in urban	The participant's strongest commitment was social justice, and teaching was her means of reaching this goal. She struggled with emotions that many beginning teachers struggle with, but her	This analysis may aid in the professional development of socially just teachers. By learning how to develop practices of critical emotional praxis in their teaching, teachers may begin to	http://aer .sagepub .com/ content/ 45/2/274 .full.pdf+ html

Author(s)	Purpose	Findings	Implications	URL
	schools through a case study of one urban educator.	emotional uncertainty created a social relationship between herself and both her students and her colleagues. *Critical emotional reflexivity* was defined as teachers' interruption of their regular teaching practices to improve the learning of students. This was found to bring about changes in teachers, relationships, socially just teaching practices, and school activism.	create room in their profession for questioning unjust practices and moving toward reform. Studying the practice of emotional navigation in relation to socially just teaching can lead to a better understanding of reform opportunities.	
Gutstein (2003)	A practitioner-researcher followed his students for two years to study teaching and learning mathematics for social justice in an urban, Latino classroom and the role of an NCTM standards-based curriculum.	The researcher's students were able to "read the world," that is, to understand complex issues related to justice and equity using mathematics. They also developed "mathematical power," new knowledge about and more positive orientations toward math.	A standards-based curriculum that employs multiple perspectives, real-life contexts, curricular coherence, investigation of situations embodying justice, and equity concerns can help students develop as agents of change.	

(Continued)

Table 8.1 (Continued)

Author(s)	Purpose	Findings	Implications	URL
Quartz & TEP Research Group (2003)	Researchers aimed to define strategies that curb urban teacher attrition. Data on urban teachers were analyzed to propose means to support and keep teachers employed in urban schools.	Several strategies were found to be efficacious in curbing urban school teacher attrition: learning to build on the strengths of urban communities, becoming a change agent, and forming a profession. It was deduced that efforts to professionalize teaching will create more learning opportunities and career development for urban teachers.	Reframing the professionalization-of-teaching debate will better fit the realities of urban schools. This will guide future research on how to facilitate and support the development of social justice for educators.	http://jte .sagepub .com/ content/ 54/2/99 .full.pdf+ html

PRACTICE

In this section, two urban teachers, **Michael Coppola** and **Aileen Zeigler,** share their experiences in implementing socially just teaching practices. Michael is a fourth-grade teacher in Providence, Rhode Island, and Aileen is a secondary Spanish teacher in Atlanta, Georgia. Aileen begins by explaining what social justice means to her.

Aileen: Social justice is equity of all things: thought, presentation, interpretation, semantics, behavior. I think it requires not just thinking that people are equal, but showing that belief in your actions. It's also viewing and treating all people with respect. Social justice contains elements of open-mindedness, tolerance, and a consciousness of the world. As a foreign language teacher, I have a great forum for talking about the whole world in a really conscious way, about different peoples and situations, and looking at things that may be different in an equitable way, even though they may seem weird, strange, or gross. Pushing students to experience the different in a safe and mature way is a great opportunity.

Both Michael and Aileen explain why the concepts of social justice and equity are important in urban classrooms.

Michael: The topics of social justice and equity are of great importance for our students. As members of their own family, school, local, national, and global communities and as future leaders, our students need to be active citizens who work toward a just and equitable society. We, as educators, have the obligation to help foster an environment where our students feel and understand that they can, may, and must make a difference for others and live life with hearts wide open.

Aileen: Simply, it's a global classroom. My classroom is the entire world; it's not just 10 kids. I believe it's my job to teach each of those kids where they are, but also push them to be everywhere, to be aware of varying perspectives and be open to changing their points of view. Also, each of my kids has a unique point of view, and creating a safe space for those things to come out requires students to deal with each other's perspectives. My room should be a comfort zone where we can deal with differences, because a classroom should be a safe space. There are nine different languages spoken in my classroom right now. I have students of many ethnicities: Ethiopian, Bosnian, Sudanese, Cuban, Argentinean, Nepali, Mexican, Ecuadorian, Peruvian, African American, American, Belgian, Australian, British, French, Haitian, Dominican. They're not all poor immigrants; some are rich or middle class; some are first or second generation. This is real diversity. Diversity should not be code for poor and Black, or migrant and Hispanic. It's more than that.

Aileen elaborates on how her commitment to teaching as a political activity developed.

Aileen: I became a Spanish teacher because I wanted to teach the other side of things. When I first found out about the tens of thousands of people who were murdered in South America, I was 18 years old at the time, thinking, "Why don't I know this?" I think it's essential that we're teaching other cultures, that we're teaching kids that there are immigrants who look like they are Mexican but who aren't. They may have escaped from a civil war in the 1990s. Their parents came here so their little boys wouldn't have to be soldiers. Instead of just reading about British and American history, let's talk about the rest of the world. Let's talk about the fact that the laws in Arizona are just like what was happening in the 1940s in Germany when the Nazis were pulling over Jews on the street. It is the same thing that is happening to Mexicans in Arizona right now, or anyone who has brown skin. And it's not just Arizona either. Recently, I was visiting a Jewish Museum viewing a Holocaust exhibit. During the course of my tour, I saw a photo of a Jewish man stopped on the sidewalk to be searched by the police simply because he was wearing a gold star. I commented on the similarities of the situation to the new laws in Arizona to the woman working at the museum. Within two sentences, she had responded with a rationalization about how it was fine. This is terrifying to me that a woman surrounded every day by the history of oppression in our world can quickly push aside something that isn't happening to her as okay. If we all continue to ignore oppression, prejudice, and intolerance, it will continue to grow until it controls our world.

Aileen goes on to describes different examples of socially just pedagogy within her own classroom. First she discusses the classroom culture she develops in her room.

Aileen: I try to create safe spaces. *Gay* and *retarded* are not synonyms for *stupid.* I share the power of the way we use our semantics. Some people may think it's not my job as a Spanish teacher to talk to students about this, but I consider it my job because the class is called Spanish Language and Culture. No language exists outside the realm of culture. I stop them every time they say *gay* or *retarded.* Sometimes it's as simple as "We don't use that word in my classroom," but sometimes it's a longer discussion about how you would feel if your brother were retarded. We even go back historically to talk about the *n*-word, the *s*-word for Hispanics, or reclamation of the word *queer.* Some people would think I was getting off topic to have conversations about the world, but if I have set my students to go out into the world as learners, then I have done my job. They need skills from me. They can learn vocabulary from many different methods.

Aileen also describes how she utilizes social justice methods in lesson planning and curriculum.

Aileen: Specifically, in my class I teach about immigration and we talk about the DREAM Act. I bring to my students' attention the fact that there are oppressed students who came to the United States as immigrants when they were two years old. They should be given a route to citizenship; they didn't do anything wrong. We also discuss that there are immigrants who are war refugees; there are many stories of immigration. I present my students with two articles to read, with two (or more) points of view, and offer an opportunity for my students to have a debate. I try to present information and have my students bring up the questions and analyze what's going on. I can preach at them all day about my views. But it won't matter if I stand up there and tell them the way to live, if they don't figure out *why* they should and develop their own views and values.

This is also why I travel with students to Costa Rica and New York City. The experience of travel took me out of a small town in the Midwest. When we travel, we can observe other people, watch how other people talk and how they sound, even if we don't understand what they say. Those experiences help us develop independent thoughts. My classroom is a conduit for those experiences.

It drives me crazy in this district because so many people think fairness equals equality. For things to be fair, they are not necessarily equal. Each student is different, learns differently, approaches things differently, sees the world differently. I do a lot of differentiating by providing multiple opportunities to prove you know something in different ways. Because foreign language is reading, writing, speaking, and listening, you have to be assessed on it all, but you don't need to be equally good in all of them. You have to participate in all of them, but by offering different chances, students can excel in some and not in others and still be successful in the classroom. I try to balance diversity with high expectations, and assessment is often a learning experience. They may struggle through the entire oral assessment in which they have to talk for two minutes about their favorite vacation, but the process of talking for two minutes might mean that, next semester when they have to talk, they will be able to. There are very few things that are "the be all and end all." But having high expectations for students is one.

Michael explains how he and his students refuse to ignore injustices by sharing a powerful lesson in his fourth-grade classroom.

Michael: "Roses are red, violets are blue. Don't let Sister Anne get any Black on you." The words flowed uneasily, yet rapidly from my mouth to the attentive ears of my 17 fourth graders. One student looked away from me. Another pupil stared incredulously and angrily at me as I sat waiting for my class to respond. I turned to the next page of Marybeth Lorbiecki's *Sister Anne's Hands* and placed the book upside down in my lap. "Fourth graders, I am noticing that some of us have very strong reactions to what just happened in the story. Who can summarize what is happening in Sister Anne's class?" I asked. Rae raised her hand, yet blurted out, "Sister Anne is Black and her class has all White kids and a White kid threw a paper plane on her desk. The note said 'Roses are red, violets are blue. Don't let Sister Anne get any Black on you.' That's messed up!" Rae's classmates turned to one another and talked about how the message on the paper airplane was "messed up." I sat back in my chair and listened in on the conversations. After a minute, Jovan called out, "Mr. Coppola, I don't mean to be rude, but why do White people always do bad things to Black people? Like to Martin Luther King and stuff."

The class was silent. All 17 pairs of eyes shifted from Jovan to me. I placed the book on the shelf and addressed the class, "When we finish reading this book, watch what Sister Anne does. She tells her class that they can live their lives with an open heart or with a heart that is closed as tight as a fist. I try to live my life with an open heart. There are some people, White and not White, who live life with an open heart. There are other people who don't. What is important is how you choose to live your life." I retrieved the book from the shelf and continued reading. After I read the last word, I looked up from the book and asked, "Who wants to live life with an open heart? Who wants to be like Sister Anne?" Seventeen hands shot up. I raised my hand, too.

I dismissed the students from the rug, and they returned to their seats. Waiting for each student at his or her desk was a graphic organizer with instructions to consider "What are some wrongs in the world that need to be right?" The fourth graders grabbed their pencils and quickly jotted down their ideas. I walked around the room glancing at student responses. Some students wrote about the need for people to recycle more, conserve energy, and help endangered animals. Others listed the need to stand up against racism, stop bullying in schools, allow gay men and women to marry, and help raise money for kids around the world who can't afford school. Students shared their ideas with partners and afterward with the whole class. Our class discussion led to the realization that kids can make a difference and that we must be "upstanders" and not bystanders for those that need support. Sister Anne was right. We need to live our lives with our hearts wide open. We can do so by helping to right the wrongs in the world.

The next week, our class met with our seventh-grade Community Service Buddies. Every Tuesday, students from both classes meet to plan, discuss, and conduct community service activities. The fourth graders found their seventh-grade buddies, and the 34 students sat in a circle on the rug. Once everyone was settled, I said, "Fourth graders, talk to your seventh-grade buddy about the lessons that Sister Anne taught us." The room buzzed loudly as the younger students animatedly summarized the story. After a couple of minutes, I asked the students to consider how we can use our time together to live our lives with our hearts open and make a difference in the world. One seventh grader suggested that we take on a project that the school's social worker wanted to start. This project was to raise money for a nonprofit organization that helps pay the salaries of doctors in some of the world's poorest countries. We talked about how many people in our world do not have the ability to get medical care, see doctors, or go to a hospital for treatment. By raising the money, we could help doctors work within their own communities and help people who need medicines and treatment get the healthcare that they need. Over the next few Tuesdays, the fourth and seventh graders created posters educating the school community about this issue, researched facts about the need for doctors and access to medicines in many parts of the world, and ran a successful drive that collected over $1,000 in change from the 150 students in our school. Sister Anne would have been proud.

Michael and Aileen's perspectives reveal that social justice and equity can be enacted in urban schools when teachers make it a priority. It is clear that their students were held to high standards, not only for academics, but also for actions.

WRAP UP

In this chapter, we have explored key orientations to teaching for social justice and equity. It all begins with a commitment to interrupting oppression. With clear eyes and an open mind, we recognize and address the injustices we see in our communities, our schools, and ourselves. Our commitments are the foundation from which we view teaching as a political act, as issues of power and opportunity drive our educational system. Understanding education and schooling in this way, we recognize the need for action and endeavor to become change agents. Pedagogy as praxis furthers our critical consciousness and helps keep the relationship between theory and practice active and fluid. As a result, we aim to work with others, collaborating in our practice and teaching against the grain in order to bring justice and equity to our students.

Rather than searching for best practices or "recipe" strategies, the challenging and important work of socially just teaching practice may be best accomplished by focusing on six principles of practice (Cochran-Smith, 1999):

Principle 1: Support meaningful academic work within communities of learners when implementing social justice.

Principle 2: Build on what students bring to school with them: knowledge and interests, cultural and linguistic resources.

Principle 3: Teach skills, bridge gaps.

Principle 4: Work with—not against—individuals, families, and communities.

Principle 5: Diversify modes of assessment.

Principle 6: Make activism, power, and inequity explicit parts of the curriculum.

You see that many of these principles overlap with earlier chapters on using students' inherent resources, bridging home and school cultures, accessing community knowledge, challenging oppressive bureaucracies, avoiding standardization, and explicitly discussing power and privilege. It is our hope that this entire book, including the theories, research, and voices from practicing educators, has been preparing you to work for social justice and equity in urban schools.

EXTENSION ACTIVITIES

Reflection

1. An important aspect of teaching for social justice is grappling with the dissonance you may feel in the classroom. Identify a source of dissonance that you are experiencing in your class or school setting. Write a reflective journal entry that honestly investigates how this dissonance can be used to help develop social justice practices.

2. Choose a lesson plan from your cooperating teacher or from the Internet. Rewrite the lesson using social justice pedagogy. Work toward collaborative resonance by sharing the changes and your rationale with your classmates and/or cooperating teacher.

Action

1. Identify an issue in your classroom, school, or community that you believe reflects an injustice. Through inquiry research (see Chapter 5), curriculum codevelopment with students, or working with the community, develop a concrete plan that begins to address this issue.

2. Identify one of Cochran-Smith's (1999) six key principles for enacting social justice pedagogy, and apply it to an area of your practice that you would like to develop. For example, you may want to address a unit of study or content area that you currently teach or your relationship with parents or your interaction within the local community. Explain why this principle is important to you and your teaching.

SUGGESTED RESOURCES

Books and Articles

Adams, M., Bell, L. A., & Griffin, P. (Eds.). (2007). *Teaching for diversity and social justice* (2nd ed.). New York, NY: Routledge.

Allen, J. (Ed.). (1999). *Class action: Teaching for social justice in elementary and middle school.* New York, NY: Teachers College Press.

Carlisle, L. R., Jackson, B. W., & George, A. (2006). Principles of social justice education: The social justice education in schools project. *Equity & Excellence in Education, 39*(1), 55–64. doi:10.1080/10665680500478809

Griffin, M. (Ed.). (2003). *Action for social justice in education: Fairly different.* Philadelphia, PA: Open University Press.

hooks, b. (1994). *Teaching to transgress: Education as the practice of freedom.* New York, NY: Routledge.

Kumashiro, K. (2004). *Against common sense: Teaching and learning toward social justice.* New York, NY: Routledge.

Oakes, J., & Lipton, M. (2006). *Teaching to change the world* (3rd ed.). New York, NY: McGraw-Hill.

Websites

Beyond Prejudice (www.beyondprejudice.com)
Aims to bring people together to reduce prejudice through commitment and education.

EdChange (www.edchange.org)
Offers a wide range of professional development, research, and resources to support teachers in addressing diversity, multiculturalism, and cultural competence.

Oxfam Education (www.oxfam.org.uk/education)
"Offers a huge range of ideas, resources and support for developing the global dimension in the classroom and the whole school."

Rethinking Schools **(www.rethinkingschools.org)**
A nonprofit, progressive education journal that balances classroom practice with theory and emphasizes issues of equity and social justice facing urban schools.

What Kids Can Do (www.whatkidscando.org)
Offers children opportunities to hear the voices of other students, as well as to contribute their own, in pursuit of social justice.

The Free Child Project (www.freechild.org/SJforALL.htm)
Advocates, informs, and celebrates social change led by and with young people around the world, especially those who have been historically denied the right to participate.

REFERENCES

Agarwal, R., Epstein, S., Oppenheim, R., Oyler, C., & Sonu, D. (2010). From ideal to practice and back again: Beginning teachers teaching for social justice. *Journal of Teacher Education, 61,* 237–247. doi:10.1177/0022487109354521

Ayers, W. (1998). Forward: Popular education—teaching for social justice. In W. Ayers, J. A. Hunt, & T. Quinn (Eds.), *Teaching for social justice* (pp. xvii–xxvi). New York, NY: Teachers College Press.

Bartolome, L. (1994). Beyond the methods fetish: Toward a humanizing pedagogy. *Harvard Educational Review, 64,* 173–194.

Chubbuck, S. M. (2010). Individual and structural orientations in socially just teaching: Conceptualization, implementation, and collaborative effort. *Journal of Teacher Education, 61,* 197–210. doi:10.1177/0022487109359777

Chubbuck, S. M., & Zembylas, M. (2008). The emotional ambivalence of socially just teaching: A case study of a novice urban schoolteacher. *American Educational Research Journal, 45,* 274–318. doi:10.3102/0002831207311586

Cochran-Smith, M. (1991). Learning to teach against the grain. *Harvard Educational Review, 61,* 279–310. doi:10.1177/0022487101052001001

Cochran-Smith, M. (1999). Learning to teach for social justice. In G. Griffin (Ed.), *The education of teachers: Ninety-eighth yearbook of the National Society for the Study of Education* (pp. 114–144). Chicago, IL: University of Chicago Press.

Cochran-Smith, M. (2001). Teaching against the (new) grain. *Journal of Teacher Education, 52,* 3–4. doi:10.1177/0022487101052001001

Donnell, K. (2004). *Learning to teach in an urban setting: The struggle to develop transformative practice* (Unpublished doctoral dissertation). Boston College, Chestnut Hill, MA.

Donnell, K. (2007). Getting to we: Developing a transformative teaching practice. *Urban Education, 42,* 223–249. doi:10.1177/0042085907300541

Esposito, J., & Swain, A. N. (2009). Pathways to social justice: Urban teachers' use of culturally relevant pedagogy as a conduit for teaching for social justice. *Perspectives on Urban Education, 6*(1), 38–47.

Freire, P. (1970). *Pedagogy of the oppressed* (M. B. Ramos, Trans.). New York, NY: Continuum.

Freire, P. (1998). *Teachers as cultural workers: Letters to those who dare to teach.* Boulder, CO: Westview Press.

Fullan, M. (1993). Why teachers must become change agents. *Educational Leadership, 50*(6), 12–17.

Fullan, M. (2001). *The new meaning of educational change* (3rd ed.). New York, NY: Teachers College Press.

Gay, G. (1993). Building cultural bridges: A bold proposal for teacher education. *Education and Urban Society, 25,* 285–299. doi:10.1177/0013124593025003006

Gutstein, E. (2003). Teaching and learning mathematics for social justice in an urban, Latino school. *Journal for Research in Mathematics Education, 34,* 37–73. doi:10.2307/30034699

Hardiman, R., & Jackson, B. (1997). Conceptual foundations for social justice education. In M. Adams, L. A. Bell, & P. Griffin (Eds.), *Teaching for diversity and social justice* (2nd ed., pp. 35–66). New York, NY: Routledge.

Irvine, J. J. (2003). *Educating teachers for a diverse society: Seeing with the cultural eye.* New York, NY: Teachers College Press.

Ladson-Billings, G. (1994). *The dreamkeepers: Successful teachers of African American children.* San Francisco, CA: Jossey-Bass.

Murrell, P. (2000). *The community teacher: A new framework for effective urban teaching.* New York, NY: Teachers College Press.

North, C. E. (2006). More than words? Delving into the substantive meaning(s) of "social justice" in education. *Review of Educational Research, 76,* 507–535.

Quartz, K. H., & TEP Research Group. (2003). "Too angry to leave": Supporting new teachers' commitment to transform urban schools. *Journal of Teacher Education, 54,* 99–111. doi:10.1177/0022487102250284

Ruchi, A., Epstein, S., Oppenheim, R., Oyler, C., & Sonu, D. (2009). From ideal to practice and back again: Beginning teachers teaching for social justice. *Journal of Teacher Education 61,* 237–247.

Schultz, B. (2008). *Spectacular things happen along the way.* New York, NY: Teachers College Press.

Sleeter, C. (1996). *Multicultural education as social activism.* Albany: State University of New York Press.

Stairs, A. J. (2010). Becoming an urban teacher in a professional development school: A view from preparation to practice. In A. J. Stairs & K. A. Donnell (Eds.), *Research on urban teacher learning: Examining contextual factors over time* (pp. 41–60). Charlotte, NC: Information Age.

Villegas, A. M., & Lucas, T. (2002). *Educating culturally responsive teachers.* Albany: State University of New York Press.

Weiner, L. (2000). Research in the 90s: Implications for urban teacher preparation. *Review of Educational Research, 70,* 369–406. doi:10.2307/1170787

CONTRIBUTING AUTHORS

Michael Coppola is a fourth-grade teacher at the Community Preparatory School in Providence, Rhode Island. He has served as a cooperating teacher, hosting student teachers, for several years. He is currently on sabbatical, earning his master's degree at Columbia University's Teachers College.

Aileen M. Zeigler is a high school Spanish teacher in Atlanta, Georgia. She received her bachelor's degree in Spanish and theatre from Denison University and her master's degree in Spanish education from Indiana University-Purdue University Indianapolis and la Universidad de Salamanca. Prior to teaching in Atlanta, she facilitated a peace education program for K–12 students in Indiana. At her school, she runs the Drama Club and the National Spanish Honor Society.

Susie Planert, whose vignette opened this chapter, completed a year of student teaching in an urban first-grade classroom in Pawtucket, Rhode Island. She graduated from Roger Williams University with a dual degree in elementary education and psychology.

GLOSSARY

Academic content-area words: words that are unlikely to be heard in social conversations and are found in one or more content areas.

Academic language proficiency: refers to learning more content-specific, less frequent vocabulary and producing more complex language both orally and in writing; also known as **CALP.**

Academic Word List: 570 word families of academic content-area words.

Accountability: the idea of holding schools, teachers, and students responsible for results in student achievement and continuous improvement.

Achievement gap: discrepancy in standardized test performance between groups of students, usually defined by race and language differences.

Acquisition: occurs when learners use language in natural communication and are not consciously aware of their acquiring L2 (see Krashen, 1981).

Action research: an inquiry approach to solving problems with others with the aim of improving practice.

Additive approach: an approach to multicultural education in which isolated lessons or units on specific cultural groups are presented without true integration into the curriculum.

Adequate yearly progress: a *No Child Left Behind* measure used to hold schools accountable for annual student improvement on the state's standardized assessments.

American Federation of Teachers (AFT): a national teachers' labor union.

Asset perspective: an ideology that views the resources and attributes students bring with them to school as positive and useful for teaching and learning.

Assimilationist teaching: an approach to teaching whereby teachers do not consider students' culture or personal characteristics and are instead concerned that students assimilate into "American" society.

Backward design: Wiggins and McTighe's (2005) framework for designing curriculum that asks teachers to indentify the results they expect of students, determine the acceptable evidence, and plan learning experiences.

Banking (or transmission) education: an orientation to teaching in which the teacher, who knows all, deposits knowledge to the student, who knows little or nothing.

Basic Interpersonal Communicative Skills (BICS): social language, also known as **conversational fluency.**

Bilingual Verbal Ability Test (BVAT): measures verbal and cognitive results in L1 and L2.

Bullying: intimidation in the form of physical, verbal, or emotional harassment; spreading rumors; Internet harassment (cyberbullying); or alienation.

Bureaucracy: a specific form of organization defined by complexity, division of labor, hierarchical coordination and control, strict chain of command, and legal authority.

Bureaucratic ossification model: a model describing school systems that are rigid and inefficient as a result of regulations and red tape.

Centralization: the process in which the school administrative authority is held completely by a small, central body, rather than in the local schools and their communities.

Change agents: teachers who develop the skills and strategies necessary to accomplish their moral goals.

Cluster: Common Core State Standards' term for a group of related standards.

Coding: the process of analyzing qualitative data, often by demarcating segments of data and assigning them terms and categories.

Cognitive/Academic Language Proficiency (CALP): academic language.

Colorblind: a personal ideology that one does not "see" or recognize racial or ethnic difference.

Common Core State Standards: national standards in K–12 English language arts and mathematics developed by the National Governors Association Center for Best Practices and the Council of Chief State School Officers.

Common Underlying Proficiency (CUP): Cummins' (1981) theory that represents the importance of L1 to L2 development.

Community teacher: Murrell's (2001) concept of a teacher who draws on diverse, urban families' cultures, communities, and identities in his or her professional work.

Comprehensible input: language delivered in L2 that is understandable to the learner.

Content-based ESL/Content-based instruction (CBI): the design of language instruction through content.

Content-specific words: words specific to a single discipline and perhaps a specific unit within the discipline that should be explicitly taught.

Contributions Approach: an approach to multicultural education in which already-planned lessons include minimal discussion of multicultural figures.

Conversational fluency: language that develops in one to two years and represents a learner's ability to carry on a conversation using social language, high-frequency words, and simple grammatical constructions; also known as **BICS**.

Critical pedagogy: educational theory and teaching and learning practices that are designed to question the status quo and to raise learners' critical consciousness regarding oppressive social conditions.

Cultural modeling theory: Lee's (2007) anti-deficit model that posits out-of-school knowledge should be used to acquire in-school-knowledge.

Culturally and linguistically diverse students (CLD): typically refers to students from non-White and/or non-English speaking backgrounds; ELLs are considered CLD students.

Culturally responsive discipline: an approach to classroom management in which teachers strive for cooperation, collaboration, and reciprocity instead of strict control and compliance.

Culturally responsive pedagogy (cultural responsiveness): the ability to teach in a way that validates their students' cultural, racial, and ethnic identities, both *what* is taught and *how* it is taught, combined with a wider transformative purpose to empower students.

Culture: a group's way of being in the world that shapes one's worldviews, values, and preferences.

Culture of power: the accepted codes or rules for participating in mainstream society.

Decentralization: the process that occurs when decision-making is passed down to individual schools and their communities.

Deficit perspective: an ideology that sees students' failure as a result of their personal, familial, or cultural deficiencies.

Descriptive review: a reflective protocol focusing on description of students and/or their work, without judgment, in order to further understand the subject.

Discrete language skills: linguistic practices learned early in language development as a result of direct instruction in grammar, letter sounds, and decoding of texts.

Domain: Common Core State Standards' term for a larger group of related standards (a group of **clusters**).

Ecological approach or orientation: an approach that views school life and classroom teaching as occurring within interconnected webs of settings and institutions that transcend classroom and school borders.

Elementary and Secondary Education Act (ESEA): a federal statute originally passed in 1965 that provides funding to public education and focuses on equal access to education for all students.

English language learner (ELL): nonnative English speaker who is in the process of acquiring English; also called **English learners (ELs)**, or **English as a second language (ESL)**, **limited English proficient (LEP)**, or **bilingual** students.

English to Speakers of Other Languages (ESOL): use or study of English by nonnative English speakers; often used interchangeably with **English as a Second Language (ESL)**.

Ethnicity: a particular group to which one belongs, as determined by an acceptance of cultural mores, origins, and customs.

First language: a student's native language, termed **L1**.

Funds of knowledge: the knowledge families pass on to their children explicitly or implicitly; this knowledge is recognized as an asset to schooling.

Highly qualified teacher: a teacher who possesses a bachelor's degree, has passed a state licensing exam in the content area he/she teaches, and holds full state teacher certification, according to the No Child Left Behind legislation.

High-utility words: words used in social language and academic language, can be learned in context and through accessible reading, and are easily explainable and translatable from L1.

Humanizing pedagogy: an orientation to teaching in which teachers respect and use the reality, history, and perspectives of students as an integral part of their practice.

Incomes-based education: a framework for teaching and learning that focuses on teacher incomes rather than student outcomes.

Individuals with Disabilities Education Improvement Act (IDEA): a federal statute reauthorized in 2004 that ensures services to children with disabilities; statute encourages response to intervention procedures.

Inquiry as stance: a habit of mind involving the systematic generation of local knowledge.

Language-as-problem: an ideology that suggests languages other than English are a social problem in the United States that should be eradicated or somehow resolved.

Language-as-resource: an ideology that values multiculturalism and bilingualism as resources that enrich the broader society.

Language-as-right: an ideology that assumes human beings have a legal, moral, and natural right to identity and language and that society is harmed when non-native English speakers lose their language and culture.

LAS Links K–12 Assessment: an assessment that measures ELLs' listening, speaking, reading, writing, and comprehension.

Learning (of a language): occurs when explicit instruction is provided in rules and error correction (see Krashen, 1981).

Merit: observable and demonstrable competence.

Meritocracy: the assumption that, with hard work and determination, all individuals can achieve whatever they desire.

Monitor theory: Krashen's (1981) theory that distinguishes between language acquisition and language learning.

Monocultural education: an approach to teaching that highlights and values one group over all others, typically that of mainstream, White, middle-class culture.

Multicultural education: an approach to teaching and curriculum that rejects discrimination and advocates the value of all racial, ethnic, linguistic, sexual, religious, economic, and ability groups.

Myth of meritocracy: the mistaken belief that that hard work always leads to success and everyone can succeed equally if they desire it enough.

National Education Association (NEA): a professional teachers' organization/union.

No Child Left Behind Act of 2001 (NCLB): Federal reauthorization of the Elementary and Secondary Education Act that increased accountability through required statewide, annual testing in reading and mathematics in grades three through eight, and one statewide test of reading, mathematics, and science between tenth and twelfth grades.

Opportunity to learn: the conditions within a classroom and school, such as curriculum, instruction, facilities, and resources, which enable all students to learn effectively and efficiently.

Oppression: the exercise of power or authority in an unjust manner.

Outcomes-based education: framework for teaching and learning that focuses on student outcomes rather than teacher incomes; also known as **standards-based education.**

Pacing guides: usually adopted at the district level, these guides dictate which content should be taught on what days over the course of the school year.

Participatory action research: a collaborative inquiry process between researchers and those expected to benefit from the research.

Political responsiveness model: a model describing school systems that respond to some groups while excluding others.

Praxis: the active relationship between theory and practice.

Problem-based learning: a student-centered methodology where students employ the habits of inquiry to learn content material, typically in collaborative groups.

Proportionate consequence: an outcome or effect of a student offense that is balanced and fair based on the committed offense.

Qualitative analysis: the process of analyzing narrative data, often through coding

Quantitative analysis: the process of analyzing numerical data, often by generating descriptive or inferential statistics.

Race: a socially constructed category that groups together those who physically resemble each other.

Reflection-in-action: the process of thinking "on our feet" and making intuitive decisions in the moment.

Reflection-on-action: the process of reflecting after an event to determine how and why things occurred as they did.

Reflection-for-action: the process of carefully evaluating problems spontaneously while they are occurring and further analyzing potential solutions, then taking action.

Reflective action: an inquiry-based reflection that focuses on the process rather than the product.

Reframing: the act of looking at a problem behavior in an objective way and changing one's response to support more positive behaviors.

Resource approach: an ideology that recognizes and builds upon students' assets (knowledge, attributes, and strengths) to make teaching and learning most effective for all.

Response to intervention (RtI): a method for identifying, defining, and resolving students' academic and/or behavior difficulties employing a continuous cycle of systematic data collection and instructional interventions.

Routine action: the everyday process of stream-of-consciousness thinking and doing.

Safe space: an environment where students can be fully themselves without fear of retribution or discrimination.

Scientifically based research: experimental or quasi-experimental research.

Scripted lessons: commercially produced lesson plans that give teachers a script to read word-for-word to students, then list what activities to do and how much time to spend on each one.

Second language: a language a student is learning in addition to their native language, termed **L2**.

Second language acquisition (SLA) theory: theory of how people acquire a second language.

Separate Underlying Proficiency (SUP): Cummins's (1981) theory that describes the belief that ELLs who are deficient in English need instruction in English only.

Sheltered English Immersion (SEI): classrooms where students learn English and academic content simultaneously before transitioning into mainstream classrooms.

Sheltered Instruction Observation Protocol (SIOP): a commonly used, research-based model for teaching ELLs content and language.

Social action approach: an approach to multicultural education in which students participate in personal, social, or civic action in ways that better their school, family, and community.

Sociocultural Theory (of language learning): the theory that second language acquisition occurs as a result of participation in social contexts, leading to internalization of language.

Standardization: the narrowing of curriculum and instruction to content and skills that appear on standardized tests, often including a pacing guide with the sequence in which standards should be taught by all teachers in a school or district; sometimes called "teaching to the test."

Standards: stated goals and objectives of what students should know and be able to do at each grade level.

Standards-based education: a framework for the cycle of teaching and learning where appropriate content standards and assessments are selected prior to designing curriculum and instruction, and continuous assessment is conducted to measure students' mastery of standards; also known as **outcomes-based education.**

Teachers of English to Speakers of Other Languages (TESOL): the global, professional education association for English language learning.

Teacher research: a form of inquiry in which teachers develop questions, systematically collect and analyze data, and articulate their theories about teaching and learning.

Teaching against the grain: a process of learning to reform teaching alongside experienced teachers who are also struggling to be agents of change.

Transformation approach: an approach to multicultural education in which diverse figures and topics become fundamental to and unified with the established curriculum.

21st-century literacies: expanded definition of reading and writing that acknowledges the influence of and necessity for competence in digital and multimodal technologies.

Two-Way Bilingual Education (TWBE): programs that include native and non-native English speakers learning content in both languages (e.g., English and Spanish).

Universal Grammar (UG): learners' unconscious knowledge and learning of language that derives from an innate understanding of language and need not be explicitly taught.

WIDA ACCESS for ELLs: annual assessment of ELLs' language development.

WIDA ACCESS Placement Test (W-APT): placement test that measures ELLs' proficiency level in English.

World Class Instructional Design and Assessment Consortium (WIDA): a non-profit group that develops ELL standards and assessments.

Zero tolerance: an approach to school discipline whereby any infraction to the school's disciplinary procedures, no matter how large or small, results in severe punishment.

INDEX

About the Authors

Andrea J. Stairs is assistant professor and chair of the Department of Literacy, Language, and Culture at the University of Southern Maine in Gorham. A former middle and high school English teacher and literacy coach, she earned her PhD in education, specializing in curriculum and instruction, from Boston College. Her research interests include urban teacher learning, teacher education in school-university partnerships, and teacher research in literacy. She is coeditor, with Kelly A. Donnell, of *Research on Urban Teacher Learning: Examining Contextual Factors Over Time* (2010).

Kelly A. Donnell is associate professor of education at Roger Williams University in Bristol, Rhode Island. A former elementary school teacher, she earned her PhD in education, specializing in curriculum and instruction, from Boston College. Her research interests include the process of learning to teach in urban settings, social justice in teacher education, practitioner inquiry, and induction for beginning teachers. She is coeditor, with Andrea J. Stairs, of *Research on Urban Teacher Learning: Examining Contextual Factors Over Time* (2010).

Alyssa Hadley Dunn is a clinical assistant professor of urban teacher education at Georgia State University in Atlanta. A former high school English teacher, she earned her PhD in educational studies, specializing in urban and multicultural education, from Emory University. At Georgia State, she works with urban teacher residents as part of the Network for Enhancing Teacher Quality grant. Her research interests include international teachers in U.S. schools, urban educational policy, and multicultural teacher education.

SAGE Research Methods Online

The essential tool for researchers

An expert research tool

- An **expertly designed taxonomy** with more than 1,400 unique terms for social and behavioral science research methods

- **Visual and hierarchical search tools** to help you discover material and link to related methods

- Easy-to-use navigation tools
- Content organized by complexity
- Tools for citing, printing, and downloading content with ease
- Regularly updated content and features

A wealth of essential content

- The most comprehensive picture of quantitative, qualitative, and mixed methods available today

- More than **100,000 pages of SAGE book and reference material** on research methods as well as editorially selected material from SAGE journals

- More than **600 books** available in their entirety online

Launching 2011!

⑤SAGE research methods online